☆
☆ Confederate Finance
☆

RICHARD CECIL TODD

CONFEDERATE FINANCE

THE UNIVERSITY OF GEORGIA PRESS

ATHENS

To my mother
ELLA BRUBAKER TODD
and my wife
CLAUDA PENNOCK TODD

Paperback edition, 2009
© 1954 by the University of Georgia Press
Athens, Georgia 30602
www.ugapress.org
All rights reserved
Printed digitally in the United States of America

The Library of Congress has cataloged the hardcover edition of this book as follows:
Library of Congress Cataloging-in-Publication Data

Todd, Richard Cecil.
Confederate finance.
x, 258 p. illus., ports. 25 cm.
Bibliography: p. 232-245.
1. Finance, Public–Confederate States of America. I. Title.
HJ254 .T6
336.75   54-9636

Paperback ISBN-13: 978-0-8203-3454-7
ISBN-10: 0-8203-3454-5

1. ALEXANDER B. CLITHERALL, Register.
2. BOLLING BAKER, Auditor.
3. EDWARD C. ELMORE, Treasurer.
4. Treasury Department, C. S. A.

Contents

	PREFACE	ix
I	THE TREASURY DEPARTMENT	1
II	LOANS	25
III	TREASURY NOTES	85
IV	TARIFFS AND TAXES	121
V	SEIZURES AND DONATIONS	157
VI	FINANCIAL OPERATIONS ABROAD	175
	APPENDIX A	195
	APPENDIX B	197
	APPENDIX C	198
	APPENDIX D	199
	NOTES	201
	BIBLIOGRAPHY	232
	INDEX	247

Preface

FROM ITS INCEPTION THE CONFEDERACY WAS ENGAGED IN A STRUGGLE for existence. The creation of its treasury and the establishment of a revenue were a concern of vital importance. In its extraordinary straits for money, the Confederacy "resorted to every expedient known to finance, even the most desperate." Federal specie located in the mints and customhouses of the South was confiscated; property of alien enemies was sequestered and military supplies were impressed; duties were placed on exports and imports; direct taxes were levied; donations and gifts were cheerfully accepted and gratefully acknowledged; and Treasury notes flooded the market while loans were floated in an attempt to stabilize the redundant currency and offer a basis for foreign exchange.

Within the following pages the writer has endeavored to show how, and to what extent, each of these financial expedients was used by the Government in meeting its obligations at home and abroad. Attention has also been focused on the organization and personnel responsible for carrying out the financial measures of the Government and on the numerous problems involved in the operation of these measures. Each of the several means of finance has been isolated and discussed relatively independently of the others.

The author wishes to acknowledge his indebtedness to the many individuals without whose aid this work would not have been completed. Gratitude must be expressed first of all to Professor Robert H. Woody, who suggested the need for this study as a doctoral dissertation and who was exceedingly considerate at all times in directing the research, offering criticism, and giving friendly encouragement. The author also is indebted to the several members of the history department at Duke University—especially to Professor William T. Laprade and to Professor Charles S. Sydnor for their kind interest.

He would like to express his thanks for the assistance given him by the staff members of the Duke University Library, the Library of Congress, and the National Archives. He would also like to express appreciation for the generous aid extended him by Miss Helen Harriet Salls, Mrs. Floyd Rhodes, Jr., and Mr. and Mrs. Malvern B. Pennock. To his wife, Clauda Pennock Todd, he owes an infinite debt of gratitude for her inspiration, cheerful encouragement, and invaluable aid from the time the first note was taken until the final proofs were read.

The author is also grateful to Duke University for the Fellowships granted him and to the United Daughters of the Confederacy for making the early publication of this study possible by awarding it the Mrs. Simon Baruch University Prize.

R. C. T.

East Carolina College
Greenville, North Carolina

CHAPTER

☆ I ☆

THE TREASURY DEPARTMENT

☆ ☆ ☆ ☆ ☆ ☆ ☆ ☆ ☆ ☆

THE PROVISIONAL CONGRESS OF THE CONFEDERATE STATES OF AMERica, originally representing six of the Southern states,[1] convened in Montgomery, Alabama, February 4, 1861. Within four days the assembly drafted a constitution which it immediately adopted to remain in force for one year. All the laws of the United States that were "in operation on November 1, 1860, and not otherwise inconsistent with the new instrument were enacted as binding on the Confederacy."[2] On February 9, Congress unanimously elected Jefferson Davis as President and Alexander H. Stephens as Vice President of the Confederate States of America. They were duly inaugurated February 18, 1861. The following day Davis announced as his choice for Secretary of the Treasury Christopher Gustavus Memminger[3] of Charleston, South Carolina — a shrewd, thrifty, and industrious lawyer. His chief qualification for the Treasury position appears to have resulted from the financial experience he gained as chairman of the Ways and Means Committee in the South Carolina House of Representatives.[4] Despite this preparation, his fitness to hold the important cabinet post has offered cause for debate. Davis, some years after the war, said:

Mr. Memminger of South Carolina had a high reputation for knowledge of finance. He bore an unimpeachable character for integrity and close attention to duties, and, on the recommendation of the delegation from South Carolina, he was appointed Secretary of the Treasury and proved himself entirely worthy of the trust.[5]

CONFEDERATE FINANCE

Henry D. Capers, biographer of Memminger and chief clerk to the Confederate Secretary of the Treasury, wrote:

> ... It is not my purpose to enter into an argument with the object in view of vindicating Mr. Memminger from charges made by some that his want of sagacity and proper administrative ability caused the unnecessary depreciation of Confederate securities. . . .
>
> It is proper, however, to call attention to the fact that Mr. Memminger was but an executive officer.
>
> At no time was he given unlimited authority to act as his judgment alone would dictate in the management of the Confederate finances. . . . On the contrary, he was never more than an officer executing the will of Congress. It is true that he had the right to appear before that body and advocate his recommendations, and to suggest such enactments as in his judgment were necessary, but beyond this he could not go. The financial legislation of Congress was, in the most vital points, opposed to his judgment and contrary to his often-repeated and strongly-urged recommendations. . . . Well would it have been for the Confederate cause if the Congress had simply followed the sound and carefully digested financial plans of the Secretary, instead of forcing on the country a policy . . . which was a jumble, resulting from confusion of ideas, and at best but a compromise between opposing factions.[6]

In contrast to these appraisals of the Secretary of the Treasury, Edward A. Pollard, severe critic of many Confederate personalities and policies, stated that "the mind of the Secretary, so juvenile in financial matters, failed . . to understand the simple idea of values, in the shape of credit, and he leaves out of account — what he appears never to have conceived in his whole financial career — the necessity of some basis for all forms and designs of currency."[7] Too, J. C. Schwab claims Memminger "had displayed no peculiar fitness for the position of organizer and head of the Confederate finances," and that, "while holding that position, his leadership evoked much hostile criticism and little commendation."[8] In passing it should be stated that there were other Southern statesmen who could have filled the highly important post,[9] but it is questionable whether any other Secretary of the Treasury would have handled the finances in any vastly different or more successful manner.[10]

From its beginning, the Confederate States of America was engaged in a struggle for existence. The establishment of revenue was of vital importance. Within a short time the organization of the Treasury Department was completed and, except for slight

THE TREASURY DEPARTMENT

modifications, it conformed to the system devised by Alexander Hamilton. Various bureaus were set up to carry on the business of the department.[11] Aiding the Secretary were a Comptroller, Auditor, Register, Treasurer, and Assistant to the Secretary of the Treasury. It became the duty of Memminger to superintend the collection of public revenue; to digest and prepare plans for its improvement and management and for support of the public credit; to prepare and report estimates of public revenue and expenditures; to decide on the forms of keeping and stating accounts and making returns, and to grant all warrants for money to be paid into the treasury, and all warrants for money to be issued from the treasury; to execute the sale of public property belonging to the Confederate States as required by law; to make reports and give information to Congress or the President concerning matters appertaining to the Treasury Department; and generally to perform all such services relative to the finances, and all such other duties as the law directed him to perform.[12]

The Comptroller was obliged to superintend the adjustment and preservation of public accounts; to examine all accounts settled by the auditor and certify their balances to the Register; to countersign all warrants drawn by the Secretary of the Treasury; to report to the secretary the official forms of all papers to be issued in the different offices for collecting public revenue, and the manner and form of keeping and stating the accounts of persons employed therein; and to provide for the regular and punctual payment of all money collected, and direct prosecutions for all delinquencies of officers of revenue, and for debts due to the Confederate States.[13]

The receipt and examination of all public accounts were entrusted to the Auditor.[14]

To the Register fell the responsibility of keeping the accounts of all receipts and expenditures of public money as well as all debts due to or from the Confederate States. He also received from the Comptroller the accounts finally adjusted, and he preserved them along with their vouchers and certificates. He recorded all warrants for the receipt or payment of money at the treasury and transmitted to the Secretary of the Treasury copies of the certificates of balances of accounts adjusted by the Comptroller.

The Treasurer received and kept the money of the Confederate States, and disbursed the same upon warrants drawn by the Secretary, countersigned by the Comptroller, and recorded by the Register. He took receipts for all money paid by him, and all receipts of money received by him were endorsed upon warrants signed by the Secretary of the Treasury, without which warrants, so signed, no acknowledgement for money received into the public treasury was valid. The Treasurer also rendered his accounts to the Comptroller quarterly, or oftener when required, and upon settlement, transmitted a copy to the Secretary.

It was the duty of the Assistant Secretary of the Treasury to examine all letters, contracts, and warrants prepared for the signature of the Secretary, as well as to perform all such other duties devolved upon him by law or by the Secretary of the Treasury.

Having perfected the organization of the Treasury Department, the Confederate Congress set about creating a clerical force to perform the duties of the various bureaus. It was enacted that the clerical force should consist of thirty-one clerks and four messengers.[15] On March 15, 1861, the bureau of the Second Auditor was added to the Treasury Department. The head of the bureau, assisted by eleven clerks, was to audit accounts for the War Department.[16]

While Congress was creating the Treasury Department and establishing a clerical force for its operation, Memminger busied himself searching for qualified men who were willing to assume the responsible positions. Fortunately, the Secretary was able to secure a number of men whose sympathies with the Southern cause prompted them to resign positions in the United States Treasury and offer their services to the Confederate Government. Philip Clayton, former Assistant to the Secretary of the Treasury under Howell Cobb, during Buchanan's administration, assumed the same position at Montgomery. Having a practical knowledge of the operation of the Treasury at Washington, he was able to render invaluable service in the organization of the Confederate Treasury. Charles T. Jones, who had worked many years in the United States Treasury, joined the Register's bureau as the Chief Clerk, bringing with him "copies of all of the forms in use in all of the several bureaus." It has been said that the Confederate Treasury was "more indebted to the willing spirit and indefatigable labors of Mr. Jones than to any other single individual for the rapid and perfect organization of the department in all of its details."[17] The Second Auditor, W. H. S. Taylor, had been in the employ of the United States for twenty-five years prior to accept-

THE TREASURY DEPARTMENT

ing appointment in the Confederate Treasury. In his report of December 31, 1861, he stated that after taking the oath to the Confederacy he returned to Washington to obtain books, forms, and precedents but was "sternly denied all access."[18] By June 30, 1861, the Treasury Department of the Confederate Government was thoroughly organized with the following officers on duty:

Executive Office—Christopher G. Memminger, *Secretary;* Philip Clayton, *Assistant Secretary;* Henry D. Capers, *Chief Clerk and Disbursing Officer;* J. A. Crawford, *Warrant Clerk.*
Comptroller—Lewis Cruger; John Ott, *Chief Clerk.*
First Auditor—Bolling Baker; W. W. Lester, *Chief Clerk.*
Second Auditor—W. H. S. Taylor; J. C. Ball, *Chief Clerk.*
Register—Alexander B. Clitherall; Charles T. Jones, *Chief Clerk.*
Treasurer—Edward C. Elmore; T. T. Green, *Chief Clerk;* Thomas Taylor, *Cashier.*[19]

But these were not all the bureaus. Following the outbreak of hostilities, more and more duties were added to those shouldered by the Treasury Department. As the exigencies of an expanding war demanded, additional offices were established. Among these were the War Tax Office, the Produce Loan Office, and the Treasury-Note Division.

The War Tax Office was created on August 19, 1861, in order to collect the tax provided by Congress for the redemption of Treasury notes.[20]

With the need for increased taxes becoming more apparent daily, Congress finally approved the Tax-in-Kind bill of April 24, 1863, and its accompanying Assessment Act. By the latter act the War Tax Office was replaced with the Office of the Commissioner of Taxes—"a species of bureau under the conduct of the Chief Clerk."[21] On July 2, 1863, Thompson Allan was appointed head of the new office being "charged, under the direction of the Secretary of the Treasury, with all . . . matters pertaining to the assessment and collection of the duties and taxes. . . ."[22]

The Produce Loan Office began as a special branch of the Treasury Department for the sole purpose of procuring the means whereby necessary funds could be raised abroad for purchasing military supplies. Arrangements for the organization of the office were conducted gratuitously by its Chief Commissioner, J. D. B. DeBow.[23]

Upon DeBow's resignation, January 3, 1862, Archibald Roane

was transferred from the office of the First Auditor to act as chief clerk in the Produce Loan Office, which had been placed under the control of Robert Tyler, Register of the Treasury. The duties of the office soon encompassed both the taking and collecting of subscriptions of produce under the Produce Loans and also entailed the purchasing of cotton and tobacco for Government use as authorized by the Act of April 21, 1862. In these operations the Produce Loan Office endeavored to become the stabilizing instrument in the Government's financial policy.[24] Acting as a curb on the inflated Treasury note currency, the office attempted to prevent the increasing redundancy of the notes by withdrawing them from circulation, giving Cotton-interest Bonds in exchange. It further attempted to restrict the inflating tendencies of the note currency by paying for its purchases of produce with Confederate Bonds. As its duties and responsibilities continued to increase with the assumption of control over the cotton and tobacco derived from the Tithe Tax, the Produce Loan Office was raised in status May 1, 1863, to that of a bureau. In the final stages of the war, the efforts of the bureau were directed towards preserving and selling all cotton likely to fall into enemy hands.

On March 9, 1861, Congress authorized the issue of Treasury notes "for such sum or sums as the exigencies of the public service may require, but not to exceed . . . one million of dollars."[25]

The notes were to be prepared under the direction of the Secretary of the Treasury, signed in behalf of the Confederate States of America by the Treasurer, and countersigned by the Register of the Treasury. Adhering to these instructions, Memminger made contracts with private contractors for the printing of the notes, while the final preparation for their issue was performed by clerks in the bureaus of the Treasurer and the Register. As the Federal forces neared Richmond in the spring of 1862, the Confederate Government was compelled to move the printing establishments to a more secure location—Columbia, South Carolina.[26] To manage better the printing and issuing of the notes under the new arrangements, a Treasury-Note Division was established in conjunction with the Treasury Department. Sanders G. Jamison was appointed principal clerk "to superintend the issue of Treasury notes" at Richmond[27] and Joseph Daniel Pope, former Chief Collector of the War Tax for South Carolina, assumed "charge of the printing of Treasury Notes" at Columbia.[28] As the war progressed, more and more emphasis was placed on Treasury notes as

THE TREASURY DEPARTMENT

the Government's means for procuring supplies at home. As a result, it became necessary to expand the Treasury-Note Division into a bureau.

Sanders G. Jamison, who formerly "had charge of the Treasury notes and coupons and of the engraving and issuing thereof from the commencement," was appointed Chief of the Treasury-Note Bureau.[29] Assisting him were two chief clerks, one of them "to reside at Columbia during such time as the engraving and printing . . . [were] conducted there," and the other to remain at Richmond.[30]

With the bureaus of the Treasury Department increasing in number, there was a corresponding increase in the clerical force. On February 13, 1862, Congress approved "An act to organize the clerical force of the Treasury Department." Under the act Congress authorized Secretary Memminger to appoint in the several bureaus of his department a total of 188 clerks and 8 messengers. The clerical force was again increased May 1, 1863.[31]

In an attempt to equalize the salaries paid employees of the Treasury Department with those paid to holders of comparable offices throughout the South and to rectify the hardships induced by scarcity of commodities and price rise, Congress periodically approved legislation granting increases.[32]

To supplement salaries further and reduce the high cost of living of the office personnel at Richmond, agents representing the clerks of the several bureaus were authorized by the Secretary to "visit the South . . . for the purchase of necessary articles of food." They were furnished "transportation, and all proper facilities for the accomplishment of . . . [their] mission." The purchasing agents apparently were successful in procuring the "necessary articles of food."[33]

To keep the office force well in hand and the Treasury organization functioning smoothly, Memminger at an early date issued to the several bureau heads a circular letter enclosing a copy of "Regulations" for the conduct of the department.[34] By a rigid adherence to these rules and a prompt enforcement of the prescribed penalties, coupled with the cooperative spirit of the office personnel, Memminger hoped to attain the most efficient service. His attempt to bring accord in the operation of the Treasury Department also resulted in creating some discord, for there were those few who did not hesitate to express dissatisfaction with the strict manner in which the department was managed. Among the dissenters was the Assistant Secretary of the Treasury, Philip Clayton, who soon began to exhibit opposition to the "restraints" and "exactions" of the Secretary. Finally, an open break occurred, and upon the failure of Clayton's friends to sustain the Assistant in his criticism of Memminger's methods, he was compelled to resign his office on the demand of the Secretary. Having announced the regulations for the Treasury Department to his subordinates, Memminger was "inflexible in their enforcement" and "no political or social influence could save a negligent or recalcitrant official."[35]

Along with the opposition to the rigid regulations for the conduct of the department, there were also other obstacles to the harmonious and efficient operation of the Confederate Treasury. Congress had granted the Secretary authority to distribute the clerks among the several bureaus as in his judgment would "best subscribe the public interest."[36] On several occasions Memminger availed himself of this power and transferred the clerks from one office to another. It appears, however, that this means of alleviating the labor shortage in one bureau only contributed to the disorganization and shortage of labor in another. On August 6, 1861, Lewis Cruger, Comptroller, wrote to the Secretary:

> I am compelled to request the favor of you either to return the Clerks whom you stated to me you desired to borrow for a few days to assist in signing Treasury notes or else to appoint others in their place as I find it utterly impossible to get on without them. The return of Mr. Ott to this office is of the *greatest importance* as he had great experience in the Comptroller's office in Washington and is therefore peculiarly adapted to this office. Mr. Sparnick can be replaced by any good clerk.
>
> The 2nd Auditor, with about ½ the business of this Office, has already *Ten Clerks,* and informs me he ought to have *double the number;* whilst this Office with about double the business has never had but 5 regular Clerks and the *two best* of these the Office is now deprived.
>
> It is consequently impossible that this utterly inadequate force can perform the Duties, or accomplish the business of this office.[37]

Memminger answered that "the Secretary of the Treasury has *absolute* controll [sic] over this subject and will appoint clerks, when satisfied they are needed."[38] Whereupon the Comptroller replied:

> I have had the honor to receive your communication of the 10th inst. in which you decline making application to Congress for Clerks

THE TREASURY DEPARTMENT

for this Office, which is now about destitute having only 3 Clerks left, instead of having Eleven, to meet the great increase of business. I have only to say in reply that I have performed my duty in making the application, and cannot be held responsible for the utter confusion and non-performance of business in my office, resulting from the want of Clerks to discharge its duties.[39]

On December 6, 1861, Cruger again called attention to the condition of the Comptroller's Office and recommended a "large increase" in the number of clerks for the efficient operation of his bureau.[40] The recommendation, however, was not approved. Thus the question of labor shortage remained until February 13, 1862, at which time Congress authorized a substantial increase in the number of clerks employed.

For a year and a quarter more the Treasury functioned rather smoothly; then, on June 3, 1863, it was confronted for the first time with what proved to be the greatest of all its obstacles—the use of office personnel for military purposes. On that date the Second Auditor was requested "to assemble immediately the clerks of his Bureau for the purpose of organizing a military company for the local defense of Richmond" and he was instructed to notify the Office of Comptroller, along with that of the Produce Loan and War Tax, "to unite with his clerks in the organization." It was expected that "all the clerks [would] unite in so essential a duty or submit an excuse to be reported to the President."[41] But such expectations did not receive the full support of the clerical force, and it became necessary to take more drastic steps "for the local defense of Richmond" as is evidenced by the following notice posted in all the offices of the Treasury Department:

NOTICE

Treasury Department, C. S. A.

Richmond, October 13, 1863

Several of the clerks of this Department have failed to do their duty in joining the organization for local defense. Any clerk not maimed who is physically unable to do the duty of drilling and preparing for local defense is *prima facie* unable to do efficient service as a clerk in this Department, and ought to be dismissed as inefficient, unless the physical disability is of such a character as to exempt him from this military duty, while it does not incapacitate him for clerical duty. Notice is therefore hereby given to each of the clerks who may not have enrolled their names that at the end of the present month he will be dismissed, clerks hereafter appointed will be subject to this regulation.

C. G. Memminger,
Sec. of the Treasury[42]

The military training of the office personnel was not without results. On December 8, 1863, Memminger addressed a circular to the heads of the several bureaus, saying:

The Secretary of the Treasury has learned from Colonel Browne, the officer in command of the troops for local defense, that the officers and soldiers connected with this Department, on their late expedition to defend the works at Chapin's Bluff, have discharged their duties with the diligence and bearing of trained soldiers, submitting with cheerfulness to privation, and addressing themselves manfully to all the duties required of them. . . .[43]

Accompanying the meritorious results of the clerical force's military activities were others far less pleasant. The absence of clerks from their desks during working hours necessitated the closing of the several offices of the Treasury Department, causing great inconvenience to the Government and public.[44] Memminger was compelled to "request the permanent detail of a sufficient number of clerks to keep up a skeleton organization for business."[45]

With the continuation of hostilities, the manpower shortage in the Army grew more critical. The threatening position assumed by the Federals surrounding Richmond in early October, 1864, rendered it "necessary for the great body of clerks in the several departments to be sent to the trenches"[46] and general orders were issued "restricting the offices to half the force."[47] Upon learning of the intention of Congress during the last months of war to remove from their desks in the Treasury Department all clerks under forty years of age, William W. Crump, Assistant Secretary of the Treasury, drew up a letter on the subject for his superior, Secretary Trenholm. He indicated the effect such legislation would have on the operation of the Treasury and offered recommendations for a minimum force which he considered necessary to carry out the "grave and responsible task" of the Treasury. Crump's opinion, "founded upon close observation and actual experience, and fortified by the earnest appeals of the Chiefs of the several Bureaux," was that the public service would "sustain permanent and irreparable injury by the contemplated conscription of all clerks under forty years of age." The Assistant Secretary wrote:

THE TREASURY DEPARTMENT

... this Department has given up to the military exigencies of the country its clerks old and young, able and disabled, month after month during the past year, and into the present year down to this period; until the business of the Department, in its several Bureaux, has been so unavoidly retarded and postponed, that the most vigorous effort is required to restore, once more, order and system to its labors, and punctuality to the dispatch of its accumulated duties.

This grave and responsible task would be almost hopeless, if the most skilful, and experienced and efficient clerks are removed—men who have been for very many years in similar Bureaux under the former government, and who have organized them under our own. Nor can any one familiar with their duties suppose that their places may be supplied from inexperienced persons over age, or disabled. Such persons require to be taught, and there will be no preceptors. Already the Bureaux are filled with as many such persons as can be profitably employed, and no multiplication of their numbers will supply the want of a skilled and expert staff in each Bureau.[48]

In order to preserve a "skilled and expert staff," Crump prepared a list of clerks required in each Bureau for the "vast business" of the Department, "making in the aggregate but forty-seven men, under forty years of age." This, he stated, was "a list of minimums," each Bureau having been scaled down to the very lowest number. He believed that with this force the current work of the bureaus could be done, but that it would be "uncandid to pretend that the accumulated business in the Bureaux will be promptly and speedily dispatched."[49]

On February 1, 1865, Secretary Trenholm forwarded the letter to W. Porcher Miles, Chairman, Committee on Military Affairs, respectfully asking the chairman's attention to the letter, saying that it embodied the views of the Secretary upon the subject with which it treated. Trenholm added:

... The indiscriminate conscription of all the clerks in this Department under forty years of age would be attended by the most serious if not fatal injury to the public interests entrusted to it; and I cannot too strongly urge upon your honorable body, to grant the few exemptions asked in the list accompanying the communication.[50]

That the correspondence had its desired effect is indicated by the absence of legislation conscripting skilled clerks in the Treasury Department under forty years of age. Nevertheless, the persistent demands upon the office personnel continued to retard the operation of the Department until the end of hostilities.

CONFEDERATE FINANCE

It should be noted that aside from the original bureaus established for the operation of the Confederate Treasury and those offices created primarily to raise funds at home and abroad (whose expanding duties in time necessitated their rise in rank to that of bureaus), there were also numerous other offices under the direction of the Secretary of the Treasury—some of greater import, others of less, but each contributing to the extensive organization of the Treasury Department. Among these were the Treasury Printing Office, Mints, Assistant Treasurers, Customhouses, and Depositories.

The Treasury Printing Office was placed under the management of S. C. Hayes, who also acted as custodian for all paper belonging to the Treasury to be used for printing purposes. The Office undertook the printing of the numerous instructions, rules, and regulations emitting from the Treasury and "no printing of any description" was "executed in the office, except for the Treasury Department, and the several Bureaux connected with . . . [the] Department."[51]

Following the secession of Louisiana, Georgia, and later North Carolina, the Federal mints located at New Orleans, Dahlonega, and Charlotte were seized by the authorities of the respective states; and the establishments, all the accoutrement, and the Bullion Fund of each mint were turned over to the Confederacy.[52]

On March 9, 1861, the Confederate Congress passed a resolution for the continuance of the mints at New Orleans and Dahlonega and "requested the Secretary of the Treasury to estimate and report to Congress the lowest amount of appropriation necessary to carry out the . . . resolution."[53]

In answer to a questionnaire from Secretary Memminger, the several superintendents revealed that the cost of operating the mints would far surpass their anticipated income.[54] Confronted with this information, Memminger was compelled to recommend to Congress an immediate suspension of the operation of the mints, since it was the policy of the Government "to make all branches of the public service self-sustaining."[55] Congress abided by the Secretary's recommendation.[56]

During the two-month period from March 9, 1861, when Congress had passed the resolution asking for continuance of the mints at New Orleans and Dahlonega, to May 14, 1861, when operation of the mints was discontinued, much attention was directed towards acquiring a new coin of the Confederate States of America.

THE TREASURY DEPARTMENT

As early as March 6, 1861, William A. Elmore, Superintendent of the Mint at New Orleans, wrote Memminger:

When the Government of the Confederate States assumes active control over the operations of this institution, I assume that it will require new dies, with new devices and inscriptions. To procure them will require time. Would it not be well to commence preparations for the new state of things?[57]

The Secretary of the Treasury replied:

I wish ... you would see some of the persons in New Orleans, who deal in engravings or designing, and procure some designs from them for the various coins, and send them here immediately. I would suggest to them to design something new and appropriate to the South, leaving to the North the Eagle and its counterpart.[58]

On April 17, 1861, Lloyd Glover of the National Bank Note Company of New York, acting upon the suggestion of Elmore, made "a model for the new coin,"[59] and five days later the Superintendent of the Mint at New Orleans forwarded by Adams Express "various designs for the coin of the Confederate States."[60]

On April 29, 1861, Elmore forwarded still another design—one which had good possibilities of becoming the accepted one for the coin of the Confederacy. Created by Messrs. Gallier & Esterbrook, New Orleans architects, the design was accompanied with the following letter of description:

... The principal figure, the Goddess of Liberty, seated, holds in her right hand a staff surmounted by the liberty cap; her left arm rests on a shield, and the left hand on the "Constitution." On the shield (there being no coat of arms yet adopted) is shown a portion of the flag of the Confederacy, unfurled; to the left of the figure will be observed sugar-cane growing, a bale of cotton, a sugar hogshead, and a bale of tobacco; to the right, cotton in its various stages of growth, as also tobacco. On the reverse side is an endless chain composed of fifteen links; South Carolina, having taken the lead, occupies the top link, and the other links represent, right and left, the other States in the order of their secession; the remaining blank links are an invitation to the border States to hasten to inscribe their names within the circle. The stars of the Confederate States are distinct; those of the border States are in the twilight, but visible, soon, we hope, to stand out as boldly as their neighbors. In the centre is inscribed the monogram, composed of the letters C.S.A. Twenty dollars has been printed to represent the denomination of the coin. Of course, the design is adaptable to any denomination of our coin.[61]

Dies for a Confederate cent were prepared by a "Mr. Lovett, of Philadelphia, and delivered to the authorities after some ten or twelve impressions were taken . . . in the United States." On the obverse side of the coin was pictured the "Head of Liberty" with the inscription, "Confederate States of America." The reverse side bore " '1 cent' in two lines, surrounded by a wreath of ears of corn and wheat, with a cotton bale at the bottom." The coin was made of nickel.[62]

With the outbreak of war, Memminger called a halt to the arrangements being made to procure designs and dies for coins of the Confederacy. Writing to the Superintendent of the Mint at New Orleans, the Secretary explained his actions, saying that since war has intervened,

. . . it is not probable that much coinage will be required, while it is certain that the Government will need the Bullion Fund for its necessities. Under all circumstances, you had better reduce immediately your expenditures in every practicable way, and dismiss workmen so as to leave the establishment merely property taken care of until Congress may pass upon such plan as I may submit under the information to be derived from you.[63]

Upon suspension of operation of the several mints, much of their material was sold to promote essential wartime industries.

Following the decision of Congress to close the mints as of June 1, 1861, frequent inquiries were made to the Secretary of the Treasury concerning the need for opening that portion of each mint referred to as the Assay Office,[64] to assay gold being mined in the South. Investigating the practicability of these inquiries, Memminger was informed by the mint superintendent at Dahlonega and Charlotte that the expense to operate the Assay Office independent of the mint was "so considerable that it did not appear . . . it could be defrayed upon the principle adopted by . . . [the] Government,"[65] namely, "that each branch of industry shall bear its own burdens, and not tax another to pay its own expenses."[66] Upon receipt of this advice, the Government "determined to abandon further consideration of this subject during the existence of the war."[67]

But on August 6, 1861, the subject was reopened in answer to the petitions of the Convention of North Carolina, asking that the mint at Charlotte be put in operation. Under the proposal made in the petition Memminger refused to recommend reopening of the mint but sanctioned the opening of the Assay Office as an experiment, whereby "The public may assist the enterprise by allowing the assayer use of the mint establishment and tools. . . ." In order "to prevent any recourse back upon the Treasury," the Secretary considered it "proper to provide that the compensation of the Assayer should arise entirely from the charges, and that the whole expense of the establishment . . . [be] at his risk."[68]

Congress approved the plans of the Secretary and on August 24, 1861, authorized the opening of Assay Offices at Charlotte and Dahlonega.[69] On January 27, 1862, an Assay Office was also established at New Orleans,[70] but despite the opening of these offices at the several mints, the amount of metal assayed proved negligible.

In May, 1862, "the machinery, implements, and other appendages of the Mint and Assay Office at Charlotte, and the occupation and use of the buildings were surrendered to the Navy Department on condition that they should be restored at a week's notice, whenever required"[71] and J. H. Gibbon, assayer, was advised to "have stored in some safe place . . . whatever . . . is not needed for the naval work."[72]

It appears that no further action was taken in regard to the mints until December 12, 1864, at which time the Senate adopted a resolution inquiring of the Secretary whether, in his opinion, the work of coining and assaying gold and silver may not be resumed at the mints without further delay.[73]

Trenholm replied that the Mint and Assay Office at Charlotte, along with all the equipment, had been turned over to the Navy Department and that he was unaware of any change in the policy of the Government that would indicate "the belief that expenses of a mint, under the existing circumstances of the country, could be defrayed from compensation to be received from the public for coining and assaying."

He concluded his reply to the Senate by saying he did not "perceive any public benefit to arise from coining and assaying of sufficient importance to outweigh the considerations that have hitherto determined the policy of the Government in favor of the inactivity of these establishments."[74] Thus, on the advice of Secretary Trenholm, the mints remained closed.

The three remaining offices of the Treasury organization—the Collector of Customs, Assistant Treasurer, and that of Depositary —were, in a sense, all depositories; that is, each was entrusted with the keeping of public funds. But if in this respect the offices were similar there were other responsibilities in which they greatly differed.

By an Act of Congress, approved February 14, 1861, anyone who held an office connected with the collection of the customs, duties, and imports in the several states of the Confederacy, at the time of the adoption of the Constitution of the Provisional Government, was reappointed to the same office; and was vested with the same powers, subjected to the same duties, and entitled to the same salaries, fees, and emoluments as had been set forth in the laws of the United States of America, provided, however, that a Collector's maximum compensation from all sources could not exceed the rate of $5,000 per annum.[75]

With the appointment of the customs personnel, Congress instructed the Collectors of the several ports "to enforce the existing revenue laws against all foreign countries, except the State of Texas."[76]

When the instructions were put into effect, an illicit traffic developed with certain of the border states. To halt the smuggling and also hasten the entrance into the Confederacy of those Southern states which had temporarily refrained from seceding, the Secretary of the Treasury was authorized "to establish additional Ports and places of Entry and Delivery" on the frontier. This Memminger did, but upon "the union of Virginia" with the Confederacy, "and the probable union in a few weeks of North Carolina and Tennessee," the customhouses established on the frontier proved of little value and the collectors were ordered to "complete all business remaining unfinished and render accounts" to the Treasury Department."[77]

The operation of customhouses was also retarded by the advent of the blockade, and Collectors of Customs at the various ports were advised that it would be "unnecessary to appoint additional officers to aid . . . in collecting the revenue."[78] As the blockade continued and the military campaigns expanded, many of the ports of entry were closed.[79] The number of customhouses fluctuated throughout the war, but it is questionable whether they ever exceeded thirty-five at one time; during the last few months of hostilities, the number decreased rapidly.

The Assistant Treasurers originally were located at New Orleans and Charleston. Upon the fall of New Orleans in the spring of 1862, Anthony J. Guirot, the Assistant Treasurer, was compelled to move to Jackson, Mississippi,[80] and later to Mobile,

THE TREASURY DEPARTMENT

Alabama. B. C. Pressley, Assistant Treasurer, at Charleston, had a somewhat similar fate. In 1863, with the enemy closing in on the port, Pressley was advised to move to Columbia, South Carolina. He prepared to do so, but shortly thereafter resigned and was succeeded by W. Y. Leitch, who later carried out the instructions, becoming "the Chief Officer of the Treasury . . . in South Carolina."[81]

The Assistant Treasurers were actually sub-treasurers of the Confederacy and were situated at strategic points to facilitate the banking operations of the Government. Like the depositaries, they received revenue from taxes, customs, and the sale of Confederate stocks and bonds, and were authorized to disburse the public funds on receipt of warrants from the Treasury Department. Too, they acted as a reservoir for "pay depositories," keeping those offices supplied with funds to meet the public demand.

The Assistant Treasurers in conjunction with the depositaries comprised the banking system of the Government. It became the objective of Memminger to extend and improve this system of banking. On March 17, 1862, in response to a resolution of the Senate directing the Secretary of the Treasury to inform that body "what depositories of funds have been established" in the Confederate States, the Secretary forwarded a list of the same, saying:

> The depositaries at New Orleans and Charleston are made so by law, being sub-treasurers; those at Wilmington, North Carolina; Savannah, Georgia; Mobile, Alabama; Nashville and Memphis, Tennessee; and Galveston and LaSalle, Texas, are appointments by this Department under the authority of existing laws.[82]

In view of the exigencies of the time, the Secretary asked for "a temporary increase of discretionary power . . . to make other depositories," stating that:

> In the present condition of the country it may be necessary to remove the funds now in the hands of some of the depositaries to other and safer localities. For such cases it would conduce to the public service to grant authority to the Secretary of the Treasury to establish depositories at other convenient places. The law only authorizes depositaries to be made of certain custom-house officers. It may become necessary to have depositaries where no such officers exist; and in interior places, even where custom-house officers exist, it may be far better to appoint some bank for the time being as a depositary.[83]

The "discretionary power" asked for was granted, and by virtue of this authority, Memminger made his sweeping appointments during the extensive funding operations under the Acts of October 13, 1862, March 23, 1863, and February 17, 1864. Because of the great increase in the number of depositories, it became necessary to separate them into two groups: Pay Depositories and Funding Depositories.[84]

The former group was composed of Assistant Treasurers, all original depositaries, and a few temporary depositaries appointed subsequent to the funding acts. Each was granted power to pay out funds on proper warrants and also receive and register notes for exchange under the funding acts. The Funding Depositories, on the other hand, were simply given authority to receive and register notes for exchange. This distinction, as the Secretary stated, was "unavoidable," for there were "250 depositaries including those appointed for funding," and it was "impossible to supply all of them in advance with funds for exchange."[85]

The inability of the Government to keep all its depositaries supplied with funds had its repercussions, and it became necessary to discontinue many of those possessing only the funding authority.[86] On March 14, 1865, Secretary Trenholm returned a list of temporary depositaries to the Treasurer, John N. Hendren, asking him to indicate those which "had been made pay Depositaries or are exercising the functions of such," adding that he was of the opinion "all others . . . had better be discontinued." He closed as follows:

. . . They are constantly applied to for the fulfilment of Government obligations, the discharge of which is no part of their appointed duty. The applicants being disappointed accuse the Government of bad faith. Their continuance in office serves, therefore, but to multiply the avenues and occasions of bringing the Government into discredit.[87]

A few words should be said concerning the banking operations of the Confederate Government. By law, estimates of expenditures for each of the several departments of the Government were periodically forwarded to the Secretary of the Treasury. The Secretary compiled these estimates and sent them to Congress along with his recommendations for procuring the means to meet them. Upon Congressional approval, funds for the specific amounts appropriated were placed in the Confederate Treasury to the credit of the respective departments.

Payment of the funds at the Treasury were then made in one

THE TREASURY DEPARTMENT

of two modes: First, upon claims regularly audited and passed and paid as demands upon the Treasury; or secondly, upon requisitions of disbursing officers. The second class was the more common of the two and was paid in the following manner: The Secretary of War, for example, made a requisition for $100,000 to be placed in the hands of a quartermaster. Upon this requisition a Treasury warrant was issued placing $100,000 of the War Department's appropriations to the credit of the quartermaster, and upon the receipt of the quartermaster, the Treasurer either handed to him, or placed to his credit in a depository, the amount, and charged him with the same. The money thus passed out of the Treasury and stood to the credit of the quartermaster as a deposit subject to his check. He drew on it at pleasure, and in accounting afterwards with the auditor, discharged himself by producing vouchers for demands paid.[88]

Unlike the central bank of the Federal Government, there was never established a Bank of the Confederate States of America. The South's lack of a central bank, however, did not result from a lack of ideas or thought on the subject. As early as April 18, 1861, there was a suggestion made for "establishing a bank similar to the Bank of England, which has been found so great a convenience to that Government." Each Southern state was expected to subscribe $1,000,000 for itself and $1,000,000 was to be disposed of by public subscription; in shares of $100 each, this would raise a capital of $14,000,000 on which it was stated the Government "could safely circulate from $25,000,000 to $40,000,000 of notes." Government accounts were to be kept in the bank, with payment of demands made in "notes of not less than $25 each, these to be negotiable in all the Confederate States." For management of the bank "each State should choose one director each year, and the stockholders in each State one director." There was to be a branch in each state and the profits were "to be paid out annually, or semi-annually, merely reserving a fund for exigencies."[89]

Frequently, during 1862, there was talk of creating a central bank on the lines of the National Bank system of the Federal Government, the objective being the same as that in the North, to stabilize the currency by improving the standing of the Government's bonds and also furnish a more reliable medium of exchange than that supplied by Treasury notes. To do this, a system was proposed whereby banks could issue notes up to half the amount of their capital, securing redemption by depositing with the bank authorities state or Confederate bonds. In event of failure of a bank to redeem its notes in specie, the Government could sell the bonds deposited and redeem the notes with the proceeds.

In June 1864, a unique proposal was made to the Secretary of the Treasury. Messrs. Emile De Erlanger and Company of Paris, J. H. Schroeder and Company of London, and others proposed to establish a Confederate bank in London, with a capital of 10,000,-000 pounds and asked the cooperation and approval of Memminger "to the extent of appointing the said bank your fiscal agent in Europe, and keeping the Government deposits with them"; also to use his influence "to enable them to obtain such charters as may be necessary to establish branches at the different cities in the South."[90]

It was claimed that:

The bank, once established, will greatly facilitate the Government in "bringing out" any new loans in Europe, and it will make liberal advances to them on the most favorable terms. The current rate of interest will be allowed them on their deposits. At the close of the war, its capital is to be used to aid in moving the various crops of the country, to encourage direct trade with Europe, and to develop the resources of the Confederacy. One-third of its capital stock will be reserved for citizens of the Confederate States, and, within a reasonable time after peace, they will be offered an opportunity for subscribing for the said stock at its par value.[91]

There were other proposals made for a Bank of the Confederate States but no action was ever taken on any of them. The Government's nearest approach to creating such an institution came February 23, 1865, when Congress in the hope of allaying the greatly increased currency authorized "the establishment of an Office of Deposit in connection with the Treasury."[92] The Office of Deposit, managed by "a Chief Clerk and such clerks as . . . [were] necessary to transact the business of the same," was to be created in the offices of the Treasurer, Assistant Treasurers, and in "one pay depository in each State." The object of the Office of Deposit was to reduce the redundancy of paper currency by receiving "on deposit, drafts on the Treasury, and current funds of all persons offering to make such deposits, and to pay the same out upon the checks of the depositors." The faith of the Government was pledged for the security of deposits. The Secretary could "lend to the Treasury part of the deposits, not . . . exceeding two-thirds of the entire sum," provided no interest would be paid on the loans, or on the deposits, the sole advantage to the depositor being that:

All Treasury notes deposited under the provisions of this act, and permitted to remain for a period not less than three months, shall be exempted from taxation, to the extent of one half the tax that may be imposed on Treasury notes, or bonds on deposit elsewhere.[93]

Before the Office of Deposit could get into full operation, the Confederacy ceased to exist.

Despite its opposition to a Bank of the Confederate States of America, Congress at all times availed itself of the wholehearted cooperation of the Southern banks with the Treasury Department. Aid rendered the Confederacy by state and local banking houses was immeasurable. They loaned the Government a large portion of their specie under the $15,000,000 specie loan of February 28, 1861, and subscribed freely to all later loans. They permitted the Government use of their bank notes until Treasury notes could be produced and gave up their supply of bank-note paper and steel plates.[94] Too, they helped the Government carry out its plan of finance based on the issue of Treasury notes by accepting the notes in payment of all dues, and aided the adoption of Treasury notes as the South's currency by taking them in on deposit and paying them out on demand. Many banks also acted as depositories for the Government and assisted in carrying out the funding measures under the acts of October 12, 1862, March 23, 1863, and February 17, 1864. Numerous bankers corresponded with the Secretary of the Treasury offering their personal views concerning financial legislation and through their action at bank conventions offered a united front in promoting the Treasury's plans and in recommending measures to improve the financial state of the Confederacy.

The esteem with which the Treasury Department looked upon the services rendered the Government by the banking institutions is perceived in the following dispatch from Secretary Trenholm to J. A. Seddon, Secretary of War, in which the former wrote:

The conduct of these institutions has been loyal and patriotic in the extreme; they have contributed their means most liberally in aid of the government and offered every convenience at their disposal to its officers.[95]

As the war progressed and the South lost the right of free access to the Atlantic Ocean and later the Mississippi River, two additional branches of the Treasury Department were created—one in Europe and the other in the Confederate States west of the Mississippi.

With the blockade proving to be something more than a "paper-blockade" and the area of warfare expanding daily, more and more emphasis was placed on procuring military supplies from abroad. To promote the financial arrangements of the Confederacy it became necessary to create depositories on foreign soil and to appoint Treasury agents to supervise the acquiring and spending of Confederate funds.

On January 10, 1862, Memminger made overtures to Jno. Fraser & Co. of Charleston, South Carolina, to have their subsidiary, Messrs. Fraser, Trenholm & Co., Liverpool, England, act as a depository of Confederate funds.[96]

On March 14, 1862, Messrs. Fraser, Trenholm & Co. agreed to accept appointment as Confederate Depository at Liverpool, England, asking for their services a commission of ½%, the same rate as was believed to be paid to Messrs. Baring Bros. & Co. by the United States for similar services. Fraser, Trenholm & Co., henceforth, remained the Confederate Depository in England.

Having established a depository for its funds abroad, Congress next approved the appointment of James Spence, Liverpool, England, as its financial agent on February 9, 1863. Spence was appointed "to negotiate and carry out such arrangements for the raising and payment of money abroad" as the Confederacy would "from time to time require."[97]

Upon authorization of the Erlanger Loan, January 29, 1863, General Colin J. McRae was sent to France by the Treasury Department as its agent to manage the interests of the Confederacy in regard to the loan, and in compliance to his request of June 19, 1863, he was appointed a depositary of the Treasury at Paris.[98]

Depositories were also established at Bermuda and Nassau in the West Indies, with Norman S. Walker being appointed to occupy the former office and Louis Heyliger the latter.[99] Following the adoption of the Government's "New Plan" for procuring supplies abroad in 1864, an additional depository was established at Havana, Cuba, and there was a reorganization of those in Europe with Messrs. Fraser, Trenholm & Co. becoming the sole depository for Confederate funds, and General Colin J. McRae the Treasury's Bursar.[100] Under the "New Plan" all funds and cotton from the Confederacy were forwarded in small blockade-runners to the depositories in the West Indies, from whence they were reshipped to Fraser, Trenholm & Co., Liverpool, England, who sold the cotton, placing the proceeds along with the other funds received to the credit of McRae. The Bursar then paid out the funds to satisfy the demands made on him by the purchasing agents of the several departments.[101] The "New Plan" for promoting the Government's financial operations abroad showed signs of great promise but its adoption came too late to save a "lost cause."

With the fall of Port Hudson, July 9, 1863, it became obvious that control of the main artery of communication between the Confederate states, east and west of the Mississippi, was lost to the North.

To counteract this loss and at the same time promote the South's efforts to wage war against the Union forces west of the Mississippi, the Confederate Congress created the Trans-Mississippi Department (composed of all those Confederate states west of the Mississippi) and placed it under the military control of General E. Kirby Smith. In order to conduct financial operations in the newly created department, Congress, abiding by the recommendation of Memminger, established an almost independent and completely organized Treasury Department at Marshall, Texas. P. W. Gray was appointed "agent of the Treasury for the Trans-Mississippi Department,"[102] and the Secretary of the Treasury was authorized to confer upon the agent power "to discharge any duty or function on the other side of the Mississippi which he, the said Secretary, is competent to discharge."[103]

On February 17, 1864, two bureaus, that of Auditor and that of Comptroller, were established in connection with the agency of the Treasury for the Trans-Mississippi Department, their duties in relation to the new agency being comparable to those of the corresponding bureaus in the Treasury Department at Richmond.[104]

When the exigencies of the country demanded, additional bureaus, offices, and personnel were added to those already established in the Agency of the Treasury for the Trans-Mississippi Department. For example, on December 27, 1864, Secretary Trenholm submitted for the consideration of Congress the expediency of creating a separate Produce Loan Bureau,[105] and on February 15, 1865, Thomas F. McKinney of Austin City, Texas, was recommended for the office of Chief of the Cotton Bureau of the Trans-

Mississippi Department.[106] An Office of Commissioner of Taxes was approved March 13, 1865, along with "such number of clerks as may be necessary to conduct the business of the office."[107] On that same day two additional bureaus were created—that of Register and that of Treasurer.

As the war drew to a close, the Agency of the Treasury in the Trans-Mississippi Department had developed into an almost completely organized and independent Treasury Department operating in its own right. That it attained a high degree of success in handling the financial operations of the Confederacy in the states west of the Mississippi is indicated in the reports of its agent to the Secretary of the Treasury.

With the Treasury Department thus organized, its personnel immediately set about finding the ways and means to sustain the Government. It should be remembered that, from its very inception, the Confederate States of America was engaged in a struggle for existence. The creation of its Treasury and the establishment of a revenue were of vital importance. In its extraordinary straits for money, the Confederacy "resorted to every expedient known to finance, even the most desperate."[108] Federal specie located in the mints and customhouses of the South was confiscated; property of alien enemies was sequestered and military supplies were impressed; duties were placed on exports and imports; direct taxes were levied; donations were cheerfully accepted and gratefully acknowledged; and Treasury notes flooded the market while loans were floated in an attempt to stabilize the currency and offer a basis for foreign exchange.

Striving to procure the funds requisite for its operation, Congress soon placed emphasis upon loans as its primary source of income; later Treasury notes were emphasized, and then, perhaps too late, taxes were stressed.

CHAPTER II

LOANS

NEEDING AN AVAILABLE SUPPLY OF FUNDS AND LACKING A CURRENCY of its own and the means of making one, the Government early turned to loans as a source whereby its monetary needs could be supplied. On February 8, 1861, two days after the six seceding states had convened at Montgomery, Alabama, the general assembly of that state appropriated a sum of $500,000 and placed it at the disposal of the Southern Congress.[1] By a unanimous agreement the $500,000 loan was accepted; thus the Congress inaugurated the use of loans as a means of financing the Confederate States of America. From the inception of the Provisional Government, February 8, 1861, to the collapse of the Confederacy, Congress showed a close attachment to, and a growing reliance upon, loans as a financial instrument to raise the much-needed funds for which it was continuously pressed.

It should be noted that Secretary Memminger was well aware of the desirability of taxes over loans as a means of securing funds for operating the Government, but he also realized that one difficulty of a direct tax lay in the time-consuming process of establishing the machinery to collect it. Hence, the urgent need for funds at home and abroad led the Secretary first to place emphasis upon public loans.

"An Act to Raise money for the Support of the Government, and to Provide for the Defence of the Confederate States of America" was approved by the Provisional Congress February 28, 1861.

CONFEDERATE FINANCE

By this legislation Congress enacted the first major Confederate loan—a loan occasionally referred to as a Bankers' Loan but more commonly called the 15-Million Dollar Loan. Under this act the Secretary of the Treasury was authorized to issue certificates of stock or bonds to the amount of $15,000,000, bearing 8% interest, payable semi-annually in specie. Bonds were issued for ten years but could be redeemed by the Government any time after five upon giving three months' public notice. The loan was supported by an export duty levied on cotton at the rate of ⅛ of one cent per pound payable in specie or in the interest coupons of the loan, and collectible after August 1, 1861. Proceeds from the duty were specifically pledged to the payment of the principal and interest of the loan with the duty to cease upon cancellation of all the stocks and bonds issued. To promote this cancellation, the act provided for the establishment of a sinking fund; this provision, however, failed to be carried out although the other provisions of the act were faithfully adhered to. The certificates of stocks and bonds were to be issued in such form and amounts as determined by the Secretary of the Treasury, provided that none would be for a sum less than fifty dollars.

Memminger immediately began arrangements for the preparation and sale of the stocks and bonds. The bonds were modeled after those then issued by the United States Government and were printed in denominations of one thousand dollars, five hundred dollars, one hundred dollars, and fifty dollars.[2]

The first public announcement concerning the 15-Million Dollar Loan was made March 16, 1861, the day Congress adjourned. In an advertisement entitled "Loan for the Defense of the Confederate States," the Secretary stated that:

Five millions of this most advantageous investment will be offered to the public on April 17th ensuing, and every citizen throughout the Confederate States will have the opportunity of taking a share of the benefit, and at the same time of sustaining the cause of the country.[3]

To aid people in all areas of the Confederacy to take a part of the loan, books of subscription were to be opened in all the leading cities and principal interior towns. Six per cent of the amount subscribed was to be paid in specie at the time of subscription, and the remainder on or before May 1, with interest to start from the date of such payment. In the event of an over-subscription, preference was to be given first to those who had paid down their

LOANS

whole subscription, next to subscribers of $50, and then to subscribers of $100.

Memminger worked diligently to place the loan, hoping that one million dollars of it would be taken in New York.[4]

The Secretary was eager to get a subscription of twice the amount offered, believing that such an expression of confidence on the part of the people would have a marked influence on European diplomacy.

The successful promotion of the loan, however, was temporarily stymied by the inability of would-be subscribers to obtain specie to meet both the 6% payment called for at the time of subscription and the remainder due on or before May 1, 1861. This inability of subscribers to obtain specie resulted from the general suspension of specie payments by many of the Southern banks during the early months of 1861.

Following the suspension of specie payment for bank notes, the rate of exchange in the several states started immediately to vary. In Mobile, New Orleans, and throughout the states of Louisiana, Mississippi, and Texas where the banking institutions refused to suspend specie payments, bank notes circulated freely and remained at par value with coin; but in Georgia, South Carolina, Florida, and the upper part of Alabama the rate of exchange varied from 2 to 4% discount, while sterling exchange brought 4 to 5% premium.

Faced with these varying rates of exchange, Memminger quickly realized the great difficulty that would be encountered in making any plan for the payment of subscriptions to the loan equally acceptable to all parts of the Confederacy. Under these conditions, it was considered best not to require payment for subscriptions in actual coin, but to accept bank notes at their exchange value.[5] This, however, proved to be only a temporary answer to the problem.

On March 27, 1861, Memminger wrote to R. R. Cuyler, banker of Savannah, Georgia:

> We are much embarrassed in our financial arrangements by the suspension of the banks in South Carolina, Georgia, and Alabama, and I write to request your assistance in removing the embarrassments. If we offer our loan, payable in current bank notes, New Orleans and Mobile will either send and make their subscriptions in Georgia and South Carolina, or if made at home will actually pay from 2 to 3 per cent more than those who subscribe where banks are suspended. To escape

this difficulty I have been compelled to direct that the bank paper shall be taken at its value in coin. But this exposes us to another difficulty, namely, that the subscribers will consider themselves paying a premium for the loan in making good the difference in value between coin and paper.

The only remedy which has occurred to me to obviate this difficulty, is to induce the banks to resolve that they will each redeem whatever amount of their paper may be taken for the loan. This will at once raise that paper to par, and will make the subscription payable in bank notes equal everywhere.[6]

Having thus stated the problem of the loan and its only remedy, the Secretary addressed a circular to the presidents of all banks suspending specie payments, earnestly recommending that each bank redeem in specie all notes paid in as subscriptions to the 15-Million Dollar Loan. The Secretary said:

It is true that this amounts to a virtual return in part to specie payments, but it is made to advance a great public interest, and the cost of providing specie for the entire loan would amount to less than $150,000, to be distributed amongst all the banks of the Southern Confederacy. But it will be far less than that to you, inasmuch as more than half the loan will probably come from the specie-paying States, and the real burden would not amount to more than $80,000, equivalent to an abatement on your annual dividends of about $\frac{1}{4}$ of 1 per cent. on your banking capital.[7]

Upon receipt of the circular, the suspending banks obligingly accepted the recommendation of the Secretary, and following the example of the Charleston and Savannah banks, resolved to redeem in coin any of their notes received in payment for subscriptions to the Confederate loan.

As a result of the banks' agreement to redeem at par, in specie, all their notes received by the Government in payment of subscriptions, interest in the loan again mounted.

To stimulate subscriptions, a Central Board of Commissioners, composed of the South's leading businessmen, was appointed in each state.[8] The Central Boards were requested to take entire charge of the subscription in their respective states and were given authority to name agents to open books at such interior places as were considered expedient while they themselves opened books in the principal cities where their offices were located.[9] Newspapers and banks heartily supported the loan and on April 17, the first

LOANS

day the books were opened, the five millions offered by the Treasury Department were immediately taken. By April 20 reports were received from a sufficient number of places to assure the Treasury that a much larger amount had been subscribed—an amount probably reaching eight millions. These figures were verified May 1, 1861, by Alexander B. Clitherall, Register of the Treasury.[10]

Following the outbreak of hostilities at Fort Sumter, Memminger wrote President Davis that due to the "present aspect of our relations [with the North] it is desirable to have control of as much money as can be raised, and I would therefore respectfully recommend that the Secretary of the Treasury be authorized to accept the whole amount which may be subscribed to the loan, instead of scaling down the subscription to the five millions called for in the advertisement of March, the 16th."[11]

Davis approved the recommendation and on April 22, 1861, the Commissioners appointed to receive subscriptions were informed that "The President . . . has determined to accept all Subscriptions to the Loan." Local Commissioners in each state were advised to reserve the original books, reporting copies thereof to the Central Board, and were reminded to receive payment of the subscriptions on or before the 1st of May, issuing receipts for the amount collected, which were to be taken up later upon the delivery of bonds or certificates of stock whenever they would be ready for delivery.[12]

No sooner had the books been closed for the first subscription than the rapidly mounting expenditures of the War Department necessitated an immediate call for the balance of the 15-Million Dollar Loan.[13] Memminger wrote to the Commissioners of the Loan, May 7, 1861, thanking them for their "zealous and effective services in procuring the amount already subscribed" and requesting them to renew their efforts to obtain the remainder. The Secretary said:

. . . The commercial community and the banks have already responded with patriotic alacrity; but they have means and loyalty which will doubtless respond again. The planting community are further removed from the centres of trade, and have not yet been reached. Permit me to suggest an effort on your part to bring the subject distinctly before them. . . . Please give notice that the books are again open . . . for subscriptions, and take such measures as, in your judgment, will be most effective in inducing the people . . . to come forward promptly. If . . . some gentlemen . . . would take the pains to explain the matter to the planting community, it would probably insure their cooperation. Few among them realize that a State Treasury, like their own rivers, will overflow by multiplying drops.[14]

Memminger apparently erred in his understanding of the planters' reticence to subscribe to the loan—the cause lay primarily in the "scarcity of money" as was attested by several commissioners when they wrote:

> Many of our planters of large means are not only willing but anxious to aid their country by taking the proposed loan, but, for want of money, they find it utterly impossible to do so. . . . We fear that we shall not be able to dispose of much more stock, unless the terms are in some way modified or relaxed. If you shall conclude to prescribe different terms from those under which we have heretofore acted, please let us know your wishes. . . .[15]

But despite a temporary lag in bringing forward the remainder of the loan, the Secretary of the Treasury did not think "any change necessary in the subscription scheme . . . adopted,"[16] and to compensate for the inability of the planters to take a portion of the loan, greater emphasis was placed on increasing the amount already subscribed by commercial and banking interests. These plans were aided by the entrance of Virginia, Tennessee, and North Carolina into the Confederacy.

To impress the urgent need for the loan upon these states, Boards of Commissioners, similar to those established in the original states of the Confederacy, were appointed to take charge of subscriptions,[17] and spokesmen for the Treasury Department addressed conventions of bankers and the state legislatures. Special commissioners were appointed to travel through the South speaking at courthouses and addressing public assemblies in the villages. As a result of these efforts, the commissioners appointed to receive subscriptions were notified on October 15, 1861, that the entire $15,000,000 had been taken up, and the Secretary extended "the thanks of the Government for the valuable services" which they "gratuitously rendered in taking the subscriptions."[18]

The success of the first Confederate Loan was unquestionably due to the support given it by the banks. Not only did they aid by redeeming, in specie at par value, all their notes used in the purchase of Government bonds, but they also donated the use of their offices for taking subscriptions and aided materially by individually subscribing to large amounts of the loan. By their support

LOANS

of the loan the banks lost control of a large amount of the specie held in the South—much of it finding its way abroad, presumably for the purchase of munitions.

According to J. C. Schwab, "The bonds of the 15-million loan were quoted at par in currency, till the middle of 1862; then they rose to 200, and ranged between 125 and 200 till January, 1865. In specie, the quotations were between 80 and 90 till the second quarter of 1862; then they fell to 33 by the winter of 1862-3, and to 20, 17, 10, 7, and 6 during successive quarters."[19]

Produce Loans

Having turned to loans as the chief source of revenue, Memminger was nevertheless skeptical as to the advisability of attempting to float another before the next crop provided the planters with funds. Having this in mind, he recommended to Congress the adoption of a $50,000,000, 8% bond issue, with the Government accepting from the investors the "tender of any resources available as a means of credit." This recommendation pointed towards a produce loan. But having observed by this time the difficulty of providing immediate funds by taxation and bond issues, the Secretary also recommended the issue of Treasury notes in anticipation of such revenue.

Congress showed its early willingness to adhere rather closely to the recommendations of the Secretary of the Treasury and by the Act of May 16, 1861, authorized the Secretary to issue $50,000,000 in bonds, payable at the expiration of 20 years from their date, and bearing a rate of interest not exceeding 8% per annum, the interest to be paid semi-annually. The bonds (after public advertisement in three newspapers within the Confederate States for six weeks) were *"to be sold for specie, military stores, or for the proceeds of sales of raw produce or manufactured articles, to be paid in the form of specie or with foreign bills of exchange."* The bonds were not to be exchanged "for Treasury notes, or the notes of any bank, corporation, or individual."[20]

Under the same act, Congress authorized for immediate use, in lieu of $20,000,000 of the bonds, the issuance of that amount in non-interest-bearing Treasury notes, redeemable in specie in two years. The notes were to be accepted by the Government in payment of all taxes except the export duty on cotton. They could be reissued, and were exchangeable at par for 10-year 8% bonds. It is evident from this early loan that Congress soon learned the popularity of a paper money policy, and most subsequent loans were accompanied by an issue of Treasury notes.

The new loan, like its antecedent, was aimed at acquiring specie, but whereas the 15-Million Dollar Loan had been directed at the bankers and commercial interests, the 50-Million Dollar Loan, being in part a produce loan, was brought more specifically to the attention of planters and farmers. Memminger was well aware that most persons in the Confederacy had no available money, but that they did possess cotton, tobacco, and other essential provisions and were willing to lend a portion of these for the Government's support.[21] As an aid in promoting the act authorizing the issue of bonds "for the proceeds of the sale of raw produce, or manufactured articles," it was considered advisable to circulate, in advance of the sale of the crops, subscription lists on which every planter could indicate the portion of his crop, the net (specie) proceeds of which he was willing to lend to the Government. The Treasury Department expected, by means of hypothecation, to use these anticipated receipts as a basis for establishing credit at home and abroad. Measures were immediately taken to canvass the rural areas for subscriptions, payable from the proceeds of the growing crops. Two types of lists were prepared, one for subscriptions of cotton and tobacco and the other for subscriptions of provisions and military stores. Copies of both lists were "placed in the hands of all members of the Confederate Congress" to be circulated among their constituents.[22] In addition to the congressmen, many prominent local residents were commissioned to circulate the lists in an effort to increase the number of subscriptions to the loan.

The lists were self-explanatory, the subscriber agreeing to contribute to the defense of the Confederate States a portion of his crop. The cotton was to be placed in a warehouse, or in a factor's hands, and sold by the planter on or before a fixed day. The net proceeds of the amount subscribed, less all charges, were to be paid to the Treasury of the Confederate States in specie in exchange for 20-year bonds bearing 8% interest.[23] Upon these pledged subscriptions the Government hoped to realize at once funds for its immediate necessities.

Origin of the Produce Loan

The origin of the Produce Loan, as an instrument to aid the Confederacy in acquiring funds, has given rise to controversy. Edward A. Pollard claims President Davis originated the scheme, but at the same time admits that "Mr. Davis, with an effort at modesty, has referred to this measure as 'one happily devised by the superior wisdom of Congress.' "[24] Additional evidence points to the responsibility of Congress for the idea. On May 6, 1861, Congress resolved that the Committee on Finance inquire into the advisability of adopting a system of finance based on:

> ... the soliciting of subscriptions of cotton, tobacco ... and sugar by agents appointed for this purpose. ... Said products to be sold for and on account of the Government, and the net amount to be accounted for the subscribers, respectively in Treasury notes or bonds. The Treasury notes and bonds to be made ... receivable for all public dues except the export duty on cotton, and to be made legal tender in the payment of all debts. ....[25]

Before action could be taken on the resolution, however, Congress, abiding by the recommendations submitted by the Secretary of the Treasury, approved the $50-Million Loan May 16, 1861, embodying the original form for the Produce Loan. This indicates Memminger to have been originator of the Produce Loan and is substantiated by Henry Capers, contemporary biographer of the Secretary, who claims, "He [Memminger] recommended still another expedient to reduce the volume of currency by dispensing with the use of Treasury notes as much as possible in the purchase of produce, and using bonds in exchange for all articles needed as supplies for the Government. This was known as the 'Produce Loan.' "[26]

Numerous other suggestions, however, were made to the Government about this time regarding various forms of a Produce Loan;[27] thus, it would appear that the establishment of the Produce Loan was not the idea of any one person but really the logical conclusion of an agricultural society.

Almost from its inception, until January 1862, it was managed gratuitously by James Dunwoody Brownson DeBow who "matured ... the whole plan of the Loan, the blanks, etc."[28] As Chief Commissioner, he maintained a separate office for the "loan" in Richmond. The handsomely furnished rooms became the "rendezvous of politicians" where "progress of the subscriptions was watched with the greatest solicitude." Newspaper reporters visited the office frequently and "published the list of subscriptions to excite the competition of particular districts."[29]

To arouse interest in the loan, rallies and assemblies were held throughout the South.³⁰ All efforts expended by the commissioners in promoting subscriptions were originally to be voluntary and gratuitous, for according to Memminger:

If these persons are paid it will destroy the whole value of their efforts. The people will not believe in a paid agent. The whole thing must be a work of patriotism. The agent himself must feel that he is above suspicion of self. Men must be procured who, like ourselves, are willing to spend their time and means for the country, and such men will command the confidence of all who hear them. . . .³¹

Playing upon the patriotism of the people and the merits of the Government bonds, the commissioners were soon able to bring forth gratifying results. The Treasury Department received numerous reports of the wholehearted manner in which planters were subscribing to the loan. Subscriptions ranged from one-fourth to offers of the whole crop, and there were instances in which subscriptions were to remain in effect yearly, during the course of the war. That the loan was well received throughout the South is indicated in a letter from Memminger to John A. Jordan:

I am pleased to learn that the prospects of the subscriptions are so favorable in your section. The Government is cheered by similar reports from every quarter and the people seem to be vying with each other in a noble rivalry of patriotic zeal and liberality. The thanks of this Department are due for the prompt efficiency with which you have organized the subscription canvass in your States.³²

The early success of the Produce Loan was also echoed by President Davis in an address to the Provisional Congress:

In the single article of cotton, the subscriptions to the loan proposed by the Government cannot fall short of fifty millions of dollars, and will probably exceed that amount; and scarcely an article required for the consumption of the Army is provided otherwise than by subscription to the produce loan. . . .³³

100-Million Dollar Loan—The Second Form

On August 19, 1861, Congress extended the Produce Loan by authorizing the 100-Million Dollar Loan.³⁴ Under this act, bonds of the type issued under the $50-Million Loan were increased to $100,000,000. This, the second form of the Produce Loan, differed only slightly from its predecessor, which it now embodied. The act approved funding the loan by placing a War Tax on property, payable in gold, silver, or Treasury notes. Unlike the

LOANS

50-Million Dollar Loan of May 16, 1861, it sanctioned the receipt of Treasury notes, as well as specie and foreign bills of exchange, in fulfilling subscriptions to the Produce Loan. The purpose of this new legislation was twofold: first, to continue to establish a basis for credit at home and abroad through additional subscriptions of the net proceeds of produce; and second, because of the inflationary tendency of the currency, to act as a stabilizer—an absorber for the surplus Treasury notes. To effect the latter, the act authorized the acceptance of Treasury notes "in payment for net proceeds of sales of raw produce and manufactured articles" subscribed to the Produce Loan and also permitted holders of Treasury notes to fund them in 8% 20-year bonds.[35] As a stabilizer of the currency, however, the loan proved a failure, and every succeeding attempt of Congress to provoke a favorable currency reaction met a similar fate.

Bonds of the new loan, valued at $50,000,000, were expected to be taken up by subscriptions to the Produce Loan. In this way the Government hoped to continue to secure a large portion of its supplies without further derangement of the currency. Notices of the loan calling for additional subscriptions of the net proceeds of the various crops and provisions appeared in the leading newspapers, but as the year 1861 drew to a close, reports of subscriptions to the loan became fewer. Nevertheless, efforts of commissioners and agents to raise subscriptions of produce during the first year proved reasonably successful. DeBow, Chief Commissioner of the loan, in issuing the first report of the Produce Loan Office, indicated the following as the nearest approximation of its achievements in consequence of the one-quarter, one-half, and two-third crops that were subscribed in numerous cases:

Alabama	125,000 bales cotton	
Arkansas	26,000 bales cotton	3,500 hhds. sugar
Georgia	75,000 bales cotton	150,000 bu. rice
Louisiana	28,000 bales cotton	3,500 bbls. molasses
Mississippi	120,000 bales cotton	
South Carolina	25,000 bales cotton	120,000 bu. rice
Tennessee	3,000 bales cotton	
Texas	15,000 bales cotton	
Virginia		(5,000 bu. wheat
		(1,000 hhds. tobacco
	417,000 bales cotton	

CONFEDERATE FINANCE

In addition, about a half-million dollars in Treasury notes was subscribed together with about the same value in other produce.[36]

Problems of the Produce Loan

While agricultural communities were contributing to the loan and Confederate authorities were expressing satisfaction over the mounting subscriptions of produce, another side of the story was being unfolded. Serious problems arose early and had to be solved if the loan was to approximate the degree of success predicted for it. As the Federal blockade became more effective, many prospective subscribers feared that the existing Produce Loan plan calling for payment of the subscribed portion of the crop on a fixed day was a financial trick—one by which the Government could compel a forced sale at prices ruinous to the planters.[37] Numerous complaints were filed with the Secretary, some expressing opposition to a specific day for satisfying subscriptions to the loans,[38] others expressing fear of a forced or compulsory sale.[39]

In an attempt to alleviate these fears, Memminger wrote to General W. W. Harllee:

> The inquiries you made as to the appointment of a day of sale in the subscriptions have been made by several other gentlemen, and for the information of all I think it would be best to make this letter public. The whole scheme of this subscription act . . . assumes that the blockade will not be continued through the winter. The date of sale mentioned in the subscription was left optional with the subscriber. It intends merely to name the time when the crops of that region are usually sold and no one contemplated or desired a forced sale. An attempt to sell while the ports remain blockaded would injure both the Government and owner. The subscription, being of net proceeds, would be destructive of its object to call for a sale when the market was closed. You may, therefore, assure all subscribers that they need be under no apprehensions on this score.
>
> If the blockade be not broken, the crop will remain unsold and neither the owner nor the Government will realize any proceeds of sale until that difficulty be removed. If this difficulty should remain permanent, or if there should be reasonable ground to apprehend the continuance of the blockade, it will become proper to adopt some other scheme of finance providing for that contingency.[40]

As the blockade continued and the planters became harder pressed for funds, another "scheme of finance providing for that contingency" was urged. From all sides came proposals for the

Government to buy the whole cotton crop and any other produce it needed, paying the average price of the last five years, and giving its bonds and Treasury notes in exchange, thus saving the debtor planters from the throes of bankruptcy.[41] To assure Government aid, the planters stressed that only by Government ownership of the entire crop could "King Cotton" really perform "its right function in the war"—that of "keep[ing] the nations of the continent and Great Britain in their good behavior towards us."[42] Other proposals importuned the Government "to simply make an advance to the planters, taking a lien on the crop in exchange."[43] At conventions of the cotton planters, resolutions were frequently passed calling upon the Government to issue notes and buy at least a part of the crop.[44]

To these numerous proposals the Secretary replied, "Congress has only authorized the exchange of the proceeds of the crops for the Government paper; not the purchase of produce,"[45] and added that:

Congress has not deemed it expedient to receive IN KIND the agricultural produce of the country [in exchange for Government Bonds]. The plan adopted is simply a subscription by the planters of the proceeds of their crops, when sold, in exchange for bonds of the Government. This plan presumes a sale. If the blockade, or any other cause, should postpone the sale, the subscriptions, of course, will remain suspended. How far, in that case, it may be expedient for the Government to make an advance to the planters is a very grave question upon which there are differences of opinion.[46]

Memminger was originally inclined to favor an advance and stated he was "endeavoring to mature a plan for lending the credit of the Government to the planters in the shape of an advance of Treasury notes, based upon the value of cotton." This, he believed, would give to the planters "all the advantages without the evils of a bank."[47]

The plan, however, failed to materialize at that time, and after further consideration of the proposals, Memminger reported that Government aid to the planter class would be unconstitutional. In a circular of October 15, 1861 to "The Commissioners Appointed to Receive Subscriptions to the Produce Loan," the Secretary declared the Government's policy was determined by its Constitution, and that under that organ "no power is granted to any Department to lend money for relief of any interest"; that the "power of Congress regarding money is limited to borrowing, and no clause can be found which would sanction so stupendous a scheme as purchasing the entire crop of cotton with a view to aid owners." The Secretary then showed such a scheme would cost 100 to 175 millions in additional Treasury notes, and would wreck the Government's finances at the beginning of what appeared to be a gigantic war. Recommending that the planters turn their attention to remedies other than Government aid, he suggested they divert a portion of their labor from raising cotton to making clothes and other supplies, prepare winter crops to ease the grain shortage, and, finally, if emergencies should demand funds, rely on the great resource of money capital in banks and private hands for individual loans.

Congress, abiding by the recommendations of the Secretary of the Treasury, refrained from legislating any measures insuring relief to the planters. Aid to the latter, however, was not to be denied, and the help refused by the Provisional Congress was soon "freely provided" by various state governments.

Mississippi, pioneering the activity, had memorialized Congress on August 2, 1861, to afford "the planters a market for their cotton and tobacco crops by the purchase of the same" or make liberal advances of Treasury notes so "the planters and others" may "carry on their business without interruption or material embarrassment during the war." The memorial added, "Such action would give the government control over a large supply of cotton with which it could coerce the Federal government into peace." But the Confederate Government remained unconvinced of the necessity for its aid to the planters, and in the winter of 1861-62, Mississippi authorized large amounts of state treasury notes to be advanced on cotton at 5 cents a pound, approximately one-half its market value, taking a lien on the crop in exchange. The cotton was to remain on the plantations.

A similar scheme for the relief of the planters was attempted in Louisiana. The original plan called for the issuance of ten millions in state treasury notes. This was then lowered to seven millions, but to the disgust of the planters and the approval of the bankers and cotton factors in New Orleans, it was vetoed by the governor. With the continuation of hostilities, other states, in an effort to gain financial relief, reacted as did Mississippi. North Carolina and Texas issued bonds and treasury notes based on the security of cotton. Expecting to redeem their bonds and treasury notes with receipts from the sale of cotton, the individual states carried on operations at home and abroad. These operations interfered with the similar cotton speculation carried on simultaneously by the Confederacy and gave rise to conflicts between the competing states and the Government.

The result of these conflicting activities was to weaken further the Confederate financial system by increasing an already redundant note currency and by jeopardizing the success of the Confederate Produce Loan—the Government's original instrument for stabilizing its finances.

Organization for Collecting Subscriptions to the Produce Loan; Its Operation

As 1862 got under way, reports were frequently circulated that planters were selling the produce they had subscribed to the loan. The Government, in an effort to insure its receipt of the subscribed portion of net proceeds, hurriedly completed plans for making collections. Adopting the arrangements made by DeBow, the Government established an organization to collect subscriptions. Explaining the organization, Memminger said:

> A principal agent or broker will be appointed at each of the principal cities where subscriptions are payable. These agents will take charge of all the subscriptions payable at that place, and also at all other places within the same State, and shall appoint subordinate agents, subject to the approval of the Secretary of the Treasury, to collect any subscriptions which may be payable at such other places; and shall superintend and direct the action of such subordinates, and cause them to account with him weekly, and shall require them to pay over weekly to such Assistant Treasurer or depositary as he shall designate, all moneys collected by them. . . .
>
> Each agent shall, on receiving payment of a subscription, issue to the subscriber a receipt exchangeable for stock or bonds. . . . These receipts shall be reported by each subordinate to this principal and by each principal to the nearest Assistant Treasurer or Depositary, and the money received shall be paid over to such Assistant Treasurer or Depositary. The Assistant Treasurer or Depositary shall deliver in exchange for such receipts the bonds or stock which they call for, and the respective agents who received the subscription shall be bound as part of the service paid for by their commission, to apply for the bonds and stock, and exchange them with the parties holding the receipts. The compensation of all the agents, both principal and subordinate, shall be a brokerage to be deducted from the amounts collected by them. . . .[48]

Having completed arrangements for collecting subscriptions, J. D. B. DeBow resigned as Chief Commissioner of the Produce Loan Office and two weeks later, January 17, 1862, accepted appointment as "General Agent to collect proceeds from the sale of subscriptions to the Produce Loan" for the city of New Orleans.[49] In announcing DeBow's resignation, Memminger insisted that the "new and onerous" duties of the Produce Loan Office be placed under the management of Robert Tyler,[50] Register of the Treasury, and he recommended that "a chief clerk with a salary of $1,500 should have the chief charge of the business, with one or two clerks under him" at a salary of $1,000.[51] In assuming the superintendence of the Produce Loan, the Register of the Treasury, believing the chief clerk "should be a gentleman of education, capacity, and integrity," submitted the name of Archibald Roane of the First Auditor's Office.[52] Memminger approved Tyler's request, and on January 21, 1862 informed Roane that "he was transferred from the office of First Auditor to the produce loan bureau, of which he will act as chief clerk" and he was instructed "to prepare a copy of the list of subscriptions for each general agency."[53]

Each General Agent was then forwarded a list covering all the subscriptions taken to the loan in his state. Accompanying each list were detailed instructions for the direction and compensation of agents collecting subscriptions.[54]

Desiring funds in England predicated upon the Produce Loan, Memminger instructed the General Agents to ascertain whether any merchants in their districts could give to the Treasury Department "a credit in England, secured by the deposit of cotton in this country, . . . upon a pledge that the cotton would be shipped to the house making the advance upon the removal of the blockade."[55] If this could be effected, the Secretary proposed that the agents procure the cotton from subscribers to the loan. "In making the purchases," he said, "it would be desirable to induce the subscribers to the produce loan to let you have, at the market price, the portion of crop which they had subscribed, and thus close the subscription. . . . You will readily perceive the advantage of exchanging the credit of the Government in a bond for commodities which will be available for foreign purchase. . . ."[56]

Having learned of these desires of the Secretary of the Treasury, the editor of the *Richmond Enquirer* wrote that a project favorably entertained by the highest authorities was under way whereby

LOANS

"It is proposed that the Government take all the cotton subscribed under the produce loan act at . . . some . . . fair price, and as much more cotton as may be subscribed on the same terms" giving Government bonds in payment. Commissioners were "to be sent to Europe with full powers to negotiate the sale of the cotton, or to make it the basis of a treaty alliance with Louis Napoleon." The editor said:

It is believed that if a million bales of cotton could be offered at a fair price, to meet the demand in France, that Government would purchase it on delivery in this country. This would necessitate the Emperor to raise the blockade and take possession of the purchase. . . .[57]

Motivated primarily by his desire to borrow funds in Europe and also hoping to induce foreign aid in raising the blockade and at the same time quiet the incessant demands of the planters to have the Government purchase the cotton and tobacco crops, Memminger recommended that Congress authorize the acceptance of articles in kind subscribed to the Produce Loan in exchange for bonds.[58]

250-MILLION DOLLAR LOAN—EXTENSION OF THE PRODUCE LOAN: THE FINAL FORM

On April 18, 1862, Congress extended the amount of Treasury notes, stocks, and bonds issued under the acts of August 19 and December 19, 1861 to $250,000,000, and three days later adopted Memminger's recommendation to accept articles in kind subscribed to the Produce Loan in exchange for the bonds.[59] Under "An Act to authorize the exchange of bonds for articles in kind, and the shipment, sale, or hypothecation of such articles," the Secretary of the Treasury was authorized "to exchange bonds or stock of the Confederate States for any articles in kind, required by the Government." Officers of the Commissary were directed "to receive, at the place of purchase, all such articles applicable to their Department, and apply same as though purchased by themselves." Section 3 of the act authorized the Secretary:

. . . to accept . . . in exchange for the said bonds or stock, cotton, tobacco, and other agriculture products in kind, which have been subscribed to the Produce Loan, or which may be subscribed in kind at such rates as may be adjusted between parties and the agents of the Government. *Provided,* That in no event shall he receive of cotton or tobacco, a greater value than $35 millions, and the said Secretary is further authorized to deposit the same at such places as he shall deem proper, and to procure advances thereon by hypothecation, or to ship the same abroad, or to sell the same at home or abroad as he may deem best; and, to assist these operations, the said Secretary may issue *PRODUCE CERTIFICATES,* which shall entitle the party to whom issued, or his endorsee, to receive the produce therein set forth, and to ship the same to any neutral port, in conformity with the laws of the Confederate States.[60]

Procuring Articles in Kind under Act of April 21, 1862

On May 21, 1862, detailed regulations were issued to the Produce Loan Agents indicating under what conditions subscriptions in kind would be accepted for 8% bonds of the Confederate states.

Under the new regulations, efforts of the Agents were to be directed almost entirely to the purchase of cotton with bonds. Any subscriber to the Produce Loan was permitted to pay the value of his subscriptions in either Treasury notes or articles in kind, both being receivable in exchange for Government bonds or certificates of stock. In case a state had made an advance on the cotton, the lien had to be removed by the planter immediately on sale to the Government. With cotton "being of a character useful to the Army or susceptible of being made . . . a basis for credit and negotiation at home or abroad," agents were ordered "to proceed with vigor to . . . every part of the state where safe deposit can be had for cotton"[61] and "purchase with 8% bonds, . . . as much as you can get."[62] Market value of the cotton was ascertained from actual *bona fide* sales, or offers, and it varied from state to state and county to county, as the cotton was near or distant from market, or more or less exposed to the enemy.

With cotton selling at fair prices, the Treasury Department requested that subscriptions to the Produce Loan be paid. Agents urged all subscribers "to immediately perform their obligation" and "comply with their terms of subscription."[63] Planters were reminded that payment of subscriptions had originally been left to the discretion of the subscriber—"The suspension being allowed by the Government due to low prices and the desire to facilitate both the interest of subscriber and Government." Now, it was stated, the planter can dispose of his crop at fair prices and satisfy his obligations in one of two ways: Take bonds of the Government for the amount subscribed, or make a sale himself and pay the portion of net proceeds subscribed in exchange for bonds.[64] To facilitate Government purchases of cotton, Memminger suggested "sending agents throughout their districts . . . endeavor[ing] to procure new subscriptions while closing the old."[65] As the cotton season advanced, more earnest efforts were made to procure a further supply of cotton for the Government. The Secretary urged upon each General Agent "the expediency of districting the region and employing an expert cotton purchaser to go through each district and make purchases instead of waiting for bids."[66] Patriotism and devotion were also played upon and the merits of the 8% bonds were stressed in an attempt to induce planters to exchange their cotton for bonds.

As the supply of Confederate funds in Europe was nearing exhaustion, difficulties in procuring additional foreign exchange mounted. Striving to overcome these difficulties, Memminger suggested "that purchases be made of a sufficient amount of cotton to meet the balance due on [military] contracts," the cotton to be stored at convenient depots according to regulations of the Produce Loan, and certificates of ownership given to contractors by way of hypothecation. Cotton thus transferred to the contractors would be shipped as neutral property whenever it could run the blockade, "the proceeds of the cotton when sold in England to be placed to the credit of the contract."[67]

As the Produce Loan Agents proceeded with their purchasing operations, complaints were made by planters of the inequality of prices paid by the Government for cotton in different states and different parts of the same state. DeBow answered these charges:

The market price of cotton is determined by the competition of private buyers and where these are willing to give 12, 15 or 17 cents it has not been found that parties are inclined to accept a lower figure from the Government. This competition is again determined by the relative safety of the article from the torch and the enemy, and whilst capital is willing to bid 15 and 17 cents in the heart of South Carolina, Georgia, and Alabama, it has not approached those figures in sections further to the West.[68]

Many planters refused to sell their cotton and other produce to the Government unless part of the transaction was paid in negotiable Treasury notes rather than non-negotiable bonds. Learning of this, Memminger informed all agents, "You are instructed to make your purchases with Bonds as *far* as practicable and whenever parties selling refuse to receive payment entirely in Bonds you are authorized to make payment partly with cash not to exceed in any case more than one-half of the whole cost."[69]

Cotton Certificates

Temporarily overcoming the difficulties retarding the purchase of cotton under the Act of April 21, 1862, the Government was able to procure a considerable amount which it stored on plantations and in warehouses. Using the cotton as a basis for security, the Treasury Department issued Cotton Certificates which it hoped to sell in Europe and thereby acquire funds for its purchases abroad. The Cotton Certificates, adopted upon the suggestion of James M. Mason, Commissioner to Great Britain,[70] stipulated that the price of cotton be fixed at 5 pence sterling per pound, receivable in Europe, or "as much Confederate currency that would be required to purchase 5 pence sterling." Each certificate was to be issued for 20 bales of cotton, "deliverable at certain ports, instead of any port at option of the holder." Since most of the cotton was in the West, and also to protect against a large portion being demanded on the Atlantic Coast, "separate certificates were issued for Gulf and Atlantic ports, in amounts that could be delivered at each." The certificates were "demandable only after peace, and within six months thereafter," as it was "impossible to deliver cotton in any great amount till then." However, in the event a purchaser desired to run the blockade, the following clause was added to the certificate: "The Government further agrees to deliver cotton called for in this certificate at any time during the pending war, at any port within its possession (if practicable to transport the cotton to the port selected) upon the payment by the holder of the cost of transportation." In case a holder failed to make his demand within the period prescribed, the certificate was not forfeited, but the Government assumed "the option to deliver cotton or return the amount paid ... with interest of 6% from issue of certificate." To "guard against capture or loss of the certificates on the way to Europe, and also to give official supervision there," an additional formality required the signature of James M. Mason, Commissioner, Confederate States, London.[71]

The Treasury Department issued 1,500 of the Cotton Certificates, 1,000 deliverable at New Orleans or Mobile and 500 deliverable at Charleston or Savannah, each valued at $1,000.[72] The

LOANS

$1,500,000 in Cotton Certificates was delivered by Captain W. G. Crenshaw to Messrs. Fraser, Trenholm and Co., Depositaries, Liverpool, who had received instructions how to dispose of them.

Believing Cotton Certificates offered the best means for raising money abroad, Memminger informed the Secretary of Navy, S. R. Mallory, of this belief, adding:

. . . The embarrassment which my agents meet with is from being obliged to purchase with bonds. This difficulty could be removed by your placing at my disposal the money which you wish to remit to Europe. With that my agents would buy cotton, and upon these purchases, Cotton Certificates could be issued and sent to Europe and their proceeds placed to the credit of your agent in Europe.[73]

Upon Mallory's approval to place at Memminger's disposal appropriations made to the Navy Department for Naval supplies, the Secretary of the Treasury hastened to fill the Navy and War Departments' needs. To effect this, Memminger appointed J. B. Gladney, a Subordinate-Agent-at-Large, to purchase cotton in Mississippi. Writing to J. D. B. DeBow, General Agent for the State of Mississippi, Robert Tyler, Register of the Treasury, said: "Mr. Gladney has made some important contracts with the Navy and War Departments and cotton to be purchased by him is to be set apart and appropriated to the payment of these contracts until they are satisfied. This appointment is somewhat irregular, but it is made to meet a special case."[74] Adhering to this example, Memminger appointed the firm of J. T. Doswell and Company, Subordinate-Agent-at-Large in northern Mississippi, Tennessee, and part of Arkansas lying between the St. Francis and Mississippi rivers, "to fill contracts for military supplies, made by the Quartermaster General with Messrs. Walker, Harris, and Fowlkes."[75] The management of the Subordinate-Agents-at-Large came under the jurisdiction of the General Agent in whose area they operated. Their activities were guided by the general instructions sent to all Produce Loan and Purchasing Agents, with one exception; namely, because of the time limit for satisfying the War and Navy contracts with cotton, the Subordinate-Agents-at-Large were not "expected like other Sub-Agents to operate in a particular district," but were authorized to make the most advantageous purchases wherever they could within the limits described in their appointments. In order to identify cotton purchased by them, the Subordinate-Agents-at-Large were instructed to endorse their "name upon the Certificates of Transfer, and place some distinguishing mark upon the cotton itself to the end that it may as far as possible be used in payment of the contracts made . . . for military supplies."[76]

For all cotton purchased by the Special Agents, Cotton Certificates were placed in the depositories, to be drawn on in satisfying the contracts. These Cotton Certificates were "valued at the expense of purchase plus the fees of agents, plus the amount cotton had appreciated since the date of purchase."[77]

As the year 1862 drew to a close, the War Department, adopting the idea fostered by the Treasury, appointed its own Subordinate-Agents-at-Large in an attempt to expedite cotton purchases and complete contracts for supplies.[78] The result, however, was not the favorable one anticipated—rather, it was a demoralizing one. The operations of the various Subordinate-Agents-at-Large competed with those carried on by the Produce Loan Agents, and both, in turn, competed with the various state and private agencies. As competition increased, prices rose, and with the rise of prices, many planters again refused to sell their commodity, hoping for a still higher price.

In the Annual Report of the Produce Loan Office, issued January 9, 1863, Archibald Roane, Principal Clerk in charge of the Produce Loan Office, summarized the activities of that office. He showed the whole amount of subscriptions to the Produce Loan, taken chiefly in the year 1861, was:

Cotton, 431,347 bales, worth $50 per bale	$21,567,350.00
Cash	608,375.00
Miscellaneous	895,180.00
Total	$23,070,905.00

To this he added "new subscriptions taken during the past year upwards of $2,000,000, making the amount of the entire subscriptions a little over $25,000,000."

Because the market for cotton had been very limited, arising from the blockade and the general condition of the country, the amount of collections was not so large as first anticipated. The following statement indicates the total amount of subscriptions actually collected:

Georgia	$1,898,950.00
Alabama	1,421,670.00

LOANS

South Carolina	886,050.00
Louisiana and Mississippi	259,864.00
Florida	170,650.00
North Carolina	63,200.00
Texas	58,450.00
Virginia	19,200.00
Total Collected	$4,778,034.00
Add to above new subscriptions collected by Produce Loan Agents in South Carolina	2,854,010.00
Total Collected	$7,632,044.00

The above amount embraced "only the payment of cash subscriptions and the proceeds of the sale of produce consisting principally of cotton." In addition to this, reports received from Agents showed "about 5,000 bales, estimated to be worth $250,000, had been purchased by the Government for bonds from subscribers to the loan." This, added to the grand total above, gave $7,882,044 as the entire amount realized from subscriptions to the Produce Loan, or "nearly one-third of its whole amount."

The cost of collecting these subscriptions was "very small, amounting only to about $19,000, or less than one-third of one per cent."

Under the act of April 21, 1862, authorizing the Government to purchase cotton and tobacco, the following purchases were made by the several agents, up to the time of the annual report:

Statement

Purchases in Mississippi	38,212 bales, costing			$1,887,159.99
" " Alabama	21,545 "	"		1,735,058.91
" " Georgia	5,281 "	"		499,172.88
" " South Carolina	2,446 "	"		252,790.27
" " Arkansas	1,023 "	"		100,218.52
Total	68,507			$4,474,400.57

Of the above amount, $46,026.75 had been paid in Treasury notes and the remainder in bonds.

The average price paid for the purchases was about $.13½ per lb., varying in different states, the average being lowest in Mississippi and Arkansas. Future prices were expected to be "without doubt, considerably higher."

CONFEDERATE FINANCE

In concluding the Annual Report of the Produce Loan Office, Roane said that only a few purchases of tobacco, under the act of April 21, 1862, had been made because a large portion of the tobacco planting region had been invaded or was under threat of invasion by the enemy. A beginning, however, had been made with 128 hogsheads, costing $38,970.17, being purchased.[79]

With the start of the new year, operations under the act of August 19, 1861, remained retarded because of circumstances growing out of the state of war and the invasion and occupation of various portions of the Confederate States by the enemy, whereas activities of the agents appointed to purchase articles in kind with bonds under the act of April 21, 1862, went on unabated.

To increase purchases of cotton, DeBow advocated buying small lots that were previoulsy ignored. "By not purchasing *small* lots," he said, "the Government loses some of the *best* and *best located* cotton . . . and causes dissatisfaction among the smaller subscribers to the loan who are among the most reliable citizens." He also suggested "buying cotton not in marketable order . . . put up in boards and under shed" saying it was "no more liable to loss than other cotton" and "if the war lasts long—cotton in rope and bagging will suffer great deterioration."[80]

Memminger approved both suggestions, saying he desired all purchases of cotton in lots of less than 20 bales to be "aggregated as much as possible" and all unbaled cotton to be purchased "at a considerably reduced rate."[81]

As the blockade continued in effect, the Government's mounting supply of cotton was considered by some to be "a white elephant."[82] The Secretary of the Treasury, however, was well aware of its merits as a basis for floating a foreign loan and in January 1863 contracted with the French house of Emile Erlanger and Company to float a $15,000,000 loan in Europe. This was known as the Erlanger Loan.

THE ERLANGER LOAN

As early as October 28, 1862, a contract to float a foreign loan of £5-million sterling had been signed in Paris by the agent for the French House of Emile Erlanger and Company, and John Slidell, Agent for the Confederacy.[83] Upon receipt of the agreement in Richmond, Memminger modified the contract and finally, on January 8, 1863, an agreement for a £3-million sterling (15-million dollar) loan was completed with Messrs. Erlanger and Company of Paris through their attorney, Jules Beer. In compliance with the requests of the Secretary, Congress authorized bonds of the Confederate States valued at 75 million francs to be issued, payable 20 years after date, with coupons attached for payment of interest abroad at 7% per year, and also Certificates for delivery of cotton in exchange for the bonds.[84] To make the loan more attractive, Article 4 stated:

Each bond shall be, at the option of the holder convertible . . . into cotton at the rate of 6 pence sterling for each pound of cotton, i.e., 4,000 lbs. of cotton for each bond of £100, . . . and this at any time not later than 6 months after ratification of a treaty of peace between the present belligerents. Notice of the intention of converting bonds into cotton has to be given to the representatives of the Government in Paris or London, and 60 days after such notice the cotton will be delivered—if peace, in the ports of Charleston, Savannah, Mobile or New Orleans; if war, at points in the interior of the country, within 10 miles of a railroad or stream navigable to the ocean. The delivery will be made free of all charges and duties except the existing export duty of $\frac{1}{8}$ of 1 cent per lb. The quality of the cotton is to be the standard of New Orleans middling. If any cotton is of superior or inferior quality the difference in value of cotton shall be settled by two brokers, one to be appointed by the Government and the other by the bondholder. Whenever these two brokers cannot agree on the value, an umpire is to be chosen whose decision shall be final.[85]

The agreement further provided for a sinking fund of 5% whereby 2½% or 1/40 of the bonds unredeemed by cotton would be drawn by lot semi-annually so as finally to extinguish the loan in 20 years from date of the first drawing. The loan was sold to Erlanger and Company at the rate of £77 per £100, anything over £77 going to Erlanger,[86] who placed the bonds on the market at £90. The bankers were also allowed a commission of 5% and when the market value of the bonds started to drop were given additional Confederate funds to sustain it.

On learning of the Erlanger Loan through Mason, James Spence, who had been appointed Financial Agent to negotiate the "$1,500,000 worth of 8% Bonds and Cotton Certificates in England," immediately went to Fraser, Trenholm and Company for a general council. It was resolved that "management of all cotton [transactions] should be under Fraser and Co. to prevent the evils of competition." Having received no offers over 60% of the face value of the Bonds, Spence stopped selling at once because of the harm he felt the "varying rates of Bonds would offer to the success of the Erlanger Loan."[87]

Thus, with a clear field before it, the Erlanger Loan was placed on the market. Evidence of its early success is undeniable. Before the prospectus of the Loan had been issued, Wednesday evening, March 18, 1863, "business had already been done on a speculative account at 2¾ to 3% premium."[88] L. Q. C. Lamar writes, "The avidity with which the Confederate Loan has been taken up, both here [London] and on the continent, has caused great rejoicing among our friends and is claimed by them to be a financial recognition of the Confederacy." Lord Campbell, in the House of Lords, March 23, said:

> And is the issue doubtful? The capitalists of London, Frankfurt, Paris, Amsterdam, are not of that opinion. Within the last few days, the Southern loan has reached the highest place in our market: £3,000,000 were required, £9,000,000 were subscribed for. The loan is based upon the security of cotton. . . .[89]

The early success of the Erlanger Loan, however, was short-lived, and the loan soon assumed the aspects of a barometer of the Southern cause, for as the tide of battle rose and fell for the Confederacy the loan took similar fluctuations. With the news of Vicksburg, "the last lingering doubts about events on the Mississippi were removed." Henry Hotze writing of its effect on the Erlanger Loan said:

> . . . the loan, despite the utmost exertion of its friends, fell with accelerating velocity, at first to 8, then to 15, until it touched the unprecedented depth of 36. . . . The slightest causes affect it sensibly without adequate reasons. . . . You have here, in the tremulous condition of the loan, a sufficiently accurate description of the state of public opinion. . . . The hopes and sympathies of an almost unanimous people incline it in one direction; the facts, as they are here interpreted, impel it in the other. . . .[90]

By February 11, 1865, approximately 5/6 of the loan was sold, the Confederacy realizing up to that date $7,675,501.25, a trifle over one-half of the face value.[91]

The reverses on the Mississippi created new embarrassments for the Treasury, for with the fall of Vicksburg a large portion of the cotton in the West would doubtless be lost or destroyed, thus increasing the deficit in meeting outstanding obligations for cotton.[92]

With the $1,500,000 in Cotton Certificates and the Erlanger

LOANS

Loan all supported by cotton presumed to be on hand, it became necessary for agents of the Produce Loan Office to increase cotton purchases and also induce planters to satisfy their subscriptions to the Produce Loan, if the Government hoped to extend its borrowing capacity abroad. With the extension of purchasing operations, competition between buyers of the various agencies grew keener and prices continued to increase. In an attempt to delay the rise in prices, Government agents were instructed **February 5 to "suspend purchases for two weeks."**[93] At the close of the two weeks of suspended operations, the order to resume purchases was not issued. Agents soon reported "planters are anxious to sell" but expressed fear that "speculators will raise prices on the Government buyers" as soon as they take the field "although they haven't done so yet."[94] On March 6, 1863, the agents were directed to resume purchases of cotton and to "pay current market prices, if it cannot be obtained for less."[95] Subscribers to the Produce Loan were reminded that "the reason for postponing sale of produce, on account of the inadequacy of market prices, no longer exists," and they were now expected "to meet their engagements with the Government."[96]

Loan of February 20, 1863

Subscribers were informed that under the loan act of February 20, 1863, the subscription list payable in 8% bonds was closed as of that date[97] and in order to receive 8% bonds the subscription had to be paid on or before July 31, ensuing, as any subscriber paying after that date would receive 6% or 4% bonds, under the currency act of March 23, 1863, depending upon the date the subscription was finally paid.

But with prices on the increase, many planters continued to refuse to sell their crops, apparently waiting for a still higher price. If the Government was to procure sufficient cotton to support its securities, additional measures had to be adopted—these measures were not long in coming.

The Tax-in-Kind and the Produce Loan Office

On April 24, 1863, Congress authorized "An Act to lay taxes for the common defense and carry on the government of the Confederate States." This Tax-in-Kind, also known as the Tithe Tax, was to be paid on or before March 1, 1864.

The provisions of the act were of vital concern to the Produce

Loan Office, for every farmer or planter in the Confederate States was compelled to pay, along with other produce, 1/10 of his cotton and tobacco as a tax-in-kind. The cotton to be "ginned and packed in some secure manner," while the tobacco was to be "stripped and packed in boxes." The producer was required to deliver the cotton and tobacco to some Quartermaster's depot within 8 miles of his residence—a 50% penalty being applied for failure to do so.

Cotton thus collected was subject to the order of the Produce Loan Agents. It was marked, weighed, classified, and stored in the Quartermaster Depot, if it could be kept there safely and conveniently; otherwise, it was stored in some warehouse or covered building, in a safer locality, in a town, village, or at a railroad depot, or upon a neighboring plantation. At the end of each month, reports were made by the General Agents to the Produce Loan Office, setting forth the number of bales of cotton collected during the month, together with their weights, marks, numbers, quality, and places where stored. All agents collecting the Tithe Cotton were compensated at the same rate of commission on its value as though it had been purchased by them.[98]

Because of the increase in its duties and responsibilities, the Produce Loan Office, under the act of May 1, 1863, relating to the organization of the Treasury Department, was expanded into "a species of bureau under the conduct of the Chief Clerk,"[99] the Register of the Treasury being "exonerated from any further charge of its business."[100]

250-Million Dollar Loan of April 30, 1863—Cotton Bonds

In its effort to supplement the Government's cotton supply and at the same time stabilize the currency, Congress approved "An Act supplementary to 'an act to provide for the funding and further issue of Treasury notes,' " April 30, 1863.[101]

Under the act the Secretary of the Treasury was authorized to issue $250,000,000 in twenty-year 6% bonds. Attached to the bonds were interest coupons payable at the pleasure of the Government in coin, or in cotton of the quality of New Orleans middling—valued at six pence sterling per pound (1 bale of 500 lbs. at 12¢, or $60 in coin). The cotton was to be delivered at the ports of New Orleans, Savannah, Charleston, Mobile, Wilmington, Richmond, or Norfolk, under such regulations as the Secretary may establish. The bonds were to be sold for all outstanding Treasury notes, at not less than par value: Provided, the Secretary of the Treasury be authorized to apply the proceeds of as many of the bonds as would be required for the purchase of agricultural products under the act of Congress, approved April 21, 1862, entitled "An Act to authorize the exchange of bonds for articles in kind, and the shipment, sale or hypothecation of such articles."[102]

To prevent any hindrance in the purchasing operations of the Produce Loan Agents while the new bonds were "in the course of preparation," the agents were directed "to make purchases with cash payable in a month or 6 weeks by which time, you will be furnished with funds realized from the sale of the Bonds."[103]

Secretary Memminger gave every indication that he was skeptical of the ability of Cotton Bonds in their proposed form to attract funds. In answer to the request of S. R. Mallory, Secretary of the Navy, for additional means to satisfy Navy purchases in Europe, Memminger said:

If they [Cotton Bonds] could be sold at fair rates abroad they would furnish the means which you desire; but in the form stated in the Act of Congress, which reserves an option to the Government to pay in cotton or coin, I think they would not sell. . . . The payment of 6% per year in coin on this side of the Atlantic does not seem to me to offer to a foreign holder sufficient inducement.[104]

The Secretary believed the most practical way to acquire funds abroad was by shipping cotton or selling cotton certificates, upon the plans already adopted by the Treasury Department. In view of these considerations, he suggested:

. . . to sell as many of the [Cotton] bonds in this country as may be necessary to purchase the requisite amount of cotton, and thereupon to issue *Cotton Certificates* in the form already adopted and offer these for sale in the European market, and when they are sold others can be sent. . . .

The Secretary said:

. . . considerable time will be required to consummate these plans. Bonds are to be engraved and prepared, and more important the market must be prepared for their sale. Then the cotton must be purchased with the proceeds of sale, and afterwards Cotton Certificates must be forwarded to Europe and sold. . . .[105]

To prepare the market for Cotton Bonds, their financial advantages were explained in the leading newspapers of the South. The Bonds were to be issued in sums of $1,000 each, interest payable annually, on June 1st, at the rate of $60 in coin or 1 bale of cotton of New Orleans middling class. Editorials stated, "At present market rates such cotton at the ports is worth at least 3 times the price set in the bonds, thus, the actual interest received by the holder is equal to 18%." A comparable advantage was also shown to attach itself to the principal, which was payable in 20 years in coin, although "the purchase money is now paid in Confederate Notes," the purchaser thus gaining "all the advantage resulting from an investment of Treasury Notes in specie security." It was indicated "that these bonds possess an intrinsic value greatly exceeding any security yet offered by the Confederate Government."[106]

Pertaining to the merits of *The New Cotton Loan*, the *Charleston Mercury* stated:

Compared with other stock or bond issues it is far superior. . . . The $15,000,000 Loan pays 8% only. It cannot rise higher. Interest on the 15-million loan is paid in currency unless the holder can use interest coupons to pay the export duty on cotton, or will await the accumulation of that in coin. The bonds now issued will give an interest to be paid in a mode which absolutely fixes its value, for it must be paid at once in coin or cotton, at a price about 1/3 to 1/4 of its present market value.[107]

The *Mercury* pointed out that when bids are accepted for the new bonds a bidder paying $1,000 in Treasury notes would receive approximately 20% interest; one paying $2,000 would receive approximately 10% interest; and one paying $3,000 would receive 6% interest.[108]

As newspapers and agents prepared the market for $5,000,000 of Cotton Bonds, instructions for bids were sent from the Treasury Department. Sealed bids were to be received by the Secretary of the Treasury any time before 12 o'clock noon, July 20, 1863. Each bid endorsed "Bid for Cotton Bonds" was to enclose a certificate of deposit in the name of the treasurer for 1% of the purchase money. The deposit was to be returned if the bid was not accepted, and if accepted, it would be applied in part payment of the purchase money if terms were complied with, or forfeited if not complied with. Accepted bids were to be paid within 10 days' notice of acceptance, in current Treasury notes, at least one-half of which were of issues subsequent to April 1, 1863.[109]

At 2 p. m., July 20, 1863, the bids were opened in the offices of the Secretary of the Treasury. Due to "certain circumstances,"

Memminger considered it desirable to keep them temporarily secret and invited J. P. Benjamin, Secretary of State, and T. H. Watts, Attorney General, to witness the opening.[110]

The following day the press informed the public of the results. No bids under 50% premium were considered.[111] The offers accepted varied, with premiums ranging from 50 to 100%—the highest premium offered being 100%.[112] Pleased with results of the first sale of Cotton Bonds, the Treasury Department, striving to establish a fixed rate at which to sell the bonds in the future, immediately advertised for bids for an additional $5,000,000, the bids to close August 5, 1863.[113]

When the bids were opened, August 5, the rate for the remainder of the $250,000,000 of 6% Cotton interest bonds was fixed at 50% premium. Purchasers at that rate were sanctioned until September 18, 1863,[114] one-fourth of the purchase money being required in Treasury notes issued after April 1, 1863, the remainder payable in any non-interest-bearing Treasury notes.[115]

Using proceeds derived from the sale of Cotton Bonds, Produce Loan Agents endeavored to purchase more cotton in an attempt to alleviate the Government's increasing obligations. But as prices continued to rise along with the premium on coin, the established interest rates of the Cotton Bonds were considered by the Secretary as too lucrative an investment, and on December 10, 1863, the Assistant Treasurers and Pay Depositaries were ordered to stop the sale of cotton interest bonds,[116] and Produce Loan Agents were instructed to devote their time to preserving and checking on the security of all Government cotton sheltered in their areas.

As early as June 3, 1863, DeBow complained of the heavy losses to Government cotton in Mississippi, estimating that 25,000 bales or about 1/7 of the total purchased had been destroyed.[117] Following the fall of Vicksburg, more and more energy on the part of the agents was expended in an effort to make secure the cotton in exposed areas. In Mississippi and Louisiana, cotton was moved inland 10 to 15 miles from all navigable rivers. With railroads suspending indefinitely the shipment of cotton, General Agents requested authority to impress wagon-trains for its removal from exposed areas.[118] Special orders were also requested "restraining the soldiery from mutilating cotton not exposed to the enemy, except in cases where its transportation in enemy lines is possible."[119] It was recommended that temporary sheds be erected on plantations because the cotton would "be safer on the plantations than in warehouses, and less expensive."[120] General Agents visited different sections of their districts "in order to communicate personally with local agents, to look after the condition of Government cotton and make arrangements necessary to its preservation."[121] Despite the precautions taken by Government agents, as the year drew to a close, complaints of cotton falling into enemy hands were lodged with the authorities, and demands were made stating such cotton "should be burned and a proclamation issued directing all selling or trading with the enemy as treasonable and obnoxious to our cause."[122]

The Produce Loan During the Year 1864

With the start of 1864, Produce Loan Agents in exposed areas were ordered to stop buying cotton and devote their "time and energies to preserving the cotton already purchased," for there was "scarcely a day that some report was not made concerning the exposed condition of Government cotton."[123] The Secretary of the Treasury was "desirous that the condition of all cotton be looked into and repairs made where needed." He suggested that a special agent be appointed "to attend to that branch of business, and that he be instructed to use boards when rope and bagging cannot be attained" to put the cotton in marketable condition.[124]

To carry out the Secretary's recommendation, Special Travelling Agents were appointed in the exposed areas "to examine as far as practicable the condition of Government cotton, reporting their observations and helping General Agents with the removal of cotton." They were informed that the Government policy was to save all cotton "within or near the enemies lines by removal and to burn all such as cannot be removed and which may fall in [to] the hands of the enemy." The Special Agents were also ordered "to report all persons undertaking interference without authority with cotton or to traffick in any manner to the end that legal proceedings be had against them."[125]

Appointment of Special Agents, however, was not the answer for ending the illicit trafficking of Government cotton, nor was it the answer for preserving and securing the cotton. Reports of cotton rotting from being unsheltered continued, and cases of fraud, stealing, and illicit trade with the enemy increased in number.[126] Planters in exposed areas resold cotton they previously had sold to the Government. In an attempt to curb some of the lawlessness, liberal rewards were offered which would:

LOANS

. . . be paid for such evidence as will lead to the conviction of any parties engaged in unlawfully appropriating the Government Cotton . . . either by removing or secreting, converting it to their own use, or trading it with the enemy, or who may be guilty of gross and wanton neglect in taking care of cotton left in their charge by the Government.[127]

Regarding the illegal trade being carried on in the exposed area of Mississippi, T. J. Wharton wrote:

. . . As many as 23 wagons loaded with cotton . . . passed through the public streets of Jackson on the holy Sabbath, in view of the whole community. I am assured that, in the district between Raymond and Utica, women (I cannot call them *Ladies,* however respectable they may have been heretofore) mount their horses, and ride over the neighborhood, buying up cotton, to sell to the Yankees and invest the proceeds in merchandize [sic] such as coffee, clothing, and, in some instances, in every kind of luxury. Parties have been engaged in this illicit and demoralizing trade whom you know personally, and whose reputation would [shelter] them from the suspicion of even harboring a thought of engaging in such disgraceful transactions. The evil has not stopped with the sale of cotton owned by the parties, but very large amounts of Government cotton have been *stolen.* The heads with the marks removed, to prevent confiscation by the enemy and then sold at Big Block, in Vicksburg. . . .[128]

In response to the many reports of unsheltered cotton, illicit trade, stealing, and fraud, the House of Representatives resolved that an inquiry be made into the "condition of Government cotton contiguous to the Mississippi and its tributaries." Answering the inquiry, DeBow, General Agent for that area, wrote:

From every source of information it is certain that the cotton in the exposed district is in the most deplorable condition. Large plantations are abandoned everywhere and the cotton has been left in sheds. These tumble down or are blown down. Stray cattle destroy the cotton; soldiers, particularly cavalrys strip it of the ropes and bagging, or make use of it for beds, scattering it in every direction; fires are of frequent occurrence from accident or incendiarism; the poor of the country take away as much as they can make use of; runaway Negroes devastate; thieves, with whom the country abounds, carry off the cotton by wholesale, trading it to the Yankees or hiding it in inaccessible places. They do it at night or even in broad daylight as there is little law in the country. Even those who have sold their cotton to the Government, in their desperate fortunes, regarding themselves as beyond the protection or reach of the Confederacy, *sell it again to the Yankees,* upon the pretext that they will replace it out of the next crop, or out of cotton in other quarters! They justify the act by their necessities—there is reason to fear that soldiers are sometimes implicated in the guilt. Parties visit the section with forged powers, represent themselves as Gov't. agents and take away the cotton, using force if necessary. General demoralization prevails throughout much of the entire section, reaching to every class. *Trade with the enemy is universal.* The temptations to fraud are overwhelming. Even our own agents are often charged with complicity. I have endeavored to procure men familiar with the country and the best recommended. They report it to be impossible to prevent the depredations. . . .[129]

Numerous representations were made to the Secretary telling of the great quantities of cotton liable to capture which "could be disposed of to the advantage of the Government."[130] In answer to these representations the Treasury Department indicated a willingness to sell the cotton in exposed districts and promised that the Confederate authorities would not burn or interfere with it as long as it did not fall into the hands of the Government of the United States."[131]

Purchase, Transportation, and Sale of Government Cotton, 1864-65

The Produce Loan Agents, having been ordered to cease buying cotton and protect from the enemy the supply on hand, new arrangements were made for the purchase, transportation, and sale of Government cotton. To enable the War and Navy Departments to fulfill with cotton their contracts for military supplies, the new regulations entrusted the purchase of cotton and its transportation by land to the War Department, since all transportation was under its charge; the shipment and sale of cotton were entrusted to the Treasury Department together with the purchase of vessels; while the planning, building, and sailing of vessels were entrusted to the Navy Department.[132]

General Agents of the Produce Loan Office were ordered to communicate with the Quartermasters and with parties willing to furnish military supplies and thus facilitate the making of contracts without actually making them themselves. It was understood that all contracts of this kind were "to be paid for with lots of cotton in danger of falling into the hands of the enemy or so situated that they cannot be removed."[133] The shipment of the cotton sold under the contract was to be provided for by the Treasury Department.

Belatedly, Congress passed a bill, February 6, 1864, giving the Government authority to regulate foreign commerce. By this act the Government was permitted ½ the stowage, and in no case could a vessel sail with less than 1/3 of her cargo on account of the Government. In event the Government could not supply ½ the cotton cargo, the owners were compelled to allow the Government part of their own cotton for the 1/3 stowage.[134] State governors, who had acquired interests for their states in many of the ships, first asked, then demanded, exemption from the regulations. A bitter and long drawn out controversy developed. On March 3, Rep. Hartridge of Georgia introduced a resolution questioning the right of the Government to regulate shipping.[135] Finally, in March 1865, an act was passed exempting state-owned vessels from the provisions of the act.

The experience the Treasury Department derived from the regulation of commerce led it to conclude that the Government should make no more contracts payable in cotton. It was believed that because of the proportionally high price of cotton in Europe compared to the small risk incurred in sending it out, the Government would do well to ship the cotton on its own account and derive the whole benefit of the enhanced price rather than make contracts payable in cotton. Under the "New Plan" all future contracts were ordered to state that payments would be made from the proceeds of cotton to be realized on sale in Europe.[136]

In order to satisfy the cotton contracts outstanding against the Government in the last half of 1864, it was necessary, according to the new Secretary of the Treasury, George A. Trenholm,[137] to supply and ship 7,000 bales of cotton per month.[138] However, as ships arrived at the Confederate ports, the cotton was invariably in need of repacking; therefore, vessels frequently cleared the ports without the Government quota.

To prevent this loss of shipping arising from an insufficient supply of marketable cotton, and also to avoid unnecessary and injurious competition in making purchases, the Chief Clerk of the Produce Loan Office was ordered to confer with Col. Thomas L. Bayne, agent of the War Department, and arrange a plan whereby purchasing of cotton could concurrently be done by both the Produce Loan Agents and the agents of the War Department. Roane was informed that in order to keep an adequate supply of cotton for shipping "it was essential to contribute the aid of the Produce Loan Bureau both by applying to the purpose any cotton on hand in the Atlantic States and by new purchases."[139]

When the Produce Loan Agents again took the field in an attempt to supplement the purchases of cotton made by the War Department Agents, their success was marred by the unmarketable condition of cotton in most of the states. Because of the scarcity of burlap and rope, the last crop in many cases remained unbaled, and the older crops which had been in marketable order were bursting and unfit to transport. In only two states, North Carolina and Alabama, was the cotton well sheltered and in marketable condition. Delays occurred in obtaining its transportation to the railroad depots, and then, while at the depots, additional delays occurred before it reached the ports, the railroads being engaged almost exclusively in bringing forward supplies for the Army.

On November 10, 1864, the Produce Loan Bureau issued its last annual report showing the following business as having been concluded by that branch of the Treasury Department:

The original subscriptions to the Produce Loan amounted to	$28,070,905
The amount collected to date	16,897,000
The amount still unpaid	$11,173,095

Further subscriptions were subsequently received and collected in the amount of $17,579,400, forming with the foregoing sum a total of $34,476,400 collected.[140]

Under the act of April 21, 1862, authorizing the purchase of cotton and tobacco, the purchases of tobacco were comparatively unimportant, the total being $1,462,558.93; of cotton, however, they were of great magnitude, the quantity of cotton purchased being 430,724 bales at a cost of $34,525,219.40. From this must be deducted the following:

	Bales
Lost by capture, burnt by C. S. A. authorities, and used for military purposes	129,771
West of Miss., and subject to be used for military purposes	67,653
Sold by the Treasury Department	6,961
Shipped to Eng. in payment of the foreign debt, and for general purposes	19,683
Expended in payment of cotton coupons	607

LOANS

Expended for Army supplies	15,000
	239,675
Which, deducted from the quantity purchased, leaves a remainder of	191,049
To which should be added for the estimated yield of the tithe	15,000
Total on hand	206,049

The report stated that notwithstanding the deficiency occasioned by the large quantity lost and appropriated to military purposes, there was no pecuniary loss, the cotton on hand being sufficient at the increased value, to reimburse the cost of the entire purchase. The value of 191,049 bales, at fifty cents per pound, was $38,000,000.[141]

GOVERNMENT COTTON AND TOBACCO FOLLOWING THE COLLAPSE OF THE CONFEDERACY

The question has often been asked, "What became of the Government cotton and tobacco upon the collapse of the Confederacy?" The following is offered as a partial answer.

Upon the surrender of the Confederate military, all cotton and tobacco owned by the Confederate States of America was to be seized by the United States Government and placed under the supervision of Hugh McCulloch, Secretary of the Treasury of the United States. Special agents of the Federal Treasury Department were engaged in the work of collecting it.[142] McCulloch hoped that all agents so engaged would "work harmoniously together to the end that *all* this cotton, wherever, and by whomever found, shall be secured to the U. S. with the least possible cost and delay."[143]

There is evidence, however, that *all* cotton belonging to the Confederacy did not reach the hands of the United States Government. In the correspondence of Charles Baskerville (Produce Loan Agent) to DeBow, the former implied that certain agents for the Produce Loan enriched themselves with some of the cotton. Baskerville wrote, "It seems that all the Cotton agents have abundant fortunes—the reapings from our labor."[144] Whether this inference bears any truth may never be known.

Nevertheless, it is known that in the very last stages of the war some of the Confederate authorities received tobacco, cotton, and other property in payment of individual debts contracted in behalf of the Confederacy. John T. Pickett, Confederate envoy to Mexico, received 2,769 boxes of tobacco in this fashion, which he immediately sold to William H. Warder for sterling bills of exchange, because he knew of Warder's "connection with a mercantile house of the highest respectability in New York," and because he had evidence of Warder's "being within the Confederate lines with the knowledge and consent of President Lincoln."[145]

Be these and other comparable incidents what they may, a great portion of Confederate cotton and tobacco was acquired by the United States Government, and with its acquisition came numerous demands from Europeans for the United States to fulfill the obligations stipulated in the various Confederate bonds which had been sold with the seized cotton as security. The United States Government, however, refused to comply with any of these claims, stating that according to the 14th Amendment to the United States Constitution:

... Neither the United States, nor any State, shall assume or pay any debt or obligation incurred in aid of insurrection or rebellion against the United States ... but all such debts shall be held illegal and void. ...[146]

In further explanation of the legality of its refusal to allow the foreign claims, the United States Government added:

Not only according to the U. S. law were the Bonds issued for an illegal and improper purpose, but in view of the law by which they must be judged, the usurping State Governments and the Confederacy were illegal corporations. If, therefore, the Confederacy was illegal, all acts were illegal; and as an illegal corporation, it could have no legal successor. It would seem, therefore, that all . . . Bonds were according to the U. S. law, that is, according to the only law that can take cognisance of them, illegally issued by an illegal corporation unknown to law and unauthorized by it, and as such have NO legal validity whatever, as Confederate Debt, against the U. S. or the present State Governments of the South.[147]

Summary of the Produce Loans

With the collapse of the Confederacy, the Produce Loans and the Produce Loan Office came to an end. Their primary purpose, as indicated, was that of procuring the means (at home and abroad) to purchase the critical supplies necessary for the Government's existence. The expanding duties of the Produce Loan

LOANS

Office encompassed the collecting of produce subscriptions under the loan acts of May 16 and August 19, 1861, and later entailed the purchase of cotton and tobacco for Government use as authorized by the act of April 21, 1862. Through its various operations, the Produce Loan Office endeavored to become a stabilizing instrument in the Government's financial policy. Acting as a curb on the inflated Treasury note currency, it attempted to prevent the growing redundancy of notes by withdrawing them from circulation, issuing long-term bonds in exchange. The Produce Loan Office also attempted to curb inflation of the Treasury note currency by paying for its purchases with Government Bonds.

As the responsibilities of the office increased with the assumption of control over the cotton, wool, and tobacco derived from the Tithe Tax, its status was raised, May 1, 1863, to that of a Bureau. In the final stages of the war, the entire efforts of the Bureau were expended in preserving the Government cotton in exposed areas, and selling that which was most likely to fall into enemy hands.

The full influence of the Produce Loans and the Produce Loan Office is impossible to relate. Monetarily, it can be estimated as follows:

Total income from Original Subscriptions to the Produce Loan, Act of May 16, 1861	$16,897,000.00
Total income from New Subscriptions to the Produce Loan, Act of August 19, 1861	17,579,400.00
Total income from the Produce Loans	$34,476,400.00
Total amount of produce received in exchange for bonds, Act of April 21, 1862	35,987,778.33
Estimated income from Tithe Tax, 15,000 bales at $75	1,125,000.00
Total business of the Produce Loan Office	$71,589,178.33

This sum, however, falls far short of indicating the true worth of the Produce Loan Office, for many of its activities are immeasurable in their intrinsic value. This is apparent by asking a few questions.

What would have been the effect on the Government's paper currency had the Produce Loan Office not been able to withdraw $34,476,400 in Treasury notes from circulation in exchange for bonds secured with cotton?

What would have been the result had the Produce Loans not

supplied cotton as security for the Erlanger Loan, from which the Government realized $7,678,501.25 in foreign exchange at a time when its funds in Europe were totally exhausted?

What would have been the result had the Produce Loans not supplied cotton for interest on the $8,372,000 of Cotton Bonds issued under the act of April 30, 1863, or established security for Cotton Certificates?

Too, what would have been the result had the Produce Loan Office failed to supply cotton to satisfy contracts for military and naval supplies under the Government's "New Plan" during the last year of hostilities?

The answers to these and similar questions are of course conjectural and it is not expected that definite answers be given—the questions have been raised simply to suggest the full significance of the Produce Loans and the Produce Loan Office as a means of financing the Confederacy.

Funding Loans

During the fall of 1862, the Confederate Congress approved the first of a series of three funding measures aimed at reducing the currency and preventing its redundancy by withdrawing Treasury notes from circulation, giving holders of the notes long-term interest-bearing bonds in exchange. The funding measures, at first voluntary in nature, gradually acquired the characteristics of a compulsory or forced loan.

The principle of funding Treasury notes in bonds was not new to the Confederacy, for every major loan which had authorized the issue of Treasury notes had also provided means for funding them in stocks and bonds. The chief objective of earlier loans, however, had been to increase the Government's supply of specie and foreign bills of exchange rather than to decrease the volume of Treasury notes in circulation.

With the continuation and expansion of war, specie and foreign bills of exchange became increasingly scarce and difficult to acquire; as a result, the Government was compelled to turn more and more to the use of Treasury notes in satisfying demands made upon the Treasury. Expenses had increased tremendously. Up to November 16, 1861, the cost of operating the Government had been placed at $70,000,000;[148] this figure rose to $165,000,000 by February 18, 1862; to $329,000,000 by August 18, 1862, and to $582,000,000 by December 31, 1862. Of the total Confederate debt, on July 19, 1861, only 10% had been represented by Treasury notes. Four months later, on November 16, the figure had increased to 66%. By February 18, 1862, unredeemed Treasury notes comprised 74% of the total Confederate debt.

Prior to the outbreak of hostilities, the amount of currency in circulation in the Confederate States was estimated at $85,500,000. By the end of 1862, over $289,000,000 in non-interest-bearing Treasury notes were circulating along with $121,500,000 in interest-bearing notes—these figures were exclusive of State notes and Bank notes, which the Secretary of the Treasury conservatively placed at $20,000,000.

While the transition from the use of specie to that of Treasury notes was taking place in the Government's financial operations, Secretary Memminger, aware of the dangers of such a policy, continually searched for means to hold back the deluge of a paper currency and the irrepressible tide of rising prices, which he believed would inevitably destroy the country's finances unless adequate absorbents were applied.

To this end, numerous measures had been adopted—each based upon the voluntary withdrawal of Treasury notes from circulation —that is, inducing holders of notes to fund them voluntarily in stocks and bonds. But the various attempts at a voluntary reduction of the currency,[149] although working well, had not proved sufficient to absorb the large issues which the exigencies of the times required, and it became necessary for the Secretary of the Treasury to recommend the adoption of more stringent funding legislation.

On October 6, 1862, Secretary Memminger wrote to President Davis, saying:

While it is proper to pursue with energy all the plans, which have thus far assisted the public credit, it is necessary to add other measures which will retire from the circulation, and absorb the very large issues which each succeeding month compels us to add.[150]

The Secretary then proposed two additional measures for relief from the inflation. The first proposal was a forced loan of 1/5 of all incomes; the second, a reduction of the interest on bonds in which Treasury notes were authorized to be funded. Explaining the second proposal, Memminger said:

The Treasury notes hitherto issued are all fundable in 8 per cent bonds; but that rate may be changed as to notes hereafter to be issued.

If after a certain date no 8 per cent bonds be issued, except to fulfill existing contracts, it is obvious that the currency now in circulation would have an advantage over that afterwards issued, and the effect would be a general effort on the part of moneyed men to get possession of . . . those notes which were fundable in bonds at the higher rate of interest.[151]

The Secretary suggested that a stimulant could be given to hasten funding by fixing a definite time after which all funding in 8% bonds should cease.

On October 13, 1862, Congress, acting on only the second of the two proposals for reducing currency, approved "An Act to reduce the rate of interest on the funded debt of the Confederate States." The act provided that all Treasury notes issued after December 1, 1862, would be fundable only in bonds bearing 7% interest. As to Treasury notes issued prior to December 1, 1862, the Secretary was authorized to require holders to fund them in 8% bonds within six months after public notice. All notes not so funded were thereafter fundable only in 7% bonds.[152] The second section of the act was a distinct violation of the terms of the contract the Government had originally entered into with holders of notes issued prior to December 1, 1862, which authorized those notes to be funded at any time in 8% bonds. Cognizant of the violation which would result from the act, Memminger recommended that the period for funding notes issued prior to December 1, 1862, in 8% bonds "should give full time to the holders of the notes to come in and claim their privilege, there would then be no just objection to the measure."[153] Setting April 22, 1863, as the date after which outstanding Treasury notes could no longer be funded in 8%, but only in 7% bonds, the Secretary immediately circulated to the public notices embodying the provisions of the act.[154]

In approving the act of October 13, 1862, Congress had failed to provide authority for issuing the required bonds and certificates of stock. To remove this obstacle in its attempt to withdraw excess notes from circulation, the legislative body approved "An Act to authorize the issue of Bonds for funding Treasury Notes" February 20, 1863. Under the act, the Secretary of the Treasury was empowered to issue 8% coupon bonds and certificates of stock, with interest payable semi-annually, for such amount as may be required in exchange for all Treasury notes which were fundable in 8% bonds. The Secretary was also authorized to issue 7%

coupon bonds and certificates of stock, with interest payable semi-annually, for such amount as may be required to exchange all Treasury notes which were fundable in 7% bonds. The faith of the Government was pledged to redeem the bonds at the expiration of 30 years from their respective dates.[155]

Under the Funding Act of February 20, 1863, Treasury notes were funded as follows: $81,668,100 for 8% Coupon Bonds, $14,912,800 for 8% Stock, $54,183,000 for 7% Coupon Bonds, and $12,758,100 for 7% Stock. The total amount of notes withdrawn from circulation under the act was $163,522,000.[156]

It is apparent from the report the Secretary of the Treasury sent Congress on January 10, 1863, that the funding act of October 13, 1862, had failed to produce the desired effect planned for it, namely, an immediate reduction of the paper currency. In his report, the Secretary again expounded upon the evils of a depreciated currency and the necessity of meeting the continual rise of prices with the issue of more notes. He reiterated that the currency must be reduced and the reduction must be prompt and effective. To correct the evils of redundancy, he proposed to extend the principle adopted in the act of October 13 by limiting the time for funding notes issued prior to December 1, 1862; that is, compel or force noteholders to exchange their notes for bonds. In this manner he hoped to reduce the amount in circulation to $150,000,000, a figure which he thought represented the proper amount of currency needed in view of the business stagnation induced by the war. Explaining his proposal to extend the act of October 13, Secretary Memminger reminded Congress that under the existing law notes issued prior to December 1, 1862, were entitled to be funded in 8% bonds and stock until April 22, 1863, after which time they could be funded in 7% securities. He said:

I propose simply to fix a period of limitation, for the exercise of this last mentioned privilege, by enacting that after July 1st, next, the privilege of funding these notes shall cease. Six months have already been allowed for investment in 8 per cent. securities, according to the contract on the face of the note. Two months more will be allowed for investment in 7 per cent. [bonds], and if, after so long a notice, the holders do not choose to avail themselves of their privilege, the good faith of the Government will stand clear of imputation.[157]

The Secretary stated that hitherto the Government had sought to absorb the circulation by inducements alone. Bonds bearing a high rate of interest had been offered, but the inducements had been lessened by the depreciation of the notes in which the interest was paid—an 8% bond, in effect, paying only 3 or 4%. He now proposed "to supply the deficiency by a small portion of constraint." Memminger believed that the "grave objections" to such "constraint" of compulsory funding would be counterbalanced by equivalent advantages resulting to the financial system.

He held that "the modification of the contract is substantially for the benefit of both parties" (the Government and the noteholder), the object being "to increase the value of the whole remaining currency." "This object," he said, "it effects by increasing the purchasing power of each note in proportion to the reduction of the whole." Thus, assuming the reduction of currency to be two-thirds, it follows that every holder of only one-third, the amount in new issues, will have the same value in money left after he shall have invested the other two-thirds in bonds. In other words, he will make a clear gain of those two-thirds.

The most obvious objection to compulsory funding, that of its being an infringement of a contract between the Government and the noteholder, the Secretary met by saying Congress had already removed grounds for this objection by approving the Funding Act of October 13, 1862. As a further justification of his proposal, he said:

A limitation of time for the performance of contracts has never been considered an infringement where sufficient opportunity is given to claim performance. Justice is satisfied by giving to the party full opportunity to receive the benefit of his contract. Upon this principle rests every change in statutes of limitation. Examples of the same principle are afforded in private matters by the laws of partnership and for the administration of assets. In public matters the history of every nation affords like precedents, which will probably find support in the laws of every State in our Confederacy.[158]

Another objection which the Secretary tried to alleviate was the declining effect of compulsory funding on the price of bonds. He admitted that "the large amount of currency turned into bonds will cause the supply to outrun the demand, and the usual consequences of such a condition on the market will follow." The Secretary said, "It cannot be denied that the price of bonds will probably fall; but this fall will in truth be merely nominal, and will find a full compensation in the increased value of the currency for which they are sold, and in which the interest will be paid." He claimed that "whatever may be the amount of depreciation on the bonds, it cannot exceed the depreciation in the value of the currency." Memminger was convinced that compulsory funding was practicable and that it would, with the assistance of a war-tax, remove all outstanding notes from circulation and afford the means for a new issue of $200,000,000 before the middle of 1863.

In his report of January 10, 1863, the Secretary also recommended the guarantee of Confederate bonds by the state governments as a means of improving the country's finances. He proposed that each state should guarantee the payment of interest and principal of its quota of the Confederate bonds, claiming this would improve the status of the funded debt and enable him to convert the 8% into 6% bonds. The saving in interest, he said, could then be applied to the reduction of the principal.

The proposal for guaranteeing the Confederate debt by the states was not original with the Secretary of the Treasury. A resolution to that effect had been introduced in the Virginia legislature in May, 1862, and again in January, 1863, but was opposed on the grounds that adoption of such a measure would tend to weaken the credit of both the Confederate and state governments. On December 1, 1862, the Alabama legislature approved a resolution, stating:

> That in the opinion of this general assembly it is the duty of each State of the Confederacy, for the purpose of sustaining the credit of the Confederate Government, to guarantee the debt of that Government in proportion to its representation in the Congress. . . .[159]

South Carolina approved a similar resolution, and went a step further, authorizing the governor to endorse the state's share of $200,000,000 of Confederate bonds.[160] On December 15, 1862, Florida, following Alabama's example, proposed to guarantee its share of the Confederate debt, provided the other states did the same. Mississippi authorized the governor, on January 3, 1863, to endorse Confederate bonds to an amount equal to Mississippi's share of $200,000,000. The Texas legislature did not go so far, but on February 27, 1863, provided that if the state for any reason was compelled to withdraw from the Confederacy, it would pay its share of the Confederate debt. In Georgia and North Carolina, where the states' rights doctrine prevailed, all attempts to involve the state in a guarantee of the Confederate debt failed.[161]

CONFEDERATE FINANCE

A bill covering the recommendations of the Secretary of the Treasury was introduced in Congress February 5, 1863, but it was unable to win support of the Senate Finance Committee and was tabled. Later, under the Funding Act of March 23, 1863, Section 8 authorized the sale of 6% bonds to the highest bidder for Treasury notes at not less than par value—the bonds to be "guaranteed by any of the States of the Confederacy upon such plans as may be determined by the Secretary of the Treasury."[162] James P. Boyce of Greenville, S. C., was appointed an agent of the Treasury Department "to proceed to the legislatures of the [states] and present the action of Congress . . . for their concurrence."[163] Nothing came of the plan, however, and the question of the state's guarantee of the Confederate debt was brought to an end as the military disasters in the summer of 1863, coupled with the refusal of certain of the states to assume their share of the debt, made it impossible to carry out the project.

Secretary Memminger's proposals regarding compulsory funding were embraced in "An Act to provide for the funding and further issue of Treasury Notes," approved March 23, 1863. This was the second in the series of funding measures aimed at reducing the currency by withdrawing excess notes from circulation in exchange for stocks and bonds. Under the act, all non-interest-bearing Treasury notes issued up to April 6, 1863, were divided into two classes: first, those issued prior to December 1, 1862, and second, those issued between December 1, 1862, and April 6, 1863. Notes of the first class were made fundable in 8% bonds until April 22, 1863, after which date—until August 1, 1863—they were fundable in 7% bonds. After August 1, 1863, they could no longer be funded, but were still receivable in payment of public dues, except the export duty on cotton, and were payable six months after the ratification of a treaty of peace. All non-interest-bearing Treasury notes of the second class were fundable in 7% bonds until August 1, 1863. After August 1, 1863, they were fundable only in 4% bonds, and continued to be payable and receivable as the first class of notes. Under the act all 8% call certificates were fundable with accrued interest in 8% 30-year bonds if presented on or before July 1, 1863. All call certificates of every description, outstanding after July 1, 1863, were to be considered 6% 30-year bonds. The Funding Act of March 23, 1863, also provided that after its passage "the authority heretofore given to issue [8% and 6%] call certificates shall cease, but the notes fundable in six per cent. bonds may be converted . . . into call certificates, bearing interest at the rate of five per cent. per annum, from the date of their issue." Each such certificate was to bear on its face the monthly date of the oldest notes it represented, and was convertible into like notes at any time within six months from the first day of the month indicated on the certificate. But every certificate not reconverted within six months from the first day of its monthly date was to be exchanged for 6% 30-year bonds. Treasury notes, which by operation of the act became fundable in bonds bearing 4% interest, could at the pleasure of the holder be converted into 4% call certificates; the 4% certificates were reconvertible at any time into notes fundable in 4% bonds, payable in thirty years and redeemable in five years at the pleasure of the Government, as were all bonds authorized under the act. The act also attempted to improve the currency by stipulating that the authority to issue notes in denominations of $5 and upwards should "cease at the expiration of the first session of Congress, after the ratification of a treaty of peace, or at the end of two years, should the war continue so long." As a further means of reducing the volume of notes in circulation to $175,000,000, the Secretary of the Treasury was authorized to sell $200,000,000 in 6% bonds at par value for Treasury notes issued since December 1, 1862. The Treasury notes thus purchased were not to be reissued if the amount in circulation should thereby be increased beyond $175,000,000 and the Secretary was authorized to use all "disposable means in the treasury" to purchase notes in order to reduce the circulation to that extent.

While the above measures had been adopted primarily to reduce the volume of Treasury notes in circulation and thus improve the value of the Confederate paper remaining outstanding, the good that may have resulted along these lines soon vanished, for the act, while authorizing the Secretary to use all "disposable means in the treasury" to reduce the amount of notes in circulation, had also empowered him to issue monthly as much as $50,-000,000 in non-interest-bearing notes. The new notes, like their predecessors, were to be receivable in payment of all taxes except the export duty on cotton, and were payable within two years after the establishment of peace. They were fundable in 6% bonds if presented within one year from the first day of the month of their issue, or in 4% bonds if presented later. The act also provided for the issue of $15,000,000 in notes of small denominations, namely, 50¢, $1, and $2, each payable six months after a treaty of peace, but not exchangeable for bonds.

Under the loan measures of the act of March 23, 1863, Treasury notes amounting to $16,740,300 were funded in 6% Coupon Bonds along with $22,300 in 4% Coupon Bonds, and $4,278,100 in 6% Stock, making a total of $21,040,700[164] in Treasury notes withdrawn from circulation. The slight reduction in the volume of Treasury notes, however, was unable to produce the favorable effect hoped for on the value of the circulating currency—the reduction being more than counteracted by the constant issue of new notes. At the start of 1863, non-interest-bearing notes in circulation totaled $289,000,000. This figure rapidly increased to over $616,000,000 by September 30, and to more than $720,000,000 by January 1, 1864.[165] The great increase in the amount of notes issued and outstanding during 1863 may be attributed to the extensive military operations of the summer and fall, which proved so disastrous to the South's cause. Confederate bonds decreased in value while the premium on gold continued to increase. Gold quoted at $1.10 in currency on May 1, 1861 rose to eight times that figure by July 1863 and to $20 for $1 by the end of 1863. Under these conditions the voluntary funding of notes in bonds presumably came to an end by July. Noteholders apparently preferring to hold notes rather than exchange them for bonds destroyed their usefulness both as a circulating medium and as a means of speculation. The Funding Act of March 23, 1863, although aiming to correct the evils of a redundant currency, merely added to them by discrediting the old issues of notes which in turn reduced the value of new issues. With old and new notes circulating together, and both being of equally doubtful value, prices quoted in them advanced to still greater heights. This called for larger and larger appropriations as well as corresponding increases in the issues of new notes.

When Congress convened for the winter session of 1863-64, it was confronted with the appalling financial condition of the Confederacy. In his report to the legislative body at the opening session on December 7, 1863, the Secretary of the Treasury stated that the voluntary exchange of notes for bonds, from which so much had been expected, had proved a failure; and the funding acts had been unable to reduce the circulation to the extent expected of them. To rectify the weakness of the funding measures, the Secretary recommended the adoption of additional compulsory legislation which would force noteholders to give up their notes and thereby correct the redundancy. More than $700,000,000 in notes, he said, were in circulation; $500,000,000 had to be retired in order to reduce the notes outstanding to $200,000,000—an amount he considered sufficient for the best interests of the public credit. Convinced of the impossibility of taxes to bring about so large a reduction in the currency, the Secretary of the Treasury said, "We are . . . compelled to resort to the only other resource presented by experience, namely: a loan,"[166] and more specifically a forced loan.

The Secretary recommended a loan of one billion dollars in 6% bonds—the principal payable in twenty years, the interest semi-annually—to be extended, from time to time, with a view to consolidating eventually the entire public debt as well as funding the excess $500,000,000 of Treasury notes. The loan was to be supported by a 5% tax on all property and credits held on April 1, 1864. To encourage noteholders to fund their notes, it was suggested that the new bonds be exempt from the 5% tax, in whole or in part, according to the promptness with which the notes were offered for bonds.[167]

As a further aid to funding, holders of Treasury notes were to be notified that notes of old issues outstanding after April 1, 1864, in states east of the Mississippi, or July 1, 1864, in states west of the Mississippi, would no longer be current or receivable by the Government, although they would still be redeemable as indicated on their face. That is, six months additional would be allowed during which time the notes could be exchanged for bonds. After the six-month funding period, notes of former issues still outstanding were to be barred from any further claim on the Government. Thus, the currency was to be forcibly reduced by compelling noteholders to withdraw their notes from circulation and fund them in bonds or face a tax of 5% along with eventual repudiation. Secretary Memminger attempted to justify his recommendations with the same arguments he used in presenting the funding measures of October 13, 1862, and March 23, 1863. He again admitted that adoption of his recommendations would constitute an infringement of the original contract between the Government and the noteholder, but held that unless such a measure were adopted all would be lost. The Secretary said:

The continuance of the notes as a circulating medium . . . in their expanded state . . . involves the ruin of public and private credit, and will deprive the Government of the means of defending the lives and property of its citizens. . . . Calamities so disastrous must certainly be averted by every means within the power of the Government. No contract, however solemn, can require national ruin; and, in such case, the maxim must prevail that the public safety is the supreme law.[168]

Evidently convinced that compulsory funding of Treasury notes was the only solution to the Government's financial dilemma, President Davis immediately seconded the recommendations of the Secretary of the Treasury.

Southern newspapers, in marked contrast to the opposition they expressed upon the passage of the Funding Act of March 23, 1863, now clamored in favor of a compulsory reduction of the currency. As early as September 3, the *Richmond Examiner* stated that "Compulsory funding of some large body of the government's currency, now outstanding, is the only cure left our government." Other newspapers frankly admitted that voluntary funding had been tried and had failed and that the only course remaining to improve the currency was to compel noteholders to give up their notes.[169]

On the other hand, certain North Carolina newspapers, although lacking a plan to improve the currency, nevertheless opposed compulsory funding, contending that repudiation of the debt would not be a solution to the existing difficulties. They held that the Government had broken its word and was being urged to do so again; as a result, its credit was ruined. They believed that since the previous funding acts had failed to drive the notes out of circulation any later and similar act would have no different effect.[170]

While the press was at work moulding public opinion, discussions concerning the financial situation were progressing in Congress. Finally, on February 17, 1864, the legislative body, adhering in some respects to the recommendations of the Secretary of the Treasury, passed the comprehensive funding measure entitled, "An Act to reduce the currency and to authorize a new issue of notes and bonds."

Provisions of the act aimed at reducing the excess currency in circulation by compelling holders of Treasury notes to fund them in 4% 20-year bonds or exchange them for new notes at the rate of $3 of old for $2 of the new issue. To carry out these provisions, the necessary bonds and notes were authorized, and the issue of old notes was to cease on April 1, 1864. New notes, which were to supersede all previous issues, were made payable two years after the establishment of peace, and were receivable by the Government for all public dues except export and import duties, and could be converted into 4% call certificates, which were also payable two years after the establishment of peace.

An issue of 6% non-taxable certificates of indebtedness was also authorized with which to pay for Government supplies, if contractors would accept them. These were not intended for general circulation and could be transferred only by special endorsement under regulations prescribed by the Secretary of the Treasury. To pay the expenses of the Government, not otherwise provided for, and at the same time reduce the amount of currency in circulation, the Secretary was authorized to float a new loan for $500,000,000. Bonds representing the loan were to be 30-year 6% bonds with interest payable semi-annually. The interest and principal of the bonds were exempt from taxation, and their payment was secured by the "nett receipts of any export duty hereafter laid on the value of all cotton, tobacco, and naval stores," plus the "nett proceeds of the import duties." To make the bonds still more acceptable, the act provided that all import duties "shall hereafter be paid in specie, sterling exchange, or in the coupons of said bonds."[171]

The effect of the Funding Act of February 17, 1864, apparently was not the one expected of it. Almost immediately following its adoption, complaints were made of the scarcity of currency and the high level at which prices remained. On February 21, 1864, J. B. Jones wrote in his diary: "The fear is now, from a plethora of paper money, we shall soon be without a sufficiency for a circulating medium."[172] Such fears were based on the continuing high prices despite the contraction of the currency. These phenomena both surprised and exasperated the people.

When the Funding Act went into operation, non-interest-bearing notes amounting to $800,000,000 were in circulation. By April 1, 1864, $250,000,000 had been funded in 20-year 4% bonds east of the Mississippi and presumably $50,000,000 more would be funded in the Trans-Mississippi Department.[173]

Efforts to float the $500,000,000 loan met with only limited success. Under section 7 of the Funding Act, the Secretary of the Treasury was authorized to sell the 30-year 6% non-taxable bonds for Treasury notes "upon the best terms he can, so as to meet appropriations by Congress, and at the same time reduce and restrict the amount of the circulation in treasury notes, within reasonable and safe limits."[174]

In order to establish a rate at which the bonds could be offered at public sale, it was considered advisable to offer $5,000,000 of the bonds at public auction Thursday noon, May 12, 1864, at Richmond, Virginia, in the auction-room of Kent, Paine & Co.[175] To arouse interest in the sale and also call attention to the many inducements offered by the bonds, notice of the loan was advertised daily from April 21 to May 12, 1864, in the leading newspapers of the South.[176] As the day approached for auction of the bonds, it became necessary to postpone the sale because of the proximity of the enemy and "the continued absence of the businessmen of Richmond from their homes by the calling out of the troops for local defense."[177] To prevent another failure from the same cause, it was considered best to hold the sale at Columbia, South Carolina, on June 21, 1864.[178] On that date the auction went off as scheduled, with bonds amounting to $665,000 being sold. Premiums ranged from 151 to 135, at which price the auction was closed.[179] Efforts were immediately made to float the balance of the $500,000,000 loan. To this end, agents were appointed to conduct private sales of the bonds throughout the Confederacy.[180]

On January 25, 1865, the House of Representatives "*Resolved,* That the Secretary of the Treasury be requested to inform Congress what amount of five hundred million non-taxable bonds have been disposed by the Government. . . ."[181] In answer to the resolution, John H. Hendren, Treasurer, submitted a statement showing $59,176,928.05 as the amount realized from the sale of 6% non-taxable bonds up to January 28, 1865. A later compilation of the 500-Million Dollar Loan placed the total amount of bonds sold at $145,755,000,[182] a figure representing only ¼ the amount expected from the loan.

The issue of 6% non-taxable certificates of indebtedness to contractors for supplies had been even less successful. Government contractors originally showed a reticence to accept them, with approximately $2,000,000 having been placed by October 1, 1864.[183] This amount, however, was increased to $38,040,000 prior to the collapse of the Confederacy.[184]

To aid the numerous Depositaries in carrying out the measures authorized by the Funding Act of February 17, 1864, Secretary Memminger asked the cooperation of the banks and treasuries of the several states. The Richmond and Charleston banks, along with other banking institutions, immediately complied with his request and notified depositors to close their accounts by April 1, 1864, or their deposits would be scaled 1/3, or credited to them in 4% bonds.[185] Notes held by the state treasuries had been specifically provided for in the 12th section of the Funding Act. Under that section, all Treasury notes received by the state treasuries prior to April 1, 1864, were permitted to be exchanged at par value for 20-year 6% bonds, if funded before January 1, 1865, and any notes received by state treasuries after April 1, 1864, were similarly fundable, but only at 2/3 face value. On June 14, 1864, this section was amended to enable the state treasuries to exchange all the old notes they held for 20-year 4% non-taxable bonds or ½ for 20-year 6% bonds and the other ½ for new notes.[186]

It is evident that certain of the state governments took advantage of both the original and the amended offer, as $6,000,000 in 20-year 6% bonds had been issued under the 12th section of the Funding Act of February 17, 1864, and an additional $4,000,000 was issued under the Loan of June 14, 1864 (amendatory of section 12 of the act of February 17, 1864).[187]

Despite the various attempts of the Government to reduce the outstanding currency, the futility of its efforts became more and more apparent with each passing month. Finally, on December 29, 1864, Congress amended the Funding Act of February 17, 1864. By so doing, it practically admitted its inability to retire the obnoxious notes from circulation. The amendment extended the term for funding the old notes in 20-year 4% bonds to July 1, 1865, and the 100% tax to be levied upon them, as of January 1, 1865, was suspended for six months, and all notes of the old issues were again made tax receivable during the same time.

To increase the desirability of bonds as a means of withdrawing excess Treasury notes from circulation, interest payments had been made regularly throughout the war. Nevertheless, the preponderance of note over bond issues prevailed. Government creditors continually showed a preference for Treasury notes, which could be circulated and used for purposes of speculation, rather than for Government bonds, the income of which was limited to interest payable in depreciating notes. Pressure on the part of the Government creditors to secure a Government obligation which could be readily circulated is evidenced by certain legislation of the last year of the Confederacy aimed at facilitating the exchange of registered bonds for coupon bonds. The act of June 13, 1864, authorized the holders of registered bonds issued under the Produce Loan Act of May 16, 1861, to exchange them for coupon bonds, which were much more easily transferred. Similarly, the act of February 23, 1865, applied the same provisions to registered bonds of the $15,000,000 Bankers Loan of February 28, 1861.

In regard to the Funding Act of February 17, 1864, it should be noted that in spite of numerous provisions for reducing the redundant currency its ultimate accomplishments must be termed a failure, as were also those of the funding measures of October 13, 1862, and March 23, 1863.

When Congress approved the measure in a form which differed essentially from the plan submitted by the head of the Treasury Department,[188] Secretary Memminger immediately made known his desire to retire from office, believing "the public service would be promoted by the appointment of a successor whose views of financial policy accorded better . . . with the legislation . . . adopted" than did his own.[189] President Davis, however, objected to the retirement, saying that the experience acquired by Memminger in the organization and management of the Treasury Department could not be immediately replaced, and that "the general welfare would be injuriously affected" by his withdrawal at that time. Representative H. S. Foote of Tennessee apparently had other ideas on the subject and, on May 27, introduced a resolution demanding the removal of Secretary Memminger from office. The resolution stated that:

Whereas the Constitution of the Confederate States has intrusted Congress . . . with control and regulation of the currency; and

Whereas, it will be impossible [to] . . . perform this duty effectively unless the office of Secretary of the Treasury be occupied by some individual of unquestioned high ability as a financier, whose views in regards to important matters of finance, and especially in regard to the currency, are in harmony with those of Congress, and . . .

Whereas the Secretary of the Treasury . . . has been made by the Constitution directly responsible to Congress . . .

Be it resolved, That without intending to call in question the honesty or patriotism of the present incumbent of the Treasury Department, it is the deliberate judgment of this House that the public welfare does demand that he should no longer be retained in said Department, but that some other individual of proper ability as a financier more likely to be successful in administering the affairs of said Department, and more likely to commend the public confidence, should be appointed in his place.[190]

LOANS

After a motion to table the resolution had been defeated 37 to 45, the resolution was referred to the Committee of Ways and Means with instructions for that body "to inquire into the expediency of adopting some such . . . resolution" and to report its findings.[191] The Committee's report was never made, perhaps because of the rumors circulating to the effect that the Secretary would resign at the close of the session.[192]

On June 15, 1864, Secretary Memminger tendered his resignation to President Davis. In so doing, he stated that his earlier retirement had been temporarily prevented for two reasons: first, he had been opposed to perform any act which could be construed into an abandonment of a post of duty during a struggle in which he felt that every citizen owed to his country whatever sacrifice or service was demanded of him. Explaining this statement, the Secretary said:

The machinery which was required for operation [of the Funding Act] was complex and extensive, and by terms of the law, just forty days were allowed to carry it into complete effect. No new head of the Department, however competent, would have been able to acquire sufficient knowledge of office details in time to have carried out the provisions of this act. The public good, therefore, demanded that I should not leave my post during this period.[193]

The second reason preventing his earlier retirement, he said, was the continued confidence placed in him by President Davis.

Contending the reasons for his remaining in office no longer governed, he said:

. . . The first is at an end. The funding of the currency has been nearly completed and the entire machinery required by the plans of Congress for taxes and finance is now in full operation. No public interest will suffer by my now giving place to a successor. The second consideration must yield to the conviction that justice to myself and the public requires me to insist on your acceptance of the resignation which I now tender in the hope that you will be successful in choosing a successor whose views shall harmonize with those of Congress, and who may, on that account, be better able . . . than I have been to do valuable service to our country.[194]

On June 18, 1864, President Davis appointed George A. Trenholm of the commercial house of Jno. Fraser & Co., Charleston, South Carolina, Secretary of the Treasury.[195] In devising the general financial policy inaugurated at the outset of the Government, Secretary Memminger had freely conferred with the leading businessmen of the South. With none had he consulted more fully than with Trenholm, whose acquaintance with large business operations was fully appreciated by Memminger. Under these circumstances, Trenholm's appointment would indicate to a large measure an endorsement of the general policy pursued by the former Secretary and a guarantee of its continuation.

When Congress met for its last session in November, 1864, Secretary Trenholm presented his report on the condition of the Treasury. He stated that compulsory funding under the act of February 17, 1864, had not permanently diminished the volume of currency nor sustained the public confidence. To strengthen public confidence in the Government's promises, he proposed that Congress reverse its policy under the Funding Act and discontinue taxing the old notes, and pledge itself not to increase the existing issues. In order to reduce the inflated currency, he recommended that 20 per cent of the Treasury notes received annually from taxes be withheld from circulation until the amount outstanding should be reduced to $150,000,000; and the tax in kind should be continued after the war, with a specific portion set aside annually for the redemption or payment of the circulation until the whole should be retired. The Secretary also proposed an additional duty of 5¢ per pound on the exportation of cotton and tobacco and the doubling of the duties on imports, with payment to be made in coupons of the $500,000,000 loan, sterling exchange or specie, as provided by law.[196]

Secretary Trenholm's proposed plan for reducing the amount of currency in circulation and restoring public confidence in the Government was immediately endorsed by President Davis in his message to Congress. A month later a bill embodying the Secretary's recommendations was prepared by the House Ways and Means Committee. Following a month of discussion and attempted substitutes, the original bill was passed by the House with one major change, but the bill met with opposition in the Senate. Upon failure of a conference commitee to bring the two houses to an agreement during February, 1865, the committee was discharged March 3 and the new bill failed enactment—the Funding Act of February 17, 1864, remaining in force until the downfall of the Government a month later.

LOANS

The Specie Loans of 1865

As in the first days of the Confederacy so in the closing days, Congress attempted to secure a supply of specie to finance Government expenditures. In both cases, the same means were used—loans. As the Confederacy began its financing with the $500,000 Alabama Loan and the $15,000,000 Bankers Loan, both specie loans, so it ended, as the tentative act of March 13, 1865, aimed at borrowing $30,000,000 in specie while the smaller loan authorized under the act of March 17, 1865, was directed at bringing $3,000,000 in specie into the Treasury. In at least one respect, however, the two sets of loans differed—the first set was a success; the last set was a failure.

Under the act of March 13, 1865, the Secretary of the Treasury was authorized "to borrow from any banks or other corporations, companies, partnerships, or individuals, specie to an amount not exceeding thirty millions of dollars." Six per cent bonds with interest payable semi-annually in specie were to be issued to each lender. The bonds were to stipulate that the repayment of the specie borrowed would take place within two years after the establishment of peace. The proceeds of the loan were to be employed by the Secretary in reducing the volume of outstanding Treasury notes.

No records are available regarding the loan but it is doubtful whether a single bond was ever issued, the act being superseded on March 17, 1865 by the smaller specie loan entitled, "An Act to raise coin for the purpose of furnishing necessary supplies for the army." The new act authorized the Secretary to borrow $3,000,000 in coin and provided for the issue of 6% bonds, payable within two years after the establishment of peace, the principal and interest being payable in specie. The loan was made secure by hypothecating 50,000 bales of Government cotton which were to be delivered at convenient shipping points to bondholders in payment of the bonds—the cotton to be valued at 15¢ per pound. All bondholders receiving cotton in payment of the loan were authorized to export the same "free from any molestation on the part of the authorities of the Confederate States, or the payment of any duty, except to the extent of one eighth per cent. now imposed by law." In the event the $3,000,000 loan could not be immediately effected, the act provided that a 25% tax-in-kind be levied on all gold and silver coin, gold dust and bullion, and foreign exchange in the Confederacy; the tax to be collected on

April 1, 1865, or as soon thereafter as possible—each taxpayer being allowed an exemption of $200. The act also provided that, "if any State of the Confederacy borrows from any bank, coin or bullion, and lends it to the Confederate Government, the bank that lends such coin or bullion shall be allowed a credit against this tax to the extent of such loan."[197]

Under this provision of the act, Secretary Trenholm urged the banks to advance their specie to the Government and succeeded in borrowing a total of $300,000 from the Richmond Banks and their subsidiaries.[198] Captain John M. Strother, financial agent of the commissary department, acting under the orders of John C. Breckinridge, Confederate Secretary of War, received the specie on or about March 27, 1865. Prior to his evacuation of Richmond on Sunday night, April 2, 1865, Captain Strother paid $25,000 of this specie fund to various officers of the commissary department. Almost immediately thereafter the Government collapsed, and the remnants of the Treasury were shipped southward to Danville, Virginia, where some of the money was disbursed for the use of Lee's army. The surrender of General Lee, April 9, 1865, drove the specie train farther South and it finally reached Washington, Georgia. The last days of the Confederate Treasury and what became of its specie has already been told by Micajah H. Clark.[199]

In concluding the discussion of the funded debt of the Confederate States of America, it should be noted that Congress resorted to loans on at least fourteen occasions as a means of raising funds to finance the Government's operations. These loans fell in one of three classes—specie loans, produce loans, or funding loans—depending upon the prime purpose for their authorization.

The following is a summary table of the total funded debt of the Confederacy.

TABLE OF THE FUNDED DEBT OF THE CONFEDERATE STATES OF AMERICA[200]

Loan		Net Amount Issued
Alabama Loan of February 8, 1861		$ 500,000
Loan of February 28, 1861		
Coupon Bonds	$10,882,750	
Exchanged for Stock	$ 245,900	10,636,850
Stock (total value of certificates issued)	$ 6,674,200	

LOANS

Table of the Funded Debt of the Confederate States of America—Continued

Loan			Net Amount Issued
Certificates erroneously issued	$ 3,650		
Transfer Certificates	2,317,400	2,321,050	4,353,150
Loan of May 16, 1861			
Coupons Bonds			958,500
Stock	$12,235,600		
Less transfers	3,870,400		
	$ 8,365,200		
Less certificates redeemed	237,100		8,128,100
Loan of August 19, 1861			
Coupon Bonds	$74,880,050		
Less Bonds redeemed	457,350		74,422,700
Stock issued	$35,389,450		
Less amount of transfers	10,241,550		25,147,900
Loan of December 24, 1861			
6% Call Certificates issued	$69,006,870		
Less certificates redeemed	12,516,400		56,490,470
Loan of April 12, 1862 (approved Apr. 18, 1862)			
Coupon Bonds			2,818,100
Stock issued	$ 448,550		
Less transfers	44,100		404,450
Erlanger Loan (French Loan) January 29, 1863			15,000,000
Loan of February 20, 1863			
8% Coupon Bonds			81,668,100
8% Stock issued	$21,372,100		
Less transfers	6,459,300		14,912,800
7% Coupon Bonds			54,183,100
7% Stock issued	$16,788,000		
Less amount transferred	4,029,900		12,758,100

CONFEDERATE FINANCE

TABLE OF THE FUNDED DEBT OF THE CONFEDERATE STATES OF AMERICA—Continued

Loan		Net Amount Issued
Loan of March 23, 1863		
Coupon Bonds		
6%'s issued	$16,740,300	
4%'s issued	22,300	16,762,600
6% Stock issued	$ 5,023,800	
Less transfers	745,700	4,278,100
Loan of April 30, 1863		
Coupon Bonds		8,372,000
Loan of February 17, 1864		
20-yr. 4% Registered Bonds (second section)	$10,198,800	
Less transfers	14,900	10,183,900
30-yr. 6% Coupon Bonds (sixth section)		145,755,000
4% Call Certificates (fifth section)		65,500,000
20-yr. 6% Bonds (twelfth section)		6,000,000
6% Non-Taxable Certificates (fourteenth section)		38,045,000
4% Coupon Bonds (eighteenth section)		16,263,500
Stock (eighteenth section)		32,040,000
Loan of June 13, 1864 (amendatory act of May 16, 1861)		
Coupon Bonds		2,164,000
Loan of June 14, 1864 (amendatory of section 12 of act of February 17, 1864)		4,000,000
Loan of March 13, 1865 (superseded by the following loan)		————
Loan of March 17, 1865		
Richmond Banks Loan		300,000
Total		$712,046,420

CHAPTER

☆ III ☆
TREASURY NOTES

☆ ☆ ☆ ☆ ☆ ☆ ☆ ☆ ☆ ☆

ALTHOUGH HAVING ORIGINALLY TURNED TO SPECIE LOANS AS A SOURCE of funds, the Confederate Congress was soon compelled to adopt a scheme of finance based on the issue of Treasury notes. This change in the Government's financial policy resulted primarily from three factors: first, the need for a freely circulating medium of exchange; second, the lack of funds during the interim incident to setting up machinery for collecting taxes and floating additional loans; and third, the inability of loans and taxes to raise the amount of income necessary to meet the mounting expenditures of a country at war.

The full responsibility for preparing the currency was shouldered by Secretary Memminger. In lieu of a Government Bureau of Engraving and Printing, the Secretary of the Treasury turned to private enterprise for the production of Treasury notes. To facilitate the printing, Memminger attempted to provide the various contractors with bank-note paper, ink, dies, steel plates, lithographic stones, presses, and other essential materials as well as skilled engravers, lithographers, and printers. As Congress turned more and more to the use of Treasury notes in meeting its expenditures, supervision over the production and preparation of the notes became quite burdensome to the Secretary, and on March 1, 1862, Sanders G. Jamison was appointed a principal clerk "to superintend the issue of Treasury notes."[1]

Memminger had at first insisted that all the establishments for printing Treasury notes be located in Richmond, where they would be under his personal supervision. In April 1862, however, as a result of the "unsettled state of the country," he thought it expedient "to remove the establishments to some place less exposed than Richmond"—Columbia, South Carolina, being selected as the new site.[2]

On May 10, 1862, Joseph Daniel Pope was tendered "a clerkship in the Treasury Department to superintend the printing of Treasury notes" at Columbia.[3]

With the removal of the printing and engraving establishments from Richmond to Columbia, two separate Treasury-Note Divisions were created. The Division at Columbia, headed by Pope, supervised the printing and engraving establishments, took charge of all bank-note paper, and trimmed, packed, and delivered daily to a courier of the Treasury all notes received from the printers. The notes were then delivered to Jamison's Division at Richmond, where they were numbered, signed, and made ready for issue.

As the demand for notes and bonds increased, Memminger reported to Congress that the large issue presented "a field of labor amply sufficient to occupy the attention of another bureau officer." He said, "I would respectfully renew the recommendation heretofore made, of establishing a separate bureau for the issue of bonds and notes, and for taking charge of all the arrangements connected with such issues."[4]

Congress finally gave way to the requests of the Secretary and on February 3, 1864, approved "An Act to organize the Treasury-Note Bureau."[5] Under the act a chief of the bureau was to be appointed with authority "to provide the materials necessary for every issue of notes and bonds, and to cause the notes and bonds to be engraved, printed and prepared for issue, and to superintend . . . all the clerks employed in and about the bureau."[6]

Sanders G. Jamison was appointed Chief of the Treasury-Note Bureau February 10, 1864.[7] In organizing the new bureau, Jamison recommended that it consist of four divisions—one in Columbia and three in Richmond. Explaining his proposed organization, he said:

> The division in Columbia, S. C., shall be under the charge of Charles F. Hanckel, as chief clerk, who shall have the superintendence of the engraving and printing of all notes, bonds, and certificates of stock executed there; shall have the notes trimmed and the notes and bonds carefully boxed for shipment to this city. . . .

TREASURY NOTES

Dr. James M. Lumpkins, chief clerk, in Richmond, shall receive all sheets of notes and bonds from the Secretary's office, and distribute the same to the principal clerks in charge of the divisions of notes and bonds respectively. The notes to be numbered by machinery will be numbered in this division. . . .

The note division shall be under the charge of Mr. Stephen Duncan, who shall receive the sheets of notes from the chief clerk, and shall superintend the numbering and signing of them. . . .

The bond division shall be under the charge of Dr. A. W. Gray, who shall receive the bonds from the chief clerk, and superintend the numbering and signing of the coupons. . . .[8]

Jamison's recommendations for organizing the Treasury-Note Bureau were approved, but before they could be put into effect, the enemy was threatening the environs of Richmond and the Bureau was ordered to evacuate the city. On April 18, 1864, Memminger instructed Jamison to make immediate arrangements for establishing the Treasury-Note Bureau at Columbia, South Carolina, and to commence removing the clerks, furniture, and presses on April 26. He was to afford proper protection and care during the journey to the several female clerks who retained their places. All clerks who did not report within one week after the Bureau's arrival at Columbia were to be considered as having resigned, and their places were to be filled by others. All male numberers and signers were to be transferred to other bureaus or informed that their services were no longer required, the only male clerks retained being those superintending the females and those whose services were required for purposes other than signing and numbering.

As was expected, a large number of the women declined to go to Columbia and resigned their appointments.[9] One of these, apparently indignant about the evacuation, expressed resentment to Memminger's order in the following manner:

> So you have turned us out of door,
> Memminger! Fie, Memminger!
> And we shall write for you no more,
> Memminger! Fie, Memminger!
> Ah! is your heart so cold and frore,
> So flinty hard your bosom's core?
> You horrid brute! You wretched bore!
> Memminger! Fie, Memminger!

No more shall we to Grace Street trip,
   Memminger! Fie, Memminger!
No more our shears the notes shall clip,
   Memminger! Fie, Memminger!
No more our pens their ink will drip
Upon your ugly sheets of scrip.
May Wigfall get you on the hip!
   Memminger! Fie, Memminger!

What you have told us well we know,
   Memminger! Fie, Memminger!
Yes! we may stay if we will go,
   Memminger! Fie, Memminger!
What, such a craven spirit show,
And turn our backs upon the foe—
We'll see you first in Jericho—
   Memminger! Fie, Memminger![10]

The removal of the Treasury-Note Bureau to Columbia rendered necessary certain changes in the Treasury's arrangements for distributing the currency. The notes being printed and registered at Columbia, it became more convenient to disburse them from that point rather than have them sent to Richmond for the same purpose. To W. Y. Leitch, Assistant Treasurer, Charleston, South Carolina, was intrusted the duty of disbursing the notes. On May 7, 1864, he was instructed to transfer as much of his office to Columbia as would enable him to receive daily from the Treasury-Note Bureau all the notes ready for issue. The notes were to be deposited in the Assistant Treasurer's vault and from time to time were to be transferred to the different depositaries as directed by transfer warrants from the Treasury. Leitch was also instructed "to cooperate with the Chief of the Treasury-Note Bureau, making all arrangements which would facilitate the issue and forwarding of the notes."[11] Despite the instructions for co-operation, friction soon developed between Leitch and Jamison, the former believing that he should have sole responsibility for both the clipping and trimming of the notes. On June 13, 1864, Memminger wrote to each saying:

Upon conferring with the treasurer in relation to the assignment of the duties connected with the clipping and trimming of the Treasury notes, the best arrangement . . . is to leave with the Treasury-Note Bureau the duty of trimming the sheets, and to assign to the assistant treasurer the duty of dividing the notes after the sheets have been completed at the Note Bureau and have been delivered to the assistant treasurer. This course exactly conforms to the practice of the two bureaus when the duties were discharged at Richmond, and it is deemed best to continue the same plan.[12]

With the differences between the two officials settled, the work of the Treasury-Note Bureau progressed rather smoothly. Jamison reported, October 31, 1864, that dating from the organization of the Bureau he had $355,378,650 in notes printed, numbered and ready to be turned over to the Treasury; $105,990,000 in coupon bonds of the $500,000,000 loan printed and numbered, along with $4,600,000 in 8% coupon bonds under act of May 16, 1861, as amended June 13, 1864; $6,000,000 in 6% coupon bonds under section 12, act of February 17, 1864, and $4,450,000 in 6% coupon bonds under act of March 23, 1863. With the above were also engraved and printed the 4% registered bonds and the 6% certificates of indebtedness issued under the act of February 17, 1864.[13]

Closing his report, Jamison said:

I must be allowed to speak in the highest terms of the ladies and gentlemen who have been associated with me in getting out the work of the office. The experiment of employing ladies in the public offices, first instituted by Mr. Memminger, has not only proved a perfect success, but has been the means of relieving the necessities of many who have been driven from their homes and have lost all by the barbarous cruelty of our inhuman foe.[14]

On January 16, 1865, Jamison was instructed to carry the issue of notes authorized under the act of February 17, 1864, to $500,000,000.[15] The issue of this amount, however, was never realized[16] for with Sherman's attack on Columbia, the Treasury-Note Bureau was forced to evacuate February 20, 1865.[17] From that day to the final surrender of the Confederate military by E. Kirby Smith, the Bureau was unable to issue a single note.[18] Having arrived at Charlotte, North Carolina, February 20, Jamison wrote to Trenholm:

I have just been able to partially ascertain what things have arrived here from Columbia—all the bonds and note plates, and the bulk of the paper. I am unable to ascertain the number of presses and material belonging to Evans & Cogswell's shop which has gotten out, as there are some trains to arrive, and there may be some here which we do not know of, the trains leaving Columbia having been loaded and sent off in such confusion that it is impossible to say what they contain until they are unloaded. As far as I can ascertain, I have thirty-five presses, with lithographic stones to each press. The amount of inks, colors, &c., saved is very small; the car on which they were loaded, I fear, was burned at the depot in Columbia. We saved nothing from Keatinge & Ball's shop but the rolls, dies, and plates, Keatinge having thrown every obstacle in the way of moving that he could. The quartermaster tells me it is uncertain when he will be able to get the effects of my office away [from here] though he assures me it will be this week. Most of the ladies have left here to go to their friends; they have been directed to report to me, to your care, at Richmond.

I shall use every effort to get to Greensborough as soon as possible. I telegraphed to you yesterday, suggesting that I be authorized to locate my bureau at Lynchburg, Va. This place suggested itself to me as the choice seemed to be limited to Lynchburg and Richmond, and the advantages appeared to be in favor of the former place, as it is less crowded than Richmond.[19]

On March 4, however, Jamison thought it advisable to locate his office at Richmond, so that the Department could "use the printing offices of Ludwig and of Dunn."[20] But with Grant's imperiling the Confederate capital and Sherman's march through South Carolina having turned eastward, it was decided to move the remains of the Treasury-Note Bureau and the printing establishment of Evans and Cogswell to Greenville. By March 16, the salvaged equipment had reached Chester, and on March 30, W. F. Miller and Stephen Duncan, principal clerks in the Bureau, were ordered to go "to Greenville, S. C., and ascertain both the practicability of procuring accommodations for the female clerks, and the necessity of continuing them in the service of the Department." If proper accommodations could be obtained and the services of the ladies were required, they were to be sent from Richmond; otherwise they would be furloughed until May 1st, and dropped from the rolls.[21] Nine female and five male clerks were furnished transportation to Greenville, but before the Treasury-Note Bureau could again be put into operation, the Confederacy had collapsed.[22]

Production of Treasury Notes

Congress having authorized the issue of $1,000,000 in 3.65% interest-bearing notes, March 9, 1861, Memminger turned to private enterprise to supply the approved issue. Through the aid of G. B. Lamar, a contract for manufacturing the notes was made with the National Bank Note Company of New York.[23]

TREASURY NOTES

On April 2, 1861, 607 sheets of Treasury notes arrived at Montgomery, Alabama. Each sheet was composed of four notes bearing denominations of $50, $100, $500, and $1,000, making an aggregate total of $1,001,550.[24] Acknowledging receipt of the notes, Memminger expressed satisfaction with the skillful manner in which they were executed, but said he believed there were too many of the $1,000 and too few of the $50 and $100 denominations. "Our calls," he stated, "will be for the smaller issues."[25]

Before more notes of smaller denominations could be had, war was inaugurated. On April 11, Memminger wrote Lamar:

> It seems from your letter and our own information that War is inaugurated. Under these circumstances would it not be well to send me immediately all the impressions and plates of the Treas. Notes and Stock certificates, lest we may be embarrassed by their seizure or detention. I had intended to order another impression of $50 & $100 Treas. Notes in place of the $1000 and to suppress most of these last. If the matter could be securely done and forwarded, I would be glad to have it done immediately and the impressions forwarded. If that cannot be done, then please forward the whole immediately by express, and I will have the work done at New Orleans.[26]

The outbreak of hostilities, however, prevented the procurement of additional notes from the National Bank Note Company, and on May 4, Joel White of Montgomery, Alabama, was requested to go to New York to "bring home the Treasury-note plates, if it can be done with safety."[27] But three days later seizure of the plates by the U. S. authorities was announced by Memminger.

The supply of Treasury notes from the North being at an end, Memminger directed his efforts to getting notes produced in the South. George B. Clitherall of Mobile, Alabama, was instructed to proceed without delay to New Orleans and "make a contract for printing Five Thousand impressions of Treasury Notes, corresponding as nearly as possible" to the $50 and $100 denominations of the National Bank Note Company.[28]

Complying with the instructions, Clitherall arrived at New Orleans on the night of May 10, and "after diligent inquiry, became satisfied that Mr. S. Schmidt, No. 12 Royal Street, was the only one there by whom the Treasury notes could be satisfactorily executed." He accordingly entered into a contract with Schmidt on May 13.[29]

Upon passage of the act of May 16, 1861, authorizing the issue of non-interest-bearing notes, the Treasury Department made a second contract with Schmidt. This one called for the engraving and printing of twenty millions of Treasury notes even though Schmidt was "but illy provided with men and tools to execute a large order."[30]

To accommodate the Government's needs while the arrangements for producing notes at New Orleans were being carried out, Memminger applied to the various banking institutions for a temporary loan of their bank notes. On May 28, he wrote George A. Trenholm:

> Congress has authorized the issue of Twenty Millions of Treasury notes of denominations as low as Five Dollars. The time necessary for preparing the plates and issue will be at least two months, and before they are ready the Government may be in want of money. To meet this exigency, I propose that the banks would allow me the use of their notes as a substitute for the Treasury notes until they can be prepared. . . . I write now to request you to see immediately the Presidents of such Banks as may be favorably inclined, and propose to each of them to let me have the use of their notes. I will deposit with them as security Treasury notes of a large denomination [$500 and $1000] which I cannot use, bearing interest at 3.65 per annum which interest they may receive, if they see fit, as compensation for the use of their notes.[31]

Similar correspondence was sent to bankers throughout the South and the desired result was soon effected. At the bankers' convention held in Atlanta, Georgia, June 3, 1861, the following resolutions were adopted:

> 1. That all the banks in the Confederacy will receive, in payment of all dues to them, the Treasury notes to be issued under the act of Congress of May 16, 1861, and will receive the same on deposit and pay them out again to customers.
> 2. That until the Treasury notes can be prepared and issued, the banks will advance to the Government, in current notes, such sums as may be agreed upon between them and the Secretary of the Treasury, the advance to be made on the deposit with the banks of Treasury notes of large denomination, or 8 per cent. stock or bonds.[32]

After approving the resolutions, scores of banks hastened to inform the Secretary that they would receive Treasury notes in payment of all dues and would lend the Government a portion of their bank notes until Treasury notes could be issued.

TREASURY NOTES

With contracts made in New Orleans for the production of 5,000 interest-bearing notes of the $50 and $100 denominations and for $20,000,000 in non-interest-bearing notes coupled with the use of bank notes until the new Treasury notes could be issued, it would seem that the problem of acquiring a Confederate currency was solved. Such, however, did not prove to be the case, for it was soon evident that Schmidt, with only the aid of his "young son and one other workman," was incapable of supplying the needs of the Treasury.[33]

Two months after the signing of the contracts not a single note had been produced by Schmidt. On July 15, Memminger wrote to James D. Dénégré, President of the Citizens' Bank of Louisiana:

> Our Treasury is entirely dependent upon these Treasury notes for its means and the want of them will reduce us to the utmost distress. It is of the last importance that they should be prepared promptly in some way or other. If they cannot be engraved, a lithograph would be the next best plan. . . . I have induced Dr. Wm. P. Reyburn to undertake a special mission to see you and Schmidt, and to arrange what had best be done, to extricate us from the dilemma in which we are.[34]

Recognizing Schmidt's inability to meet the needs of the Treasury, Reyburn recommended that he give to the lithographic establishment of J. Manouvrier, at New Orleans, 10,000 sheets of bank-note paper for the lithographing of notes. Reyburn also recommended that Schmidt should continue to produce engraved notes as fast as possible in order to withdraw the lithographed issue from circulation at the earliest moment.

Confronted with Schmidt's inability to meet the needs of the Treasury, and being obliged to accept lithographed notes as a circulating currency, Secretary Memminger was compelled to search for other ways to increase the production of Treasury notes. Agents were sent abroad to procure skilled workmen, machinery, and materials, while financial inducements were offered to individual contractors to set up note-making establishments in Richmond. Major Benjamin F. Ficklin was sent to England to employ engravers, lithographers, and printers, as well as to purchase steel dies, presses, lithographic stones, inks, bank-note paper, and other materials needed in the production of notes.[35]

Thomas A. Ball, later of the firm of Leggett, Keatinge & Ball, was sent to New York for a similar purpose, and a contract for lithographing notes was made with Hoyer & Ludwig at Richmond.[36]

Following the issue of lithographed notes, numerous complaints were made of the inferiority of the workmanship and the ease with which they could be counterfeited.[37] Since the banks had agreed to receive Treasury notes in payment of all dues, they asked that the issue of lithographed notes be stopped until a sufficient number of engraved notes could be printed to take their place. In the interim the banks offered the Government an additional loan of bank notes at 5% interest.[38] Congress temporarily refused the new loan, but with arrearages in the payment of Government expenditures increasing, the additional loan of bank notes was accepted.[39]

With expenditures mounting, Congress turned more and more to the use of Treasury notes in meeting its debts. To supplement production of the currency, Memminger urged Colonel Blanton Duncan of Nashville, Tennessee, to set up a lithographic establishment in Richmond and also attempted to make a contract with the firm of Evans & Cogswell, Charleston, South Carolina.[40]

During the latter part of April 1862, the establishments producing Treasury notes were moved to Columbia, South Carolina, as a precaution against attack from the enemy.[41] By this time several changes had taken place in the list of firms manufacturing the Government's currency. Samuel Schmidt, proprietor of the Southern Bank Note Company, at New Orleans, completed his first contract for 5,000 engraved interest-bearing notes on August 26, 1861.[42] Two days later he was asked to take all his tools to Richmond and join an establishment which the Government was creating for engraving notes or else remain at New Orleans and speed up production of the $20,000,000 in notes authorized under the act of May 16, 1861.[43]

Shortly thereafter the American Bank Note Company, of which Schmidt's establishment was the Southern branch, was declared an alien enemy, and its "materials, paper, and tools" at New Orleans were seized, moved to Richmond, and placed in the engraving and printing establishment of Leggett, Keatinge & Ball.[44] Upon the intercession of James D. Dénégré, Schmidt was permitted to retain as many presses and tools as he could work himself,[45] but because of his continued slow rate of production, he was ordered, November 16, "to give up the plates, and send them by special messenger" to Richmond where his number could be "more than doubled."[46] Giving up the last of his equipment, Schmidt ended his services with the Treasury Department.[47]

The lithographic firm of J. Manouvrier, New Orleans, also had but brief employment with the Treasury Department. Manouvrier had made a contract to lithograph notes of small denomination, but due to carelessness in packing printed notes for shipment to Richmond, some were stolen, and, with signatures forged, put in circulation. As a result, notes of the stolen denominations were never issued; the Manouvrier contract was ended, and the company disbanded, some of the skilled workmen and equipment being transferred to Hoyer & Ludwig at Richmond.[48]

Just prior to the removal to Columbia, personnel changes occurred in several of the other firms contracting to manufacture Treasury notes. On March 12, 1862, Leggett, Keatinge & Ball received the following communication from Secretary Memminger:

> The connection of your Mr. Leggett with Captain Leonard, who has been arrested as a spy, renders it impossible for the Government to continue the arrangement heretofore made for your engraving and printing Treasury notes. The most perfect confidence in your establishment is necessary in order to carry on so confidential a work. I give you notice, therefore, that unless you immediately arrange your establishment so as to exclude Mr. Leggett from any further agency, I will suspend the whole contract, and withdraw from your hands all the materials, plates, and machinery over which I have control.
>
> You will please inform me within twenty-four hours after you receive this letter whether you have succeeded in arranging for Mr. Leggett's removal. At the expiration of that time, if not notified by you, I shall give directions to take possession as above stated.[49]

The necessary arrangements were made and the firm henceforth was that of Keatinge & Ball.

Dr. James T. Paterson, of Richmond, wrote Memminger, April 28, 1862:

> I contemplate purchasing the whole or part of the lithographic establishment of Messrs. Hoyer & Ludwig, that is to be moved South. The present proprietors, for special reasons, decline going themselves.
>
> Before entering into any definite arrangement with them, I desire to consult your wishes in the matter, and ascertain, if I should purchase, whether you would extend the same business arrangement to me as at present exists between you and them, and would prefer a personal interview with you on the subject.[50]

The interview was granted, more definite arrangements were made, and Paterson purchased the branch of Hoyer & Ludwig that was being transferred to Columbia.

With J. T. Paterson & Co., Keatinge & Ball, and Blanton Duncan locating in the South Carolina capital, Columbia became the center for the engraving, lithographing, and printing of Confederate currency. To Hoyer & Ludwig, Archer & Daly (later Archer & Halpin), and Dunn & Co., lithographic firms remaining in Richmond, fell the task of manufacturing the major portion of the various issues of government stocks and bonds. The Richmond firms also made occasional contracts for lithographing and printing notes of small denominations and postage stamps. In lieu of coin, postage stamps were used for small change just as United States postage stamps were used for the same purpose at the same time in the North.[51]

Soon after Blanton Duncan arrived in Columbia he expanded his firm by buying out the Charleston establishment of Evans & Cogswell.[52] As a result of the inability of the several establishments to produce the amount of notes required by the Treasury, Secretary Memminger wrote to B. F. Evans of Evans & Cogswell on October 8, 1862:

. . . I desire to see you engaged in the printing of Treasury notes and bonds for the Government. If you will make arrangements for commencing the work, and provide yourself with material, presses, and workmen, I will undertake to contract with you for such amount of work as you can accomplish upon as favorable terms as are offered other contractors. I will also assist your arrangements by transferring to you, whenever the same can be done with advantage to the work you may undertake, as many of the printers detailed by the War Department as can be properly employed in your establishment.[53]

Evans & Cogswell immediately proceeded to set up a lithographic establishment in Columbia. By April 1, 1863, forty-three lithographers were in their employment and the proprietors believed that they were prepared to do all the lithographic work required by the Treasury.

In answer to a Treasury communication requesting new proposals for lithographing notes, Evans & Cogswell wrote, "Our price will be fifteen dollars ($15) for each one thousand notes, complete, with backs and fronts, or at the rate of one and a half cents for each complete note."[54] J. T. Paterson & Co. proposed to lithograph the notes at $16, and Blanton Duncan at $20 per thousand notes. On April 7, 1863, Secretary Memminger accepted the offers of Evans & Cogswell and J. T. Paterson & Co. and rejected that of Blanton Duncan.[55] Dating from April 7, and continuing until the collapse of the Confederacy, Evans & Cogswell were the Government's principal lithographers, while Keatinge & Ball continued as the chief engraving establishment.

More than a month had been consumed in moving the currency producing establishments to Columbia, and it was hoped that all obstacles to increased production were at an end; such, however, was not the case. Jealousy and friction developed among the proprietors almost upon their arrival at Columbia. The feeling was intensified by the monopolistic tendencies of certain establishments, and by the charges of favoritism brought against the Treasury Department by others. To bring harmony among the proprietors, Memminger considered setting up a single Government establishment, with all the contractors working under the same roof.[56] Concerning this proposition, J. D. Pope, head of the Treasury-Note Division at Columbia, wrote:

I do not think we will mend the matter a great deal by putting three or four contractors in one house and calling them a Government establishment. They would quarrel still, and perhaps worse than ever. All want to be masters, and all want the profits. This is the whole truth, and all the trouble they have been giving me has been in their efforts to outdo each other. All wish to dictate just as soon as you do not yield to their particular schemes. Duncan took up an idea to break up everybody but himself, and because I would not let him, he got terribly provoked, as you know. Now Keatinge & Ball have a scheme, and are just as much out with me because I would not yield to their whims; and Paterson is equally so. In fact, if it was not that I feel that I would not be doing my duty to my country, I would kick them all over together and quit. I never have been so annoyed in my life. They deliberately desire to use me to outwit each other. It is impossible for you at a distance to see the "will and won't" policy of these contractors. Keatinge is much the most intelligent and practical workman of them all, and would make a capital director, but I fear he is too deeply interested as a contractor to give up the profits and take a salary. These contractors have no idea of doing anything that will take away the profits. To counteract all of this, I would with great deference propose that a real Government establishment be inaugurated (for long after a peace these notes will have to be used), and to this end I have suggested that paper in large quantity be imported, and lithographic material, as well as steel-plate material and presses, and men in sufficient quantities to put the Government beyond the control of contractors.

. . . In the meantime, take the Scotch engravers, who are here, and Archer, in Richmond, and carry them all to Richmond and make them prepare such plates of notes as will please you, and have everything in readiness to commence immediately as the material and workmen arrive. At present, let me work on here to supply the present necessities of the Government. Mr. Keatinge told Mr. Jamison that he would not furnish plates to be used by any one else, and he would not use anybody else's plates. Let us take our own men and make our own plates. When the establishment is complete, let no one but an official go into it; then it will be entirely under your own control. From my observation, nothing else will work. . . .[57]

But because of the Government's dire need for funds and the length of time required to move the equipment and men back to Richmond, it was decided to leave the establishments at Columbia and continue the production of Treasury notes by private enterprise.

Along with friction between contractors, there were other obstacles hindering the manufacture of Government currency. Shortages of supplies and skilled manpower plagued the production of Treasury notes during most of the existence of the Confederacy. Proprietors of the Treasury-note establishments were also troubled with strikes, drunkenness, and incendiarism.[58] The transmission of notes to the numerous depositories located throughout the Confederacy also offered its problems, for the distribution of currency by Special Courier and the Southern Express Company was both costly and slow.[59]

On several occasions the War Department impeded the production of Treasury notes. A temporary seizure by the military of one of the establishments afforded an opportunity for abstraction of some notes, causing that specific issue of currency to be cancelled and the plates made valueless to the Treasury. The military also hindered the production of notes by frequently refusing the Treasury Department the use of details.

Perhaps the most serious of all the obstacles confronting the production of Treasury notes was that of counterfeiting. Regardless of the threat of death or heavy fines and long-term imprisonment at hard labor, the evil continued throughout the existence of the Confederacy.[60] To aid in the apprehension and conviction of persons engaged in forging or circulating counterfeit, the Secretary of the Treasury was authorized to offer rewards up to $5,000. Too, a detective agency, under the supervision of Colonel G. W. Lee, was established at Atlanta, Georgia.[61] Numerous arrests were made but in only a few cases were the parties found guilty.[62] As Detective W. H. Gilbert wrote:

... whenever I arrest a party implicated, which I have done a good many times, I find it is very hard to hold them, as the law is altogether on the side of the criminal. It is almost impossible to prove that a man passes a counterfeit knowing it to be so, as the law requires.[63]

Other measures were also considered in the hope of finding a way to prevent counterfeiting of the Confederate currency; some were mechanical in nature, some legislative. A suggestion was made to foil counterfeiting by producing a bank-note paper bearing the "water-print" CSA. This failed fulfillment due to the great amount needed and the degree of difficulty experienced in producing bank-note paper in the South. Later pink paper was used to stymie the efforts of counterfeiters, but this, too, proved of little protection.

Originally, notes were printed in black on only one side of white bank-note paper. Following the early appearance of counterfeit, the notes were produced in two-tones; i.e., a green background on white paper with black print, or a blue background on white paper with black print. The reason for producing the two-toned notes was that the additional time, plates, stones, and ink required in preparing the new issues would delay and perhaps prevent their being counterfeited. The same reasoning was adopted later when the Treasury had its notes printed on both sides.

The first notes issued by the Confederacy bore the autograph signature of the Treasurer and Register as a protection against counterfeit. With the large amount of notes approved under the act of May 16, it became impossible for the two officers to sign them personally. On July 24, 1861, Congress authorized the appointment of clerks to sign Treasury notes for the Treasurer and Register.[64] As the amount of notes continually increased, more and more "signers" were appointed until their great number, like the great number of plates used in printing the notes, lost all aspects of protection and merely added to the ease of counterfeiting the currency.

Measures were not only taken to prevent the counterfeiting of

CONFEDERATE FINANCE

new issues but also to remove from circulation all former issues which had been counterfeited. To this end, Secretary Memminger ordered the depositories to exchange 6 per cent call certificates for the circulating notes of any counterfeited issue. The call certificates were to be redeemed as speedily as "the great deficiency of mechanical force and paper" would permit.[65]

Because of the South's lack of skilled workmen, equipment, and materials, few, if any, of the illicit notes were ever made in the Confederacy. It is true that legitimate Treasury notes were stolen on different occasions from several of the lithograph establishments and were put in circulation with forged numbers and signatures, but in these cases the notes were of a bona fide issue. Practically all the counterfeit was produced abroad and smuggled into the Confederacy. During the first three years of war, most of it was produced in Louisville, Kentucky, New York City, and Philadelphia.[66] In the last year of hostilities, some counterfeit was made in Havana, Cuba, and having run the blockade, entered the South at Mobile, Alabama, or passed through Matamoros, Mexico, into the Trans-Mississippi Department.[67]

Perhaps the most famous of all the counterfeiters was Samuel C. Upham, of Philadelphia. Strangely enough, Upham never represented himself as a counterfeiter of Confederate currency; rather, he advertised his lithographed notes as "fac-similes" and "mementos of the rebellion." Some years after the war, Upham wrote of his earlier activities:

. . . I printed from the 12th of March, 1862, to the 1st August, 1863, one million five hundred and sixty-four thousand and fifty fac-simile Rebel notes, of denominations ranging from five cents to one hundred dollars, and presume the aggregate issue, in dollars and cents, would amount to the round number of fifteen millions of dollars.

In the year 1863 two individuals in New York (Haney & Hilton, the former since deceased) copied several of my fac-simile notes, and I have been told, sold large quantities to bogus Jew cotton brokers and other scalawags, who passed through the Confederate lines and purchased cotton from the Rebel planters. . . .

[The lithographed notes] sold like "hot cakes," at one cent each. I supplied the trade at fifty cents per hundred notes. On the margin of each and every note was printed "Fac-Simile Confederate notes sold, wholesale or retail, by S. C. Upham, 403 Chestnut Street, Phila." . . .[68] I made no distinction in price in consequence of the high denomination of the note. I sold a $100 fac-simile note at the same price I charged for a five-cent shinplaster. I sold the notes as curiosities—mementos of the rebellion—and advertised them as such in several of the most widely circulated papers in the Union. . . . I printed in all twenty-eight different varieties of fac-simile Rebel notes and shinplasters, and fifteen different postage stamps.

During the publication of those fac-simile notes I was the "best abused man" (by the rebels) in the Union. Senator Foote, in a speech before the rebel Congress, at Richmond, in 1862, said I had done more to injure the Confederate cause than General McClellan and his army. . . .[69]

It was Upham to whom Secretary Memminger alluded when he said:

. . . Organized plans seem to be in operation for introducing counterfeits among us by means of prisoners and traitors, and printed advertisements have been found stating that the counterfeit notes, in any quantity, will be forwarded by mail from Chestnut street, in Philadelphia, to the order of any purchaser.[70]

To repress the introduction of counterfeit by prisoners of war and other enemies of the Confederacy, Memminger recommended that a law be passed providing for their punishment by military commissions. On October 13, 1862, Congress adopted the Secretary's recommendation and approved "An act to punish and repress the importation, by our enemies, of notes purporting to be notes of the Treasury of the Confederate States."[71]

Proposals were also made to have a permanent issue of notes produced in Europe. On January 19, 1864, S. G. Jamison wrote to Memminger: "The style is so different in the two countries that we may be sure of obtaining a note which will be as difficult for the American counterfeiter to imitate as it would be for the European to counterfeit the American style."[72] Finally, late in the war, the firm of S. Straker & Sons of London, England, was engaged to prepare plates of new designs, using a process of engraving by chemical action.[73] The chemicograph plates were to be used in printing the backs of a proposed new issue of Treasury notes and were in denominations of $5, $10, $20, $50, $100, and $500. While they were in the hands of blockade-runners, some, if not all, of the plates were seized by the North; as a result, none were ever used by the Confederacy. Some impressions taken from the chemicograph plates are in existence, but they probably are the work of Northerners.[74]

Despite the numerous attempts of the Confederate Government

to prevent counterfeiting of its currency, the inferior quality of Treasury notes and the ease with which they circulated offered counterfeiters the proper conditions to ply their evil. Of their victims, the Government was not among the least. Having adopted a system of finance based upon the issue of Treasury notes, Congress, at the same time, had tried to increase the desirability of notes as the South's circulating paper by making them acceptable in payment of all taxes due the Government except the export duty on cotton. It was primarily in the receipt of taxes that collectors, depositaries, and assistant treasurers fell prey to counterfeit. On May 1, 1863, Congress enacted its first legislation in regard "to the receipt of counterfeit Treasury-notes by public officers." Under the act, any treasurer, assistant treasurer, depositary, or tax collector who had received counterfeit or forged notes prior to January 1, 1863, in the course of his business and who could establish proof that the receipt of such notes was not the result of "neglect, carelessness or want of attention to his duties" was relieved from all "liability on account of any counterfeit or forged treasury notes so received."[75]

The act was amended periodically to relieve liability for counterfeit notes received after January 1, 1863.[76] Later, the provisions of the act were extended to include relief of postmasters who had received counterfeit in payment for postage stamps and sequestration receivers who had accepted counterfeit or forged notes in the course of their business. The amount of counterfeit and forged notes received by the various tax collectors and officers of the Treasury is not known, but from the records available, it was unquestionably very large.

Despite the numerous obstacles retarding the manufacture and issue of Treasury notes, production of the currency continued unceasingly, and in due time, the Government, instead of facing a scarcity of negotiable paper, was confronted with an over-abundance, and measures had to be taken to compel its withdrawal from circulation.

Treasury Note Legislation

Congress approved the first issue of Confederate Treasury notes March 9, 1861. Under "An Act to authorize the issue of Treasury notes, and to prescribe the punishment for forging the same, and for forging Certificates of Stock, Bonds, or Coupons," the Secretary of the Treasury was empowered "to cause Treasury notes to be issued for such sum or sums as the exigencies of the public service may require, but not to exceed at any time one million of dollars. . . ."[77] The notes were to bear interest at the rate of 3.65% per year and were redeemable one year from their date of issue. They were to be of denominations not less than $50, and were receivable in payment of all duties and taxes laid by the Government, except the export duty on cotton. When received by the Treasury, the notes could be reissued up to March 1, 1862, provided the amount outstanding did not exceed one million dollars. On August 3, 1861, the amount of 3.65% notes was increased to two million dollars.[78]

It is evident, both from their large denominations and from the fact they were transferable only by endorsement, that the notes were intended as an investment rather than a circulating currency. In recommending the issue of interest-bearing notes, Secretary Memminger believed that receivers finding it advantageous to hold the notes as an investment would withdraw them from circulation, thus preventing their redundancy.

Later, upon the adoption of non-interest-bearing notes, the issue of 3.65% notes came to an end, the total issued being $2,021,100.[79] Practically all the 3.65% interest-bearing Treasury notes were withdrawn from circulation under the funding acts of October 12, 1862, March 23, 1863, and February 17, 1864.

In his comprehensive report of May 10, 1861, Secretary Memminger stated that according to the estimated appropriations for operating the several departments, the Government would face a deficit of $38,000,000 on February 18, 1862. "This sum," he said, "will, in all probability, be increased by the increased dimensions which the war is assuming." Believing that the threatened blockade would prevent any material assistance from import and export duties, the Secretary looked to loans and direct taxes as the chief sources of revenue. Cognizant of the time required to establish the machinery necessary to collect taxes and float loans, Memminger suggested the issue of $20,000,000 in three-year Treasury notes as a means of deriving funds for immediate use. The notes were to be of two classes: those of small denominations—$5 and $10—to be without interest, and those of larger denominations—$20 and upwards—to bear 8% interest. It was believed that the interest-bearing notes would appeal to investors and be retired from circulation; whereas, the non-interest-bearing notes would act as a circulating medium of exchange.

Approving the act of May 16, 1861, Congress adhered to the recommendations of the Secretary by authorizing the issue of $20,000,000 in Treasury notes—it digressed, however, in that it made all the notes non-interest-bearing, and payable in specie at the end of two years.[80]

The new Treasury notes were to be issued in "denominations of not less than five dollars" and were "receivable in payment of all debts or taxes due to the Confederate States, except the export duty on cotton." They were not to be received in exchange for 20-year 8% bonds of the Thirty Million Dollar Loan authorized under the act, but in order to prevent the notes from becoming redundant, they were exchangeable at par for 10-year 8% bonds, an issue of which was authorized for that purpose. All of the "two-year" notes redeemed by the Treasury could be reissued, provided the amount of such notes outstanding together with the amount of 10-year 8% bonds issued did not exceed $20,000,000.

In this, its first major issue of non-interest-bearing Treasury notes, Congress apparently sensed the popularity of a paper money policy. Despite the difficulties confronting the Treasury, by November 16, 1861, $17,347,955 in two-year notes had been issued.[81]

On July 29, just four days after the first of the two-year notes had been issued, Secretary Memminger advised Congress that the enlarged dimensions of the war necessitated the raising of additional funds. He said, "The fact that so much of the first Loan remains undisposed proves that Bonds cannot be relied on as a resource immediately available," adding that, "it will, therefore, be necessary to have recourse to [additional] Treasury Notes."[82]

To allay the fears of inflation which some held would result from increasing the issue of notes, Memminger said:

> The apprehension of danger to the currency does not appear to be well founded. Taking an average of six years, up to 1858, the circulation and deposits in the banks of the eight Confederate States where banks exist was about eighty-five millions, with eighteen and a half millions of coin. It would be not unreasonable, therefore, to assume that at present a circulation could be sustained of one hundred millions. . . .[83]

To prevent inflation, two plans were recommended for removing the notes from circulation. The first was to allow the notes to be funded in 8% bonds; the second, to give interest on notes of denominations of fifty dollars and upwards. Secretary Memminger said he preferred the second plan "because in an agricultural community, there are many persons who would hoard up notes which bore interest, who would not undertake the trouble of exchanging them for Bonds; and secondly, because the Banks themselves and all the moneyed capital usually employed in short loans would absorb these notes." He recommended that the notes be issued "at 2 or 3 years, bearing an interest at two cents per day on each hundred dollars."[84]

Congress adhered to the recommendations, August 19, 1861, and authorized the issue of $100,000,000 in Treasury notes—it digressed again, however, in that it made all the notes non-interest-bearing. The new notes were to be issued in any denomination not less than $5 and were receivable for payment of the war tax provided under the act and for all other dues except the export duty on cotton. Unlike their predecessors, the new notes could be received in satisfying subscriptions to the Produce Loans and were fundable in 20-year 8% bonds. The notes were redeemable "six months after the ratification of a treaty of peace between the Confederate States and the United States," and could be reissued any time during that period provided "the whole issue outstanding at one time, including the amount issued under former acts, shall not exceed one hundred millions of dollars."[85] On December 24, 1861, the issue of non-interest-bearing Treasury notes was increased to $150,000,000.[86] In an attempt to prevent inflation of the notes, Congress authorized an issue of $30,000,000 in 20-year 6% Call Certificates with interest payable semi-annually. The Call Certificates were exchangeable for notes issued under the acts of August 19 and December 24, and holders of the certificates could reconvert them into Treasury notes at any time. This issue apparently aimed at combining the attractive features of an investment with those of a circulating currency.

As the year 1861 drew to a close, the Government was fast adopting a policy of finance whereby expenditures were to be met largely from the issue of Treasury notes. Of the total Confederate debt on July 19, 1861, 10% represented outstanding notes; by November 16, 1861, the fraction had risen to over 63%.[87] Total expenses for the fiscal year ending February 18, 1862, were $165,-490,576.91; the receipts, $139,051,004.32; the difference, $26,439,-572.59, represented notes remaining in the Treasury to the credit of disbursing officers. Of the total receipts, $105,603,795.49 or 76% had been derived from the issue of Treasury notes.[88]

With the area of warfare continually expanding, expenditures continued to increase. To meet them in the years ahead, issue after issue of notes was authorized.

On March 14, 1862, at the first meeting of the Congress of the Permanent Government, Secretary Memminger reported on the condition of the Treasury. He estimated expenses for the remainder of 1862 at $214,004,427.10. To meet this figure he counted on $18,000,000 in bonds, the balance of the $100,000,000 loan, and approximately $20,000,000 as the proceeds of the war tax levied on August 19, 1861, and collectible during 1862; the remainder, approximately $176,000,000, he proposed to raise by new taxes and by the further issue of notes and bonds. In regard to the issue of Treasury notes, the Secretary said, "Experience has established that this is the most dangerous of all methods of raising money," and that $108,000,000 was then outstanding—$8,000,000 more than he previously considered a safe limit. He said:

> . . . evidence of redundancy begins to appear in the freedom with which call-deposits are made, and the high prices of specie and foreign exchange are partly the result of the same cause. But, on the other hand, the freedom with which Treasury notes are circulated at par with bank notes, indicates an equal confidence in both, while the capacity they have of being funded gives them a superior claim on public confidence.
>
> Under existing circumstances it seems . . . that Congress might venture to authorize an issue of fifty millions more if they will provide means for absorbing redundancy similar to those already provided for existing issues. This will raise the issue to two hundred millions, an amount at which we should pause . . . until we can see the effects upon the country.[89]

The Secretary also recommended that he be authorized to keep a reserve of $10,000,000 in Treasury notes, to be issued to holders of deposit certificates upon any sudden and unexpected call.

On April 12, 1862, Congress acted on the recommendations, adopting those pertaining to the issue of notes and bonds, but refusing for the time being to add to the war tax. The act, approved April 18, 1862, authorized the issue of $165,000,000 in 30-year 8% bonds and also provided for an additional $50,000,000 in Treasury notes, $10,000,000 of which were to be held as a reserve fund to pay any unexpected call for deposits. The notes and bonds, being an extension of those approved under the acts of August 19 and December 24, 1861, were issued under the same forms, conditions, and restrictions as those of the former acts. To prevent expansion of the currency, the notes were exchangeable to the extent of $50,000,000 for 10-year 6% Call Certificates, the certificates being reconvertible into Treasury notes at the pleasure of the holder.[90] On September 23, 1862, the issue of 6% Call Certificates was "extended from fifty millions to one hundred millions of dollars."[91] The theory of preventing a redundant currency by the interchangeability of notes and Call Certificates, presumably to the advantage of the note-holder, proved rather successful. Up to August 1, 1862, $37,585,200 in 6% Call Certificates had been issued.[92] This figure rose to $59,742,796 by December 31, 1862,[93] and under the funding act of February 17, 1864, the Treasury redeemed 6% Call Certificates amounting to $70,729,000.[94]

The Government's attempt to make Treasury notes as attractive an investment as bonds and yet keep them out of circulation is further illustrated by the interest-bearing notes authorized under the act of April 17, 1862. Similar in many respects to the 3.65% notes issued under the act of March 9, 1861, the new issue was made even more attractive by bearing interest at the rate of 7.30%. The 7.30% notes, issued in the denomination of $100, were payable six months after the ratification of a treaty of peace. They were "receivable in payment of all public dues except the export duty on cotton" and were issued in lieu of a part or all of the $165,000,000 in bonds authorized under the act approved April 1862.[95]

Regarding it as very important not to add to the general circulating medium more than what was absolutely necessary, Memminger desired to substitute 7.30% notes as far as possible for the general circulation.[96] On June 4, he advertised that:

. . . the Treasury Department is now ready to issue Treasury notes of the denomination of one hundred dollars, bearing interest at the rate of two cents per day, in payment of dues or in exchange for ordinary [non-interest-bearing] Treasury notes of every denomination. . . .

These notes, being receivable for all dues in the same manner as ordinary Treasury notes, offer to the holder the double advantage of an interest of $7.30 per $100, while retained in his hands, and the capacity of being used as currency whenever he may desire to pay them away. They thus afford an opportunity for investments of small sums at short dates, at the will of the holder.[97]

According to the amount issued, it is evident that the 7.30% notes were well received. On August 1, 1862, the value of the notes outstanding was approximately $23,000,000 [98] and the figure mounted to $113,740,000 by January 1, 1863.[99] But despite the large issue, the desirable effect expected of the 7.30% notes in reducing the currency was not realized. Instead of being withdrawn from circulation and held as an investment, the notes circulated freely, adding to the redundancy of the currency. Under the funding act of February 17, 1864, they were declared no longer tax receivable and were considered bonds payable two years after a treaty of peace. Nevertheless, the 7.30% notes continued to circulate and on November 28, 1864, a final attempt was made to drive them out of circulation by making them exchangeable for 30-year 6% bonds. It is questionable, however, whether this attempt to drive them out of circulation was any more successful than the former, for, by this late date, it was generally more profitable to circulate the notes than to hold them in the form of bonds.

The act of April 17, 1862, also provided for an issue of $5,000,000 in notes of $1 and $2 denominations. The notes did not bear interest but were receivable in payment of all public dues except the export duty on cotton, and were payable six months after the ratification of a treaty of peace. Due to the great demand for notes of small denomination, their amount was increased to $10,000,000 on September 2, 1862.

On August 18, 1862, Secretary Memminger advised Congress that the authority to issue $200,000,000 in Treasury notes was almost inadequate, that requisitions totaling $28,000,000 remained unpaid, and that provision for an additional $209,000,000 was required to make good the deficiencies and support the Government to January 1, 1863.[100]

In response to a resolution of the House of Representatives requesting what legislative measures were necessary to provide the required funds, Memminger stated that the chief means furnished by Congress to pay requisitions had consisted of bonds which could not be sold to the extent desired, and that if the requisitions were to be paid in Treasury notes, the first legislation must grant authority to extend the amount of their issue.[101]

Under the act of September 23, 1862, Congress made sweeping provisions for the issue of notes, stocks, and bonds. Secretary Memminger was authorized to issue "such additional amount of the same as may be required to pay the appropriations made by Congress, at its last and present sessions." The notes, stocks, and bonds

TREASURY NOTES

were to be similar to those issued under previous acts—the stocks and bonds to be given preference in all cases where they could be used; and where they could not, the deficiency to be supplied by Treasury notes.[102] On October 13, 1862, the amount of Treasury notes authorized to supply "the deficiency" was fixed at $90,000,000, but evidence indicates that a total of $140,400,800 was issued under the act.[103]

On October 3, the Secretary wrote that the great increase in the issue of Treasury notes rendered it the duty of Congress to provide some additional means to sustain their credit. He showed the amount of issues on September 30 to be $283,226,890, and said that about $150,000,000 must be added to cover expenditures to the end of the year, making a total of $433,000,000. Allowing a large reduction for interest-bearing notes, the amount of currency left in circulation, he said, would be $340,000,000.[104]

Three days later, the Secretary again referred to the expanded condition of the currency:

When it is remembered that the circulation of all the Confederate States before the present war was less than one hundred millions, it becomes obvious that so large an increase must produce depreciation and final disaster, unless sufficient remedies are provided.[105]

He said it was not only "proper to pursue with energy all the plans which have thus far assisted the public credit," but that it was also "necessary to add other measures which will retire from the circulation, and absorb the very large issues which each succeeding month compels us to add." Memminger then proposed two new measures of relief against depreciation of the currency. The first was a forced loan of 1/5 of all incomes and the second was a reduction of the interest on bonds in which Treasury notes were fundable.

Congress ignored the first of the recommendations for improving the currency, but on October 13, 1862, approved "An act to reduce the rate of interest on the funded debt of the Confederate States." This was the first of the Government's three compulsory funding acts, each of which aimed at curbing the inflationary tendencies of the currency, and to this end, each increased the severity of the compulsory funding measures over those of its predecessor. But the compulsory measures for reducing currency failed to meet their objective, as did the voluntary measures preceding them. It is true the compulsory funding acts of October 13, 1862, March

23, 1863, and February 17, 1864, withdrew huge sums of Treasury notes from circulation, but the amount withdrawn was always exceeded by the amount of new notes issued. With the amount of paper currency increasing, prices rose. During 1862, food prices climbed to four and six times their 1860 level. As prices mounted, Government appropriations grew correspondingly and necessitated the issue of additional Treasury notes to meet the increased expenses. Each new issue of notes resulted in a corresponding advance in prices and appropriations; thus, a vicious cycle—ever increasing in dimensions—was in constant operation. For the period February 18, 1862, to December 31, 1862, the total expenditure reported by the Secretary was $417,000,000—almost twice the amount he had anticipated at the start of the year. Of the receipts during the same period, 80% were comprised of interest-bearing and non-interest-bearing Treasury notes.[106]

In his report of January 10, 1863, Secretary Memminger again expounded upon the evils of an inflated currency:

... the mere fact that its actual volume has been increased threefold would lead us to expect a corresponding increase in prices. Such increase, although eventually certain, does not usually appear at the same moment with the expansion. Like the moon's attraction upon the ocean, the time of high-water is postponed for a certain period beyond the moment at which the influence has been exerted ... but, although there may be delay, the event is certain. Prices will reach the height adjusted by the scale of issues, and they can only be restored to their usual condition by a return to the normal standard of currency. In other words, the only remedy for an inflated currency is a reduction of the circulating medium.[107]

The Secretary added that the remedy to be effective must be prompt and must withdraw two-thirds of all the outstanding currency. To promote the remedy, he suggested that the compulsory funding measures approved October 13, 1862, be extended by adopting a time limit beyond which the privilege of funding notes issued prior to December 1, 1862, should cease. To insure payment of the principle and interest on the funded notes, he recommended that a 10% war-tax be collected, and to protect any new issue of Treasury notes from growing redundant, he urged Congress to approve the states' plan for guaranteeing payment of the Confederate debt. Despite the expanded condition of the currency and the remedies suggested to improve it, Secretary Memminger was compelled to request authority to issue an additional $200,000,-

TREASURY NOTES

000 in Treasury notes in order to meet the Government's expenses up to July 1, 1863.[108]

On March 23, 1863, Congress acted upon the recommendations of the Secretary. He was empowered to issue monthly up to $50,000,000 in non-interest-bearing Treasury notes. As under former acts, the new notes were receivable in payment of all public dues, except the export duty on cotton, and were payable within two years after the ratification of a treaty of peace. The notes were to be of a denomination not less than $5 and were fundable any time during the first year of their issue in 30-year 6% bonds; after that period they were fundable in 30-year 4% bonds. The act also authorized the issue of non-interest-bearing notes of the denominations of 50¢, $1 and $2, "to such an amount as, in addition to the notes of the denomination of one dollar, heretofore issued, shall not exceed the sum of fifteen millions of dollars." The small denomination notes, payable six months after a treaty of peace, were receivable for all public dues except the export duty on cotton, but were not fundable.[109]

Under the funding measures of the act only $21,000,000 in notes were withdrawn from circulation[110]—the reduction being far surpassed by the issue of new notes. On January 1, 1863 non-interest-bearing notes in circulation had totaled $289,000,000.[111] This figure increased rapidly to over $616,000,000 by September 30,[112] and to more than $730,500,000 by January 1, 1864.[113] The great increase in the amount of notes issued and outstanding resulted from the huge expenditures necessitated by the extensive military operations in the summer and fall of 1863. During the operation of the funding act of March 23, 1863, more than $517,000,000 in non-interest-bearing notes were issued.[114]

When Congress convened for the winter session of 1863-64, it was confronted with the appalling financial condition of the Confederacy. Secretary Memminger reported that more than $700,000,000 in notes were in circulation, and that $500,000,000 had to be retired in order to reduce the notes outstanding to $200,000,000 —an amount he considered sufficient for the best interests of the public credit. He reiterated that the voluntary exchange of notes for bonds, from which so much had been expected, had proved a failure, and added that the compulsory measures for funding under the acts of October 13, 1862, and March 23, 1863, had also failed to reduce the circulation to the extent expected of them. To rectify the weaknesses of the previous funding measures, Memminger recommended the adoption of additional compulsory legislation —legislation which would *force* noteholders to give up their notes for bonds, thus correcting the redundancy. In order to prevent the evils incident to too rapid a contraction, the Secretary proposed that "two hundred millions of new currency be issued from time to time during the period of contraction, and only in substitution of that called in; so that when the 1st of April shall arrive, at which time the old circulation shall become uncurrent, there may be a new currency to take its place." To guarantee payment of the principal and interest of the bonds, and also to make the bonds and new currency more desirable, a tax of 5% was proposed on all property and credits, payable July 1, 1864, one-half in coin or coupons of the bonds, and one-half in the new notes.[115]

On February 17, 1864, Congress passed "An Act to reduce the currency and to authorize a new issue of notes and bonds." This was the third and last of the compulsory funding acts. As indicated in its title, the act was aimed primarily at reducing the redundant Treasury notes. Under the act non-interest-bearing notes were divided into four classes: those of denominations of 50¢, $1, and $2; those of the denomination of $5; those of denominations above $5, except the $100 notes; and those of the denomination of $100. In the order of their classification, the degree of severity with which the notes were treated increased.

Notes of denominations of 50¢, $1, and $2 were not affected by the provisions of the act; they were to remain current and receivable as formerly.

Notes of the denomination of $5 were received at par, both for public dues and for funding in 20-year 4% registered bonds, until July 1, 1864, east of the Mississippi or until October 1, 1864, west of the Mississippi, after which dates they were receivable and fundable at two-thirds of their face value until January 1, 1865, when they would be abolished by the tax of 100%. The specific requirement of funding notes in "registered bonds" aimed at impeding their easy transfer.

All notes of denominations above $5, which composed by far the greater portion of the currency, were receivable at par, both for public dues and for funding in 20-year 4% registered bonds, only until April 1, 1864, east of the Mississippi and until July 1, 1864, west of the Mississippi, after which dates they were receivable and fundable at two-thirds of their face value until January 1, 1865, when all notes of the old issues were taxed 100%.

TREASURY NOTES

The non-interest-bearing $100 notes were treated even more severely. Those not presented for 20-year 4% bonds by April 1, 1864, east of the Mississippi or by July 1 west of the Mississippi ceased being receivable by the Government, and in addition to the tax of 33 1/3% placed on other notes, were also taxed 10% of their face value each month until funded. Moreover, the $100 notes were not exchangeable for new notes.[116] To avoid too sudden a contraction in the currency, the funding act of February 17, 1864, provided for a new issue of notes to be made during the period April 1, 1864, and January 1, 1865. Any holder of non-interest-bearing Treasury notes issued under former acts, and of any denomination of $5 or more (except $100 notes), could, after April 1, 1864, east of the Mississippi and after July 1, 1864, west of the Mississippi, exchange them for notes of the new issue at the rate of $3 of the old for $2 of the new. To prevent further inflation of the currency, holders of the new issues or of the old (except $100 notes), after the latter had been reduced by the 33 1/3% tax, could convert the notes into 4% Call Certificates, payable two years after peace, unless reconverted earlier into notes.

Thus the act attempted to reduce the currency by compelling noteholders to (1) fund their notes in 20-year 4% registered bonds or (2) exchange them at the rate of $3 in old for $2 in new notes. To promote its plans, Congress authorized the necessary notes and bonds. Authority to issue notes under former acts was revoked April 1, 1864. The new notes, which it was hoped would supplant all previous issues, were payable two years after a treaty of peace, and were receivable by the Government for all dues except the export duty on cotton. To prevent the notes from becoming redundant they were exchangeable for 4% Call Certificates.

When the funding act of February 17, 1864, went into effect April 1, 1864, Secretary Memminger estimated that non-interest-bearing notes totaling $800,000,000 were in circulation.[117] On April 30, Robert Tyler, Register of the Treasury, reported that the amount of all classes of Treasury notes issued under former acts and outstanding on that date totaled $951,500,000. Of this figure, $851,000,000 represented non-interest-bearing notes. The Register also reported that by April 30 an additional $48,000,000 had been issued under the act of February 17, 1864.[118] During the early operation of the funding act a large number of old issue notes had been withdrawn from circulation, thus improving the value of the remaining currency. The improvement, however, was short lived, for as soon as the Treasury began to issue new notes and exchange them for old ones at the rate of $2 for $3, the value of the currency again declined, and with old and new notes circulating together each discredited and continued to depreciate the value of the other.

The changing value of currency was reflected in the fluctuating premium on gold. At the time the act of February 17, 1864, was approved, the value of a gold dollar was $23 in Treasury notes. The exchange rate remained the same during March, but dropped to $22, $18, and $17 during the next three months, only to turn upward in July and again reach $23 in September as it continued its climb, reaching $45 by the end of the year.

Unable to cause a permanent reduction of the currency, the funding act had the ill effect of impairing popular confidence in the Confederate Government. Concerning the ill effect of compulsory funding, Secretary Trenholm wrote to Governor M. L. Bonham of South Carolina on August 5, 1864:

. . . However patriotically intended, it is not to be denied that the [compulsory] measures adopted by Congress for the reform of the currency had the unhappy effect of inspiring the public mind with feelings of fear and distrust as to the course that would ultimately be pursued in relation to that part of the public debt that is represented by the Treasury notes. Apprehensions of ultimate repudiation crept like an all-pervading poison into the minds of the people, and greatly circumscribed and diminished the purchasing power of the notes . . . it must now be universally admitted that the policy was erroneous.[119]

With prices continuing to rise, noteholders found it to their advantage to withhold the old notes from the Treasury and circulate them. That Congress failed to reduce the currency by compulsory funding is evidenced by the act of December 24, 1864. The act extended the time for exchanging old notes for 20-year 4% registered bonds to July 1, 1865; it suspended for six months the 100% tax due on the notes; and again declared notes of old issues tax receivable during the same period.

When Congress convened for its last session in November, 1864, Secretary Trenholm presented the final comprehensive report on the condition of the Confederate Treasury. The report showed the expenditures and receipts for the six months' period ending October 1. On that day the public debt totaled $1,148,000,000. Interest-bearing notes and Call Certificates amounted to $301,000,

000, which with $608,000,000 in non-interest-bearing notes comprised 81% of the debt. Of the non-interest-bearing notes, $324,000,000 were old notes still in circulation and $284,000,000 were new notes issued in exchange for old ones at the rate of $2 for $3.[120] Turning to the inflated condition of the Treasury notes, the Secretary stated that the compulsory funding measures of February 17 had not permanently diminished the volume of the currency or sustained the value of the notes. He said, "The depreciation of the currency, proceeding from redundancy and the want of confidence in its ultimate redemption, can only be corrected by measures that shall both diminish its volume and sustain the public confidence." To this end, he recommended that Congress reverse its policy and discontinue taxing old notes; pledge the faith of the Government against increasing the existing issues; apply 1/5 of the annual taxes to the redemption of current notes until the amount outstanding is reduced to $150,000,000; and continue the tax-in-kind after the war, appropriating an ascertained portion of it annually to redeeming the circulation until the whole shall be retired. Trenholm then elaborated upon each recommendation showing how it would beneficially affect the currency, if adopted.[121]

President Davis immediately endorsed the Secretary's plan for improving the currency and restoring public confidence in the Government,[122] but Congress after three months of intermittent debate finally dismissed a joint committee of both houses March 3, 1865, when it failed to reach an agreement on the Secretary's recommendations, the bill thus failing enactment.[123]

At this late date the belief was becoming prevalent that the Government's paper money policy had gone too far to be reversed; that nothing would be gained by trying to reduce the currency; and that Congress might as well continue to pay its expenses with further issues of notes, which probably would be worth something if the Confederacy succeeded, but would be worth nothing if it failed.[124]

This was apparently the view held by Congress when it rejected the plan of Secretary Trenholm, and later when it overrode the President's veto by approving the act of March 18, 1865, which provided for a new issue of $80,000,000 in Treasury notes to pay the arrears due the army.[125] The new issue, however, was never realized since the Treasury Note Bureau and the contractors for producing the Government's currency were unable to issue a single note after they evacuated Columbia on February 20, 1865.

CONFEDERATE FINANCE

It should be noted that the monetary disorder of the Confederacy was abetted by the increasing quantity of notes issued by corporations—public and private—as well as by individuals. Each vied with the other and the central government to supply the popular demand for more paper, and each, knowingly or unknowingly, added to the evils of a redundant currency.

Taking their cue from Alabama, following that state's issue of notes, February 9, 1861, practically every state in the Confederacy fell in line and made issues of its own.[126] Although the amount of state treasury notes outstanding during the war has never been determined, it probably was very high. As early as January 10, 1863, Secretary Memminger reported that approximately $20,-000,000 in state treasury notes and banknotes were in circulation,[127] but in view of the financial legislation enacted by the several states,[128] this amount unquestionably rose to a much higher figure before an end was brought to the hostilities.

Numerous cities of the South, adopting the example set by the states, issued municipal treasury notes of small denominations as an aid in making change. Of the cities assuming this privilege, Richmond, Charleston, Pensacola, and Augusta were perhaps the most notorious. Like the cities, many private corporations eagerly resorted to the issuing of notes in the hope of supplying a receptive public with currency of small denominations. Railroad companies, factories, turnpike companies, savings banks, and insurance companies were among the private corporations to issue notes. Of this type of circulation the greatest amount was probably that issued by railroads. Following in the footsteps of the large private corporations, independent business men issued personal notes of small denominations in order to give change to customers. These "shinplasters" were signed and circulated by bankers, grocers, milk dealers, and innkeepers, and were usually redeemable in the goods or services of the individual issuing them. Although the notes of individuals and private corporations circulated freely in the South, the Confederate Congress never adopted measures to suppress them. Several of the states, on the other hand, approved legislation in an attempt to prevent the circulation of personal and corporate notes, but their efforts apparently met with little success.

The inflated condition of the Confederate currency was further aggravated by the free circulation of counterfeit Treasury notes and banknotes, coupled with the constant infiltration of Federal "greenbacks." It was claimed that the circulation of "greenbacks"

TREASURY NOTES

had done more harm to the Southern cause than had the Federal arms.[129] On February 6, 1864, Congress passed "An Act to prohibit dealing in the paper currency of the enemy." The act forbade under heavy penalty any person to "buy, sell, take, circulate, or in any manner trade in any paper currency of the United States." The act, however, did not apply to the purchase of Federal postage stamps nor "to any person acting in behalf of the Government of the Confederate States, by special authority from the President, or any of the heads of Departments."[130]

The various kinds of currency in the South, circulating side by side, became so muddled that people were frequently compelled to revert to barter in order to escape the monetary confusion. As with taxes and subscriptions to the Produce Loans, payment was frequently made in produce or manufactured articles. Upon the collapse of the Confederacy, the following lines written on the unprinted back of a Treasury note by Major A. L. Jonas of Mississippi attests to the status of the Government's currency "from the birth of the dream to its last":

The Confederate Note

Representing nothing on God's earth now,
    And naught in the waters below it,
As the pledge of a nation that passed away,
    Keep it, dear friend, and show it.
Show it to those who will lend an ear
    To the tale this paper will tell,
Of liberty born of a patriot's dream,
    Of a storm-cradled nation that fell.

Too poor to possess the precious ores,
    And too much of a stranger to borrow,
We issue to-day our promise to pay
    And hope to redeem on the morrow.
The days rolled on and the weeks became years.
    But our coffers were empty still,
Coin was so scarce the Treasury quaked
    If a dollar should drop in the till.

But the faith that was in us was strong indeed,
    Though our poverty well we discerned,
And this little note represented the pay
    That our suffering veterans earned.
They knew it had hardly a value in gold,
    Yet as gold our soldiers received it;

> It gazed in our eyes with a promise to pay
>   And every true soldier believed it.
>
> But our boys thought little of price or pay,
>   Or of bills that were over-due,
> We knew if it bought our bread to-day,
>   'Twas the best our poor country could do.
> Keep it. It tells all our history over,
>   From the birth of the dream to its last;
> Modest and born of the Angel Hope,
>   Like our hope of success—it passed.[131]

In concluding the discussion of Confederate Treasury notes, a few words should be said regarding adoption of a legal tender act as a means of improving the value of currency. The advisability of such a measure attracted much attention during the existence of the Confederacy, but Congress persistently shied from adopting a legal tender act, viewing it as being inexpedient and unconstitutional.

The first serious discussion concerning the expediency of making Treasury notes a legal tender occurred with the convening of the First Permanent Congress, and Secretary Memminger was afforded an opportunity to express his views on the subject. In response to an inquiry from L. J. Gartrell, Chairman of the House Judiciary Committee, the Secretary listed his reasons for opposing a legal tender act. First, he said, "Treasury notes are now the accepted currency of our whole country, and circulate at par with banknotes. They therefore need no assistance at present to enable them to perform the function of legal tender." In fact, he said, any law to compel their acceptance would immediately arouse suspicion, shake public confidence, and depreciate the value of the notes. Second, a legal tender act could neither prevent depreciation of the notes nor alleviate the injury done by such depreciation. And third, "If the Government should attempt to constrain the receipt of notes by penalties, they have before them the experience of all nations as to its utter failure." Secretary Memminger ended by saying, "Extreme pressure may compel our Government to adopt in the future extreme measures; but it seems to me that at present it is our best policy to avoid every possible shock to public credit. . . . My judgment is against the passage of the law at the present time."[132]

Proponents of a legal tender act endeavored to sway those who held such a measure unconstitutional, saying that the Constitution gave Congress the power "to declare war" and "to raise and support armies"; that it also granted to Congress the authority "to make all laws which shall be necessary and proper for carrying into execution the foregoing powers"; thus the constitutional right to declare Treasury notes a legal tender was established.[133]

Discussion over a legal tender currency aroused the leading newspapers to take sides on the issue. Among those advocating a legal tender were the *Richmond Examiner* and the *Charleston Courier*. Those constantly opposed to a legal tender were the *Charleston Mercury* and the *Augusta Constitutionalist*.

During the first three years of the Confederacy, numerous legal tender bills were introduced in Congress, but Secretary Memminger's opinion in regard to their inexpediency and the strict constructionist views held by a majority of the Congressmen prevented any of the bills from becoming law. On December 24, 1863, Senator A. G. Brown of Mississippi in urging passage of a legal tender bill offered all the arguments previously used, but to no avail. With this failure, the question of a legal tender came to an end. Following adoption of the funding act of February 17, 1864, Congress relied upon its plan of compulsory funding and taxing of Treasury notes to correct the evils of a redundant currency; when this failed, all hope of curbing inflation by legislative measures ended.

The following table is a summary of the total amount of Treasury notes issued by the Confederate Government:

TABLE SHOWING AMOUNT OF EACH ISSUE OF CONFEDERATE TREASURY NOTES[134]

Act of March 9, 1861		$ 2,021,100.00
Act of May 16, 1861		17,347,955.00
Act of August 19, 1861		
Total	$292,101,830.00	
Less notes stolen, destroyed, &c.	140,000.00	291,961,830.00
Act of April 17, 1862		
Total	$128,561,400.00	
Less 100's destroyed . . .	320,000.00	128,241,400.00

CONFEDERATE FINANCE

TABLE SHOWING AMOUNT OF EACH ISSUE OF CONFEDERATE
TREASURY NOTES—Continued

Act of October 13, 1862
    Total $140,403,200.00
    Less one's & two's,
      never issued 2,400.00   140,400,800.00

Act of March 23, 1863
    Total $517,995,278.50
    Less ten's printed
      but never issued . . .   24,000.00   517,971,278.50

Act of February 17, 1864 . . .   456,142,990.50

      Net amount issued . . $1,554,087,354.00

CHAPTER

☆ IV ☆

TARIFFS AND TAXES

☆ ☆ ☆ ☆ ☆ ☆ ☆ ☆ ☆ ☆

FROM THE BEGINNING, THE CONFEDERATE CONGRESS HAD ASSUMED that import and export duties would furnish the basis for a substantial revenue. On February 9, 1861, the Congress enacted that all the tariff laws of the United States, in force and in use in the Confederate States on November 1, 1860, and not inconsistent with the Constitution of the Confederate States, should be continued in force until altered or repealed by Congress.[1] In order to carry out the act, it was resolved that the officers connected with the collection of Federal customs in the several states of the Confederacy at the time of the adoption of the Provisional Constitution be appointed to their respective offices under the Confederate Government. They were to "have the same powers, be subject to the same duties, and be entitled to the same salaries, fees and emoluments" as provided by the laws of the United States until April 1, 1861, at which time a plan was to go in effect whereby "the expenses of collecting the revenue at each Custom House" were to be "diminished at least fifty per cent."[2] With this in mind, Secretary Memminger requested of the various collectors information and suggestions as to dispensing with some of their officers. The smaller customhouses informed him that there could be no reduction in personnel and the larger ones stated that an increase in the staff was necessary.[3] Whereupon, Memminger appointed C. C. Walden of Savannah, Georgia, as Special Agent of the Treasury Department "to visit the customhouses'. . . . at the seaport towns, and make rigid examination into all the modes of conducting business there, and report fully as to all details." Walden was particularly to inquire and report whether the manner of conducting business could be improved; whether the number of officers could be diminished; and whether the expenses of collecting could be lessened. He was "to have in view the direction of Congress requiring these expenses to be abated 50 per cent, and report the best means of doing so."[4] While Walden went about his assignment, the collectors of customs were instructed "to enforce the existing revenue laws against all foreign countries, except the State of Texas."[5]

As a means of enforcing the tariff and preventing smuggling, the Secretary of the Treasury was empowered to establish such additional ports of entry as he considered necessary. He was also authorized to change, alter, and abolish the ports and places of entry at any time the public interests required it. Memminger, therefore, immediately created places of entry along the frontier and appointed officers to collect the duties. This action brought protests from those who believed that "collectors . . . on the interior borders would work some inconvenience and irritation of feeling that might delay the act of secession of North Carolina, Tennessee, and other States." It was suggested that the Secretary "suspend the execution of the revenue laws against the interior portion of the border States as long as propriety would permit."[6] Despite these protestations, C. P. Cooper was appointed a Special Agent of the Treasury April 4, 1861, to visit the Revenue Depots on the interior border for "the purpose of organizing the Customs business, and putting into operation the Revenue Laws."[7] But following the outbreak of war and the establishment of the Federal blockade, it was found "expedient to delay organizing the new revenue depots," and Cooper was ordered to return to Montgomery and await further developments.[8] On May 17, Secretary Memminger wrote that "the union of Virginia with our Confederacy, and the probable union in a few weeks of North Carolina and Tennessee, has rendered unnecessary the custom houses now established on the frontiers," and the several Collectors were ordered to "complete all business remaining unfinished, and render accounts to the Treasury Department."[9] With the closing of the frontier customhouses, the collection of duties was handled by officers at ports of entry and delivery on the seacoast, as approved under the act of February 14, 1861, and by certain officers appointed June 26 to collect customs in Virginia, North Carolina, and Tennessee following the union of those states with the Confederacy.[10] Except for an occasional withdrawal necessitated by the loss of a port of entry to the Federal forces, it befell this group of officers to collect the customs during the existence of the Confederacy.[11]

As stated previously, the Confederate Congress on February 9, 1861 temporarily adopted the United States Tariff Act of March 3, 1857, and the House Committee on Finance was "instructed to report, as soon as possible, a tariff for raising revenue for the support of the Government."[12] Nine days later a list of free articles was approved. The list included living animals of all kinds, all agricultural products in their natural state, meats, and war materiel. Also included were all the goods, wares, and merchandise imported from any one of the United States not then a member of the Confederacy, provided the articles had been purchased before February 28, and shipped prior to March 15.[13] On the latter date, Congress enacted the first of two distinctly Confederate tariffs. The new law levied a 15% *ad valorem* duty on imports of iron, coal, cheese, paper, and lumber,[14] and a day later a duty of 5¢ per ton, called "light money," was placed on all ships entering a Confederate port after May 1.[15]

In his report of May 10, Secretary Memminger stated that he expected to raise over $25,000,000 by import duties during the year. To do this he proposed that Congress "enact a tariff on imports at a rate averaging at least $12\frac{1}{2}$ per cent."[16] Congress obliged the Secretary May 21, 1861 by approving "An act to provide revenue from commodities imported from foreign countries." The new tariff act, slightly amended August 3 and put into effect on August 31, became the basis for the tariff policy adhered to by the Confederacy throughout the war. As might be expected, Congress enacted a tariff from which practically all traces of protection were removed. In fact, both Confederate Constitutions prohibited a protective tariff, the Permanent Constitution specifically stating that "no bounties shall be granted from the Treasury; nor shall any duties or taxes on importations from foreign nations be laid to promote or foster any branch of industry."[17]

The tariff of May 21, 1861, being primarily a revenue measure, was based upon the United States tariffs of 1846 and 1857 rather than upon the protective measures advocated in the Morrill Tariff of 1861. All imported articles came under one of seven schedules of duties. Five of the schedules levied *ad valorem* duties of 25%, 20%, 15%, 10%, and 5%; a sixth levied specific duties, and the seventh contained a list of free articles. In each schedule the rate of duty was aimed at deriving the largest revenue from the particular articles to which it pertained. In application of this principle, some of the rates of the ante-bellum acts were lowered while others were raised. Duties on textiles and metal manufactures were reduced from 24% to 15%, and coal, coke, raw hemp, tobacco, leather, iron ore, and pig iron were reduced from 24% to 10%. On the other hand, a duty of $1.50 per ton was placed on ice, which article had been on the free list under the two previous United States tariffs.[18]

Until the new tariff went into effect on August 31, all goods imported into the Confederate States were subject to duties under the tariff of 1857, except for the few exemptions provided by the Acts of February 18 and March 15, 1861.[19] As stated above, Memminger expected to receive $25,000,000 during the year from imports. His plans, however, were never realized, for the vigilance of the Federal Navy prevented the Treasury from acquiring the anticipated revenue from customs. On April 19, 1861, President Lincoln declared the Confederate coast blockaded south of North Carolina and eight days later extended the blockade to include the coasts of North Carolina and Virginia. In a short time, Wilmington, Charleston, Tampa, Mobile, and other ports were blockaded by Federal men-of-war. That the blockade interfered most effectively with the trade of the South cannot be denied. On October 18, 1861, A. B. Noyes, Collector of Customs at St. Mark's, Florida, informed Secretary Memminger that he did not believe a single vessel had knowingly been allowed ingress or egress from that port since the start of the blockade.[20] Similar reports were made by customs collectors located all along the coast.[21] Regardless of the watchfulness of the Federal fleet, the possibility of large profits from importing foreign goods and exporting cotton stimulated ingenuity and daring in blockade-running; nevertheless, the amount of imports proved insignificant and Secretary Memminger's plans for a substantial revenue from customs duties were doomed to failure, the total receipts being less than $3,500,000.

The accompanying table exhibits the amount of customs collected during the existence of the Confederacy.

TARIFFS AND TAXES

TABLE SHOWING THE AMOUNT OF IMPORT DUTIES COLLECTED IN THE CONFEDERACY[22]

Date	Amount Collected
Feb. 17, 1861 to Feb. 18, 1862	$1,270,875.48
Feb. 18, 1862 to Dec. 31, 1862	668,566.00
Jan. 1, 1863 to Sept. 30, 1863	934,798.68
Oct. 1, 1863 to Apr. 1, 1864	441,094.32
Apr. 1, 1864 to Oct. 1, 1864	59,004.33
Oct. 1, 1864 to collapse of Confederacy, say	50,000.00
Customs collected in the Trans-Mississippi Dept.	56,278.51
Total Customs	$3,480,617.32

EXPORT DUTIES

Brief as is the story of import duties, that concerning the duty on exports is briefer. An export duty on cotton had been conceived early by the Confederate Congress. In fact, the Provisional Constitution, unlike the Constitution of the United States, completely omitted the prohibition against export duties whereas the Permanent Constitution of the Confederate States sanctioned such a duty if approved by a two-thirds vote of both Houses of Congress.[23] The legislature was not long in making use of its authority to lay an export duty. As has been seen, the first major loan approved by the Confederate Congress—the $15-Million Loan of February 28, 1861—provided for an export duty of one-eighth of one cent per pound on all cotton shipped from the Confederacy after August 1, 1861. The duty, payable in specie or in the interest coupons of the loan, was expected to furnish the Treasury with a large specie revenue. One advocate estimated the amount to be realized from the export duty on cotton at $20,000,000,[24] but, as in the case of import duties, the severity of the blockade permitted only meagre returns, the total export duty received by the customs collectors being approximately $30,000 in specie.

Although the one-eighth of one cent per pound on cotton was the only export duty authorized by Congress, the question of increasing the rate and also of extending the duty to cover additional articles was raised on several occasions.

On May 1, Secretary Memminger estimated the value of cotton, rice, tobacco, and other articles to be exported during 1861 at $237,000,000 and recommended that Congress authorize an export duty of 10 to 12½%, which would net approximately

$25,000,000. "In framing the Constitution," he said, "it was foreseen that the necessities of War might compel a resort to export duties, and the power exists in Congress to raise money from export as well as import duties." The Secretary admitted that a duty on exports was open to the objection that it was paid by only a portion of the community—the producer, and proposed to remove this objection by indemnifying the producer from revenue derived from import duties. He suggested that "when the export duty is paid, a Custom House Warrant for the amount paid, assignable to order, be delivered to the exporter; and that such Warrant be receivable in payment of duties on imports, within a limited period." He also recommended that an interest be allowed on the Warrant during the time it was receivable in payment of import duties.[25]

Congress refused to adopt the Secretary's recommendations regarding a 12½% duty on exports, but on May 21, 1861, it approved his recommendations of May 10 for a similar duty on imports.

On April 7, 1863, with a view to improving the value of the bonds issued under the Funding Loan of March 23, 1863, Secretary Memminger again raised the question of an export duty, proposing for the security of the bonds that an export duty payable in coin or in the interest coupons of the bonds be laid on all agricultural products. The Secretary said:

> If it be asked how an export duty on goods which cannot be exported can aid the public credit, the fifteen-million loan answers the inquiry.
>
> This whole loan has always been above the par of Treasury notes, and very little of it is ever for sale in the stock market. The bonds at the last quotation of a sale were as high as 135. This high premium is owing to the fact that the coupons are receivable at the customhouse for the export duty on cotton, and the high price of the whole loan is owing to its being secured by this export duty. It is manifest therefore that if the same privilege be extended to other bonds a similar result will follow. . . .[26]

Memminger then recommended that an export duty of 2¢ per pound be laid on the principal agricultural products. He said at that rate the duty on the cotton and tobacco on hand in the Confederacy, along with the duty on the anticipated crops for the next two years, would furnish the Treasury with $48,000,000—more than enough to pay the interest on the loan up to April 1, 1865.

Notwithstanding the Secretary's recommendations for improving the value of the bonds issued under the act of March 23, 1863, Congress again refused to authorize an extension of the export duty. Later, however, upon adoption of the $500-Million Loan of February 17, 1864, the way was prepared for increasing the duty on exports. The loan stipulated that for the payment of interest on the bonds "the entire net receipts of any export duty hereafter laid on the value of all cotton, tobacco, and naval stores, which shall be exported from the Confederate States . . . or so much thereof as may be necessary to pay annually the interest, are hereby specially pledged."[27] Despite this provision of the loan, Congress continued to refrain from increasing the export duty.

On November 7, 1864, Secretary Trenholm proposed a duty of five cents per pound on the exportation of cotton and tobacco, and the duplication of the duties on imports, payment to be made in specie, sterling exchange, or in the interest coupons of the $500-Million Loan. "These measures," he said, "would enhance the value and enlarge the demand for the five hundred-million loan."[28] But Congress failed to act on the proposal, and attempts to increase the duty on exports came to an end.

The accompanying table exhibits the amount of export duty collected during the existence of the Confederacy.

TABLE SHOWING THE AMOUNT OF EXPORT DUTIES
COLLECTED IN THE CONFEDERACY[29]

Date	Amount Collected
Feb. 17, 1861 to Dec. 10, 1861	$ 1,311.65
Dec. 10, 1861 to Dec. 31, 1862 (none reported collected)	
Jan. 1, 1863 to Sept. 30, 1863	8,101.78
Oct. 1, 1863 to Apr. 1, 1864	14,322.50
Apr. 1, 1864 to Oct. 1, 1864	4,320.12
Oct. 1, 1864 to collapse of Confederacy, say	2,000.00
Export duties collected in the Trans-Mississippi Dept.	9,012.15
Total export duty collected	$39,068.20

FREE TRADE, PROTECTION, AND EMBARGO

Although the Confederate Congress adopted a tariff based on the principle of procuring revenue, the question was frequently raised as to whether the commercial policy of the Government should be one of free trade, protection, or embargo.

During the first year of the Confederacy, a policy of free trade was especially advocated. It was believed that restrictions on foreign trade would be injurious to the Southern cause, and the repeal of all tariff laws was earnestly discussed. In the fall of 1861, planters and merchants, convening at Macon and Charleston, advocated the suspension of all duties and the adoption of a policy of free trade with all nations at peace with the Confederacy.[30]

The *Richmond Examiner* also strongly advocated a policy of free trade. Its editor maintained that a Confederate tariff at the time of a Federal blockade was an absurdity and recommended the repeal of all tariff laws as a means of encouraging foreigners to break the blockade.[31]

The agitation for free trade was not without effect. Before the end of the year two bills for the repeal of all tariff laws had been introduced in Congress but, after being discussed in secret session, the measures failed adoption.[32] The last legislative attempt to adopt a free trade policy occurred April 3, 1862. On that date a bill approving free trade with foreign nations other than the United States was passed by the House, but the Senate refused to act on the measure.[33]

With the Senate's failure to act on the bill, vigorous discussion in behalf of free trade ended, and in its place developed a public opinion in favor of trade limitations. This transition in thought regarding a trade policy resulted primarily from three factors: 1. The severity of the blockade which made insignificant any legislative restrictions on trade. 2. A growing desire to protect Southern industries. 3. The spreading conception that by restricting trade foreign powers could be coerced into recognizing the Confederate Government.

As formerly stated, the Confederate Constitution prohibited a protective tariff. The prohibition, however, could not prevent the growth of a strong protectionist feeling. Three months after the institution of the blockade, it was being claimed that the blockade was a blessing in disguise and that it was educating the South to promote and encourage the development of its own boundless resources.[34] Industries previously neglected were called into existence, and as the war progressed, lists of factories were published in testimony of the South's industrial advancement.[35] During this time many of the arguments in support of a protective tariff were voiced,[36] and there was a growing feeling that the blockade would accomplish both the national and commercial independence of the South. This latter feeling found expression in the movement to forbid exports and adopt an embargo policy.

TARIFFS AND TAXES

When the Provisional Government convened at Montgomery in 1861, there were some who believed that the North and Great Britain could be brought to terms with the Confederacy by cutting off the supply of cotton. This group, therefore, looked upon an embargo with favor.[37] The movement for a cotton embargo gained impetus during the summer of 1861 as cotton factors at Charleston, Savannah, Mobile, and New Orleans urged planters throughout the South to withhold their cotton from market until the blockade was ended. In the spring of 1862, the Governor and Council of South Carolina passed a resolution prohibiting the exportation of cotton, but suspended its operation when Secretary Memminger objected on the grounds that the state should refrain from action until Congress had expressed a definite policy on the embargo question. Later varying forms of an embargo policy were proclaimed by other states.

The movement for an embargo policy, like most controversial issues, found both proponents and opponents. Some viewed the embargo as a powerful military weapon which the South would be foolish not to use. In February of 1862 the *Charleston Mercury* claimed that England was already beginning to feel the power of the Confederacy to withhold cotton and must inevitably intervene. Others held that it was not England nearly so much as New England that gained by obtaining raw cotton for its mills and it was contended the latter could be coerced by cutting off the cotton supply.[38]

The *Charleston Courier*, on the other hand, strongly opposed the prohibition of exports advocated by correspondents in its columns. The editor declared that a Confederate embargo would simply aid the enemy to enforce its blockade, and stated that the wisest policy for the South to adopt was one which would increase her exports, not decrease them, and thus furnish the means for obtaining the needed imports at the lowest possible cost.

Confronted with the numerous arguments relating to the prohibition of exports, the Confederate Congress continually refrained from adopting an embargo act. True, on February 6, 1864, and again on February 18, 1865, legislation was passed forbidding the exportation of cotton, tobacco, military and naval stores, rice, sugar, and molasses, except under regulations of the Treasury Department, but this legislation was no part of an embargo policy. It was aimed specifically at supplying the Government's needs for articles from abroad by placing at the disposal of the Confederate authorities one-half the tonnage of all privately-owned incoming and outgoing vessels. In this way the Treasury hoped to curb the excessive profits of blockade-runners, prevent the importation of luxuries, and, at the same time, avail the Government of facilities to export its cotton and tobacco.

WAR TAX OF AUGUST 19, 1861

The Confederate Congress, as we have seen, originally emphasized loans as the means of supplying the necessities of its existence. Later the use of Treasury notes was stressed. During the first two years of the Confederacy, direct taxation, although frequently advocated by the Secretary of the Treasury, was almost completely neglected. The reluctance of Congress to adopt a direct tax resulted primarily from the notion held by many that the war would be of short duration and that the revenue to be derived from export and import duties would more than supply the Government's financial needs. As it was, the war continued, expenditures mounted, and the effectiveness of the Federal blockade greatly diminished the revenue from duties. Congress was, thus, gradually compelled to place more and more emphasis on taxes. This was done in an effort to create a sound foundation for its financial policy. It was believed that by laying a direct tax adequate funds would be raised to pay the principal and interest on the various loans, and by making the tax payable in Treasury notes, it was hoped the desirability of notes as a currency would be increased and their redundancy decreased. The action of Congress, however, throughout the existence of the Confederacy failed to achieve the desirable objectives expected of it.

As early as May 1, 1861, Secretary Memminger informed Congress that a resort to Internal Taxes seemed to be a necessity:

When war is waged upon a country and its citizens are called to the defense of their homes from foreign aggressions, it is every man's duty to contribute of his substance to that defense. . . . The most certain and the most enduring resources are those which should be sought out by the Government, and Taxes afford the only certain reliance under all circumstances. Loans, from their nature, are contributions from only portions of the community; duties, although reaching further, do not reach all; but direct taxes pervade the whole body politic, and bring forth the contributions of the willing and of the unwilling, if there be any such.[39]

James D. Dénégré, well-known New Orleans banker, urged Memminger to recommend the adoption of a direct tax which would produce $30- to $40-million annually from owners of real estate, slaves, and invested capital.[40] Others, thinking a direct tax too cumbersome, looked to the revenue from customs duties to suffice the Government's needs.[41]

In his report of May 10, 1861, Secretary Memminger recommended that Congress impose a direct tax of $15,000,000, payable in specie or in Confederate Treasury notes. He proposed that the tax be assessed and collected prior to October 1, by the tax machinery then existing in the several states, and suggested that a discount be allowed to each state immediately paying its quota.[42]

Congress, however, was reluctant to adopt a system of direct taxation and merely pledged the faith of the Confederate States to provide a sufficient revenue to pay the interest and principal of the $50-Million Loan, approved May 16, 1861.[43] To carry out this pledge, Secretary Memminger was directed to collect information regarding "the value of property, the revenue system, and the amount collected during the fiscal year in each of the Confederate States, and to report the same to Congress . . . so as to enable it to lay a fair, equal and convenient system of internal taxation" for the purpose of raising $10,000,000 during the year 1861.[44] The states were urged to pay into the Treasury, in anticipation of the tax, any sum greater than $100,000 in specie or its equivalent— the amount, along with a discount of 10%, if paid before July 1, to be deducted from the tax quota assessed the respective states.

Memminger immediately set about collecting the information requested by Congress[45] and on July 24 reported his findings to that body. The Secretary stated that the revenue system adopted by each of the states was so different that Congress would be compelled to adjust a scheme of its own. In respect to the amount of tax to be raised, he said, "events have occurred since the adjournment of Congress which require a larger sum than was originally supposed. At least twenty-five millions of dollars ought to be raised for the wants of the Government, and to sustain its credit in taking up the loans which will become necessary." To raise this amount, he recommended that a tax of 54¢ per $100 be placed on the value of slaves, real estate, merchandise, bank and other corporate stock, and money at interest. The assessed value of the taxable items the Secretary placed at $4,632,160,501, approximately one-half representing slaves, and nearly two-fifths real estate.[46]

CONFEDERATE FINANCE

Adhering rather closely to the recommendations of Secretary Memminger, Congress provided for a direct war tax by approving the loan act of August 19, 1861. The act stated that "for the special purpose of paying the principal and interest of the public debt, and of supporting the government, a war tax shall be levied," at the rate of fifty cents per one hundred dollars, upon the assessed value of the taxable items recommended by the Secretary of the Treasury along with a number of luxury items added to the list by Congress. In the event the taxable property of the head of a family was valued at less than $500, it was declared tax free as was the case with all property belonging to educational, charitable, and religious institutions. To aid in assessing and collecting the tax, each state was to constitute a tax division under the supervision of a Chief Collector. The state or tax division was to be divided into districts headed by tax collectors who were empowered to appoint assessors for their respective districts. An assessment of all taxable property was to be made on or before November 1, and assessment lists were to be completed and delivered into the hands of each tax collector by December 1, 1861. Collection of the tax was to take place on May 1, 1862, and to guarantee prompt payment, the act prescribed severe penalties for delinquents. To ease the burden of the taxpayer, the several states were authorized to anticipate the amount of taxes assessed against their citizens by paying the amount, less 10% discount, into the Treasury at any time prior to April 1, 1862.[47]

Arrangements for collecting the War Tax moved forward slowly. By September 17, 1861, Secretary Memminger had selected his Chief Collectors and recommended them for President Davis' approval;[48] by September 28, a War Tax Bureau under the supervision of Thompson Allan had been created in the Treasury Department;[49] and by October 15, printed instructions for the assessment and collection of the War Tax had been sent to all Chief Collectors.[50] On November 20, Secretary Memminger reported that preliminary arrangements for collection of the War Tax had been completed; Chief Collectors had been appointed in all of the states, and the states had been divided into districts. He added, however, that the great extent of the country, together with the condition of the times, had rendered it impossible to comply with the requisitions of the act fixing Monday, November 1, as the day for making assessments, and recommended the time be extended to January 1, 1862.[51] On December 19, 1861, Congress not only accepted Memminger's recommendation and extended the time of assessments to January 1, 1862, but also authorized the Secretary to make further postponements if circumstances so warranted.

Numerous difficulties were encountered in assessing uniformly similar items of property in the several states, especially slaves.[52] By July 1862, only two of eleven states had made complete assessment returns while six states made no returns at all.[53] When finally completed, the assessments proved to be somewhat less than Secretary Memminger's estimate, amounting to $4,220,755,834.21. Of this figure, approximately 1,500 millions represented slaves; 1,400 millions, real estate; 500 millions, money at interest; and 94 millions, bank stock.[54]

Under the act of December 19, 1861, which extended the time of assessment, the time for collecting the tax remained unchanged, but by the later acts of April 19, September 30, and October 13, 1862, either the time was extended, or the collection was temporarily suspended, as in the case of Missouri, Kentucky, and portions of other states which had been overrun by the enemy.[55] During the first year of the Confederacy, no revenue was realized from the tax, but during the five months ending August 1, 1862, $10,538,910.70 had been collected.[56] This figure rose to $16,664,513 by the end of the year.[57] In November 1863, the War Tax Bureau issued its last comprehensive report covering the ½% tax levied under the act of August 19, 1861. The report stated that of the $19,418,392.49 to be collected, $17,446,736.28 had been paid into the Treasury by July 1, 1863.[58]

The balance was represented mostly by tax on property lying in Arkansas, Tennessee, Texas, and Virginia, where the presence of the enemy or the distance from Richmond made its collection difficult and frequently impossible. The delay in collecting the tax in the other states resulted primarily from the dependence of Congress upon the state governments to either collect the tax assessed their citizens or pay the quota, less 10%, into the Confederate Treasury.

It was this privilege granted the states of paying the quota assessed their citizens which prevented the tax from assuming its true character. Of the eleven states paying the assessment, only three—South Carolina, Mississippi, and Texas—actually collected the tax. The other states borrowed the amount they believed due, paid it into the Confederate Treasury, and then replaced the

Treasury notes withdrawn from circulation with issues of state treasury notes.[59] By assuming payment of the War Tax, the states hoped to protect their citizens from hardship and inconvenience, but in so doing competed with the Confederate Government in floating loans and weakened the central power's measures to prevent a redundant currency by issuing state notes. Only three of the states assuming payment of the tax paid their quotas in full; they were: Georgia, Louisiana, and North Carolina. In fact, Louisiana and North Carolina overpaid the assessment and were reimbursed for the amount of excess.[60]

Of the states collecting the tax, South Carolina first floated a temporary loan to raise funds to pay the assessment. The state then obtained the books prepared by the Confederate assessors, collected the tax with the aid of the state tax machinery, and used the proceeds to cancel the loan.[61] In only Mississippi and Texas was the War Tax collected by Confederate officers. These two instances, however, showed that the 10% discount allowed the states for assuming payment of the tax, presumably to cover the expense of collection, was much too large—in Mississippi, the actual cost being less than 2%. In the border states of Missouri and Kentucky, no attempt was made to either assess or collect the tax.

The following table shows the total assessments made under the act of August 19, 1861, the net tax levied, and the amount paid into the Confederate Treasury by each of the states up to July 1, 1863. Available records indicate that the balance, represented largely by the tax on property lying in areas held by the enemy, was never collected.

TARIFFS AND TAXES

War Tax Assessments under Act of August 19, 1861 and Payments Made up to July 1, 1863[62]

States	Total Aggregate	Tax—½ One Per Cent	Net Tax	Amount Paid
Alabama	d$ 459,659,497.47	$ 2,298,297.47	$ 2,068,467.73	$ 2,000,000.00
Arkansas	f 122,579,117.00	612,895.58	551,606.03	400,000.00
Florida	49,480,561.00	h 251,232.19	226,109.88	225,374.11
Georgia	564,173,946.82	2,771,236.01	2,494,112.41	2,494,112.41
Louisiana	534,921,329.01	h 2,693,527.10	2,424,174.39	2,424,174.39
Mississippi	447,616,073.00	2,241,003.20	2,241,003.20	2,094,990.23
North Carolina	286,405,625.00	1,432,028.12	1,288,825.31	1,288,825.31
South Carolina	399,468,798.00	1,997,343.99	h 1,798,076.52	1,651,528.55
Tennessee	n 490,000,000.00	2,450,000.00	2,205,000.00	1,499,766.77
Texas	318,286,671.00	1,654,278.05	1,654,278.05	1,242,964.51
Virginia	o 548,164,215.91	2,740,821.07	2,466,738.97	2,125,000.00
	$4,220,755,834.21	$21,142,662.78	$19,418,392.49	$17,446,736.28
Not including unassessed tax in Lawrence and Franklin, estimated at And same in Winston				$72,119.74 500.00
				$72,619.74

d Not including unassessed tax in Lawrence and Franklin,
  And same in Winston
f Eight counties not returned.
h Double tax included.
n Estimated, as no organization of State was made.
o Inclusive of assessments of sequestered and non-rendered property, (unclassified)—

	Tax	
Rendered property	$303,941,360.00	$1,519,706.80
Non-rendered property	12,568,939.00	125,689.39
Sequestered property	1,776,372.00	8,881.86
	$318,286,671.00	$1,654,278.05

· 135 ·

Judging by the $17,446,736.28 collected, it would appear that the war tax of August 19, 1861, was a success. Such, however, was not the case. As we have seen, little more than one-fourth of the amount raised by the war tax was actually a tax. In all the states except South Carolina, Mississippi, and Texas, the tax had been transformed into a loan in order to protect the people from hardship and inconvenience. On July 11, 1861, Alexander Stephens gave voice to the early feeling prevailing in the South regarding taxation. The Vice President of the Confederacy stated that the Government's policy was to make the burden of the war fall as lightly as possible upon the people. To this end, he said, Congress proposed to get along with as little taxation as possible, and would resort to that means of raising a revenue only when loans failed to supply the Government's needs.[63] That this policy was adhered to is readily seen. Aside from the war tax of August 19, 1861, no other tax was passed during the first two years of war. In the same period, seven loans had been floated and numerous issues of notes were approved. As the war expanded, the volume of supplies increased and expenditures mounted. To meet the growing needs, additional issues of Treasury notes were approved, and to curb the growing redundancy of the currency, additional loans were authorized in an attempt to withdraw the excess notes from circulation by funding. To secure payment of the principal and interest on the loans, taxes had to be increased. Thus it was that Congress was compelled to approve the first real tax act of the war—the tax of April 24, 1863—commonly referred to as the Tithe Tax or Tax-in-Kind.

The Tax Act of April 24, 1863

Despite the general opposition to taxation during the first two years of the Confederacy, Secretary Memminger repeatedly urged upon Congress the approval of additional tax laws. In reading the reports of the Secretary of the Treasury, one can readily sense that officer's growing anxiety in regard to the Government's tax policy. He stressed the need of a substantial revenue from taxation as a basis for loans and called attention to the insufficiency and weaknesses of the tax act of August 19, 1861, which had distributed the quotas among the several states and permitted the tax to be raised in any manner agreeable to them, subject to delay and uncertainty.[64]

The persistent efforts of Secretary Memminger in behalf of

TARIFFS AND TAXES

increased taxes were not without effect. On September 23, 1862, Representative D. F. Kenner of Louisiana, Chairman of the Ways and Means Committee, reported a bill providing for the levy of a uniform income tax of 20%. The tax was to be assessed January 1, 1863, on the gross products of the year 1862. All sources of income were taxable except bonds and Treasury notes. When the gross products or income of an individual totaled less than $500, it was to be exempt from taxation. In return for paying the tax, the payer was to receive an equal amount of Government bonds, called "Income Tax Bonds," bearing 6% interest and payable from 10 to 30 years. Thus, the proposed tax was really not a tax, but was actually a forced loan under the disguise of a tax. In support of the bill, Kenner stated that the Government's financial measures had been going smoothly, but the time had come for vigorous action. He said that but for one slight exception (the war tax of August 19, 1861) the credit of the South had been based almost exclusively on loans and issues of Treasury notes, and added that the issue of notes could no longer carry on the war, but that well defined revenues based on taxation had to be created if the Government was to be sustained. He reminded Congress that its first duty was not necessarily to lighten the financial burdens of the people, but rather to devise measures which would meet the growing expenses of the war.[65] The urgent need for increased taxes, however, had not yet permeated the thinking of Congress, and action on the relief measure was postponed until the next session.

The failure of Congress to pass an adequate tax law did not escape condemnation by the press.[66] As the issues of Treasury notes mounted, the condition of the currency received increasing public attention and the growing demand for heavy taxation to secure the bonds which would relieve inflation developed a public opinion favorable to tax legislation.

In his report of January 10, 1863, Secretary Memminger stated that $450,000,000 in Treasury notes was then outstanding and said the amount had to be reduced to $150,000,000—a figure he considered adequate to meet the needs of the country. He recommended that the reduction be made by loans, and urged Congress "to provide ample means to secure and pay the principal and interest of the securities in which the holders are required to invest." He said, "This can only be effected by an ample and permanent tax. . . . Without it the scheme has no foundation and can secure neither public confidence nor success."[67]

CONFEDERATE FINANCE

The Southern press rallied to the aid of the Secretary in demanding higher taxes in order to correct the redundant currency and reduce prices.[68] The *Richmond Enquirer* called for a tax of $200,000,000, criticized the inaction of Congress, and charged that the South had "representation without taxation." It stated that the Revolutionary note issues had depreciated because there was no central power to lay taxes, whereas the Confederacy had the power to lay taxes, but held it as a means of last resort.[69]

The plan of taxation proposed by Memminger followed the system used in the war tax of 1861 and levied a tax on property and income. Submitting his recommendations to Congress, the Secretary said:

> It seems to me that a tax upon property and income is so much to be preferred to stamp duties, excises, licenses, and other like taxes which call for a machinery vexatious in its character and expensive in its operation, that there will be little hesitation on the part of Congress in its acceptance. The direct tax heretofore levied has set in operation all the machinery necessary to levy another, and an income tax could be collected by the same means. It seems to me that both these forms of tax should be adopted. To lay a sufficient tax upon property alone would require too large an increase in the rate of last year. Such an increase would operate with peculiar hardship upon property producing no income. On the other hand a tax upon income is so easily evaded that of itself it would furnish an insecure resource. It is proper, however, that incomes should be taxed; otherwise the whole profits of speculation and trade, together with those resulting from skill and labor, would escape contribution. I propose therefore that a tax be imposed upon property, and upon the gross amount of income of every kind, excepting those below some minimum to be adjusted by Congress.[70]

Outlining his plan, the Secretary said that the amount of revenue to be raised must be gauged by the interest demands of Treasury notes and the funded debt, an amount then equal to $48,360,000. To raise this sum, he recommended a property tax of 1%, based on the war tax returns for 1862, which he estimated would yield $36,000,000, with deductions allowed for occupied territory. The probable yield from the income tax was arrived at by valuing the property of the South at $4,000,000,000, allowing 7% interest on that sum as earned income, then laying a tax of 10% on the earned income, thus returning $28,000,000. Allowing deductions for expenses and other contingencies, the Secretary expected the tax on

TARIFFS AND TAXES

property and incomes to raise a sum total of $60,000,000. Any excess after paying the interest obligations of the Government was to be applied to the yearly redemption of a portion of the debt. This was the principle upon which the $100,000,000 Loan of August 19, 1861, was based, but which had been omitted from subsequent loans.

Despite the urgent need for adequate tax legislation, it was not until February 25, 1863, that Congress gave the Secretary's recommendations serious thought. On that day the House Ways and Means Committee reported a bill providing for a 1% tax on all property, an income tax, and a system of licenses. After a month of debate, the measure was passed with only minor changes. The Senate, however, took a strong stand against the property tax, holding it to be unconstitutional since direct taxes under the permanent constitution had to be levied according to representation, and the limit for taking a census had been placed at February, 1865. Too, the Senate changed the grading of the income tax. Instead of 14% on incomes up to $10,000, and 24% on excess of $10,000, as provided by the House, the Senate proposed 5% on incomes from $500 to $1,500, 10% on incomes from $1,500 to $10,000, 12½% on $10,000 to $15,000, and 15% on all excess.

It was at this point in the discussion of tax legislation that Secretary Memminger sent a special report to the Senate, recommending the adoption of a tax-in-kind upon agricultural income.[71] Arguing strongly in favor of such a tax, the Secretary said that it would: 1. Afford abundant subsistence to the Army, in bread and forage, and would distribute the same all over the country, so that it could be conveniently collected wherever wanted. 2. Relieve the Government from the necessity of resorting to impressment, a measure which, however judiciously conducted, tended to produce odium and discontent. 3. Relieve the Government from the exactions and imposition of those who speculated upon its necessities. 4. Withdraw from the market the Government as a purchaser of articles of prime necessity, thus enabling individuals to purchase at much lower rates. 5. Relieve the currency from an issue of the amount necessary to purchase the articles levied in kind, and assist greatly in restoring all prices to their usual and normal condition. 6. Render much more productive the tax itself, not only because it would be less easily evaded, but because being certain in quantity it would not be subject to the fluctuation which would attend any further expansion of the currency.[72] Abiding by the recommendation of Secretary Memminger, the Senate also provided for a tax-in-kind—a tax of one-tenth of the agricultural products.

With so many changes made in the original bill, a joint committee of both Houses was compelled to work weeks for an acceptable adjustment. An agreement was finally reached and the tax bill was approved April 24, 1863. The "Act to lay taxes for the Common Defense and Carry on the Government of the Confederate States" avoided the objectionable features of the former war tax and was planned to be exhaustive, with only real estate, personal property, Negroes, and the income from educational, charitable, and religious institutions being exempt. The taxes were to be assessed on July 1 and collected on October 1, 1863, unless otherwise indicated, and were arranged in the following classes:

I. An ad valorem tax of 8% was levied on all naval stores, salt, wines, liquors, tobacco, cotton, wool, flour, sugar, molasses, syrup, rice, and all other agricultural products held July 1, 1863. The tax was retroactive in order to cover the output of 1862 and allowed deductions for articles necessary for home use. A tax of 8% was also placed on the value of all kinds of money, bank notes, and credits on hand or on deposit and not used in business, but a tax of only 1% was applied to credits held abroad, on which interest had not been paid, and which represented capital not employed in business.[73]

II. A tax of 10% was placed on profits resulting from the purchase and sale in 1862 of flour, corn, bacon, pork, oats, hay, rice, salt, iron or the manufactures of iron, sugar, molasses made of cane, leather, woolen and cotton clothes, shoes, boots, and blankets. This tax was directed at the gains from speculation, which were so popularly denounced, and did not apply to the regular retail business.

III. A license tax was levied upon a large number of occupations, trades, and businesses. Among those taxed were bankers, brokers, auctioneers, wholesale and retail dealers in liquors, pawnbrokers, distillers, brewers, innkeepers, theatre and circus owners, jugglers, butchers, bakers, apothecaries, physicians, tobacconists, peddlers, lawyers, photographers, and confectioners. The rate of the license varied according to the supposed lucrativeness of the occupation, the rate being $50, $100, $200, or $500. In many of the occupations there was a double levy of a license and a percentage of the gross sales; i.e., apothecaries were taxed $50 license

TARIFFS AND TAXES

fee and 2½% on gross sales as was the case of auctioneers, tobacconists, cattle brokers, peddlers, photographers, and confectioners. In other cases, the percentage tax was rated at 5%, 10%, or 20% of gross sales. Each business was required to register within 60 days after passage of the act, and on or before January 1 each year thereafter, at which time the license and special tax were payable.

IV. A graded income tax, payable every January 1, was laid upon salaries and net incomes from sources other than salaries. In regard to the tax on salaries, an exemption of $1,000 was allowed after which a tax of 1% was laid on the first $1,500, and 2% on the excess. The tax on net income from sources other than salaries was graded in the following manner. Incomes not exceeding $500 were exempt. Those from $500 to $1,500 were taxed 5%; those from $1,500 to $3,000 paid 5% on the first $1,500, and 10% on the excess; $3,000 to $5,000 paid 10%; $5,000 to $10,000 paid 12½%; and all over $10,000 paid 15%. Taxes levied on incomes were to be paid January 1, 1864, and on each January 1 thereafter.

V. A tax-in-kind of one-tenth of the agricultural produce grown in the year 1863 was provided. Each farmer and planter after reserving for his own use 50 bushels of sweet potatoes, 100 bushels of corn or 50 bushels of wheat, and 20 bushels of peas or beans, but not more than 20 bushels of both, was compelled to pay to the Government one-tenth of his wheat, corn, oats, rye, buckwheat or rice, sweet and Irish potatoes, cured hay and fodder, sugar, molasses made of cane, cotton, wool, tobacco, beans, peas, and ground peas. In addition to the above, every farmer, planter, or grazier was taxed one-tenth of all slaughtered hogs, the tax being payable in bacon at the rate of 60 pounds of bacon to 100 pounds of pork.

The tithe was to be delivered by the tax payer to a post-quartermaster's depot located not more than eight miles from the place of growth. Officers at the depot then distributed the food products direct to the army and the cotton to agents of the Treasury Department. The money proceeds from the other four classes of taxes were to go to the regular tax collectors. The act of April 24, 1863, was to remain in force until the end of 1865, except for the 10% tax on profits made in 1862 and the 8% tax on surplus naval stores and agricultural products for the same year, which were to be assessed only during 1863.

Since the new tax law was expected to yield heavy returns and bring relief from the inflated currency, its adoption immediately met with popular approval. Later, however, when it became evident that these expectations were not to be fulfilled, objections were raised against certain features of the measure. The chief objection to the tax was perhaps that which centered around the tax-in-kind levied on agricultural products.

The plan of taxation, although embodying a complex system of many valuations and varying times of payment, was believed equitable in that the tax was levied upon the actual products on hand rather than on land which was then largely unremunerative. Many of the farmers, however, became dissatisfied and contended that the tax should be placed on the profits of their crops and not on the gross value. The farmer believed that a graduated tax, payable in currency, should be applied to the income from his products in the same manner in which it was applied to the income from salaries and other sources. To him the tithe or tax-in-kind looked large and discriminatory in comparison with the 2% currency tax on salaries over $1,500.[74] As a result of this dissatisfaction, public meetings were held during the summer of 1863 and resolutions were drawn up denouncing the tax-in-kind. One of the resolutions passed by the farmers stated that the act of April 24 in "taking from the hard laborers of the Confederacy one-tenth of the people's living, instead of taking . . . currency, is unjust and tyrannical, and we solemnly protest against that act." Another pictured the tax as being "oppressive, and a relic of barbarism, which alone is practised in the worst despotisms." Still another stated that "We are in favor of a just and equitable system of taxation so that all classes may bear their burden equally; [but] we are . . . opposed to the tithe system . . . discriminating against and taxing the labor and industry of the agricultural classes."[75]

It should not be inferred from the above that opposition to the tax-in-kind was unanimous. On October 30, 1863, John T. Donald of Thomastown, Mississippi, wrote to Secretary Memminger, "The tax in kind, or tithe tax, was fortunate; you hit the nail slap on the head—a good deal of trouble and expense. No matter, the planters generally . . . have made abundant crops. You know that, where such is the case, we are apt . . . to be careless and waste a good deal. The tax in kind makes us careful, and we shall not miss what we give to the Government."[76] The unpopularity of the tax unquestionably resulted from the Government's attempt to substitute a tax-in-kind for one payable in money. The agricultural classes were willing to pay any just and equitable tax in currency, but they resented parting with their produce.[77]

TARIFFS AND TAXES

Objections to the tax act were also raised concerning the license and percentage tax on gross sales of occupations. These taxes were originally commended in that they were paid by the consumer, but the right of the central Government to levy a license tax was opposed early as a distinct encroachment on the rights reserved to the states.[78] In this matter, the sovereignty of the Confederate Congress was determined by the exigencies of the times. Regarding the taxes on occupations, the range of license fees was small, and the assessment on gross sales was by no means in accordance with the real profits of the business.

Other objections to the act of April 24, 1863, arose from the fact that a large amount of the tax returns was expected from a year already past. The tax on surplus products and profits of trade for 1862 would be difficult to determine, and the possibility of evasion would be very great. The whole system of direct taxation was practically impossible to equalize; as a result it aroused strong opposition.

The new tax was subject to the limitations of the Permanent Constitution which contained a provision similar to the one in the United States Constitution, stating that:

Representatives and direct taxes shall be apportioned among the several States . . . according to their respective numbers by adding to the whole number of free persons, including those bound to service for a term of years, and excluding Indians not taxed, three-fifths of all slaves.[79]

On November 11, the *Charleston Mercury* declared the tax unconstitutional, claiming it was direct and not apportioned because no census had been taken since adoption of the Permanent Constitution. President Davis answered the charge in his message of December 8, stating "The special mode [of apportionment] for levying a tax is now impracticable, but Congress is not excused from the general duty." The President argued that until the Confederate Census, as called for by the Constitution, was taken, direct taxes need not be apportioned.[80] Although the position held by President Davis prevailed, the question continued to be a subject of discussion throughout the existence of the Confederacy.

In order to carry out the provisions of the act of April 24, 1863, Congress approved "An Act for the Assessment and Collection of Taxes," on May 1, 1863. Under the act an Office of the Commissioner of Taxes was created "for the purpose of superintending the collection of internal duties or taxes imposed . . . by laws, and of assessing the same."[81] On July 2, 1863, Thompson Allan, Chief Clerk of the War Tax Bureau, was appointed Commissioner of Taxes. In his new position Allan was charged "with all . . . matters pertaining to the assessment and collection of the duties and taxes which may be necessary to carry the laws . . . into effect."[82]

As stated earlier, two separate organizations were created to collect the tax. The appraisal of all property and the collection of the money tax were to be conducted by officers of the Treasury Department, whereas the collection of the tax-in-kind was to be carried on by agents under the supervision of the War Department.

The machinery for assessing and collecting the money tax was similar to that set up under the act of August 19, 1861. Each state became a tax division under the supervision of a state collector who divided the state or tax division into districts headed by district collectors. The district collectors then appointed appraisers to assess all taxable property in their respective districts. As a result of the similarity of the organizations for collecting and assessing taxes under the acts of August 19, 1861, and April 24, 1863, six chief collectors of the first war tax were reappointed.[83]

To avoid some of the weaknesses of the tax of 1861, all assessments and collections under the new act were to be made by officers of the Confederate Government. Following the assessment, the appraisement returns were open to appeal for fifteen days, after which time notices of the dates and places of collection were posted and payment of the assessed taxes was guaranteed by a two-year lien on the assessed property.[84]

The Treasury Department promptly set up its new machinery, appointed officers, and sent out instructions and printed forms. But the new undertaking was far more complex than the earlier one when there was merely a uniform tax levied on twelve items. Now there were scores of articles listed under various headings. The object of the tax schedule was to reach items of which no tangible evidence of liability existed except the word of the taxpayer. The different times for making returns and receiving collections further complicated the system. The act called for almost immediate assessment, the date of July 1 being set for the commodities on hand produced in 1862, and for profits made on purchases and sales during the same year. These taxes were to be collected October 1, 1863. Tax payments on retail and wholesale business were to be made quarterly, while many other collections were postponed to 1864.

The administration of the money tax required a multiplicity of executive directives. In practice the tax law proved ambiguous on many points; hence, the rulings of Commissioner Allan had vast scope and authority. On December 23, 1863, a complete set of instructions replaced all previous orders in order to minimize further causes for delay in collecting the tax. But regardless of the numerous directives from the Commissioner, numerous obstacles blocked the satisfactory operation of the tax machinery. Speculators, distillers, and traders evaded the tax on profits, while many other frauds and failures were noted.[85] Within a few months, it was readily admitted that the money tax would not supply the Treasury with an adequate revenue. This resulted partly from tax evasion and from weaknesses in the system itself, but mostly from the increased needs of the Government, coupled with mounting prices.

By February 1, 1864, $27,402,423.70 had been collected in eight states; two weeks later the amount collected in the same states totaled $34,731,592.92, with the largest collection, $10,876,876.62, being reported by Georgia.[86] As of April 29, 1864, taxes totaling $82,262,349.83 had been collected from 338 collection districts in ten states. Reporting this amount to the Secretary of the Treasury, Commissioner Allan wrote:

. . . when we consider that out of four hundred and seventy-one collection districts one hundred and thirty-three have been so much interfered with by the public enemy as to prevent any organization, and that the area embraced by these districts thus exempted is occupied by over two millions of population—or nearly one-third of the whole population of the States—the results of the execution of the law appear very satisfactory.[87]

Of the $82\frac{1}{4}$ millions collected in currency up to April 29, each state contributed the following amount: Georgia, 22 1/3 millions; Virginia, $21\frac{1}{2}$; South Carolina, $12\frac{1}{2}$; North Carolina, 10; Alabama, $9\frac{1}{2}$; Texas, 3; Mississippi, 2; Florida,1; Louisiana, $200,000; Tennessee, $141,000, and Arkansas, nothing.[88]

The tax-in-kind, having been planned to provide supplies mainly for the army, was placed under the supervision of the Quartermaster General's Department. On May 23, 1863, Colonel Larkin Smith, Assistant Quartermaster General, was put in charge of the tithe, and a corps of 68 assistants was stationed in the several states.[89]

Heading each state was a Controlling Quartermaster, with the rank of Major, who assigned a Post Quartermaster, with the rank of Captain, to each congressional district in the state where it was found practicable to collect the tax.[90] The Post Quartermaster was assigned the duty of receiving the tithe from the producer, protecting and preserving the tithe while in his possession, and distributing the tithe to the issuing depots of the army. To promote this assignment, congressional districts were subdivided by the Post Quartermasters in charge of them into sections in which depots were established for the convenient delivery, by the taxpayer, of his quota of produce.[91] Agents were then appointed by the Post Quartermaster to take charge of the depots established in each section.[92] The tax law required an assessor of the Treasury Department to visit the farmers and planters, and to determine the quantity, quality, and value of produce to be received under the act.[93] Making his estimate in duplicate, the assessor left one copy with the producer and transmitted the other to the Post Quartermaster. The Post Quartermaster then forwarded the estimate to his agent at the depot nearest the producer and as soon as possible thereafter made public notice to the producer that the agent was ready to receive the Government's quota of agricultural products. Should a producer fail to deliver any part or all of his quota within two months after the assessor's estimate was made, he became liable to a penalty of 50%.[94] The tithe was not allowed to accumulate at the receiving depots. Special attention was directed to the importance of transferring the produce as soon as possible to the distributing officers of the army. All quartermaster's stores (corn, oats, rye, hay, fodder, and wool) were sent to the nearest quartermaster; whereas all commissary stores (sweet and Irish potatoes, wheat, buckwheat, rice, sugar, molasses, peas, beans, ground peas, and bacon) were forwarded to the nearest commissary.[95]

Quartermasters who had been appointed to purchase supplies, and who had means of transportation at their command, were directed to assist the Post Quartermasters receiving the tax-in-kind by transporting the supplies collected from the depots of collection to the issuing depots of the army. The purchasing quartermasters were also directed to permit use of their storehouses for storage of articles received from the tax-in-kind. Every possible precaution was taken to prevent stored grain and other produce from heating and spoiling. In case these precautions failed, the Post Quartermaster made application to the Controlling Quartermaster of the state for authority to sell the commodities at public auction.

To expedite delivery of the tax-in-kind to the army, commissaries appointed to purchase supplies were authorized to receive from the producer that portion of the tax consisting of commissary stores, giving a receipt to the producer as evidence that so much of his tax was paid. Too, quartermasters and commissaries serving with the troops could receive the tithe tax from producers when authorized to do so by the Chief Quartermaster or Chief Commissary of the army in which they served. As a protection against fraud, the names of such authorized officers were reported to the Quartermaster General; nevertheless, there were frequent reports of unauthorized persons collecting the tax-in-kind.[96] Where the exigencies of the army compelled impressment or purchase of the whole of any one article or all of the planter's taxed-in-kind, the Post Quartermaster of the district was directed to transfer to the District Collector the assessor's estimate of the tithe, and the tax, valued at the rate of purchase or impressment, was to be collected in money.[97]

Because of the difficulties of transportation, Congress, by an act of December 23, 1863, permitted the payment in money of the tithe on sweet potatoes. This transferred the administration of that part of the tax-in-kind from the War Department to officers of the Treasury. On January 30, 1864, a somewhat similar act was approved, whereby the collection of the tobacco tithe was transferred from the War to the Treasury Department—the tobacco, along with cotton, forming the basis for the Government's export trade.

Although the tax-in-kind had aroused much opposition, it was re-enacted on February 17, 1864, with only few modifications. In passing "An Act to Levy Additional Taxes for the Common Defense and Support of the Government," Congress provided for more liberal exemptions, especially in the case of small farmers' and soldiers' families.[98] Later, under an act approved June 10, 1864, further concessions were granted payers of the tax-in-kind by extending the time of delivery of the tithe three months, by allowing the corn tithe to be commuted in money when the quantity of corn was not sufficient to supply the actual needs of the producer, and by exempting products of gardens intended solely for family consumption and "crops destroyed by fire or any other accidental cause or by the enemy."[99]

From all available records, it is practically impossible to determine the exact amount of produce collected by the tax-in-kind. On November 30, 1863, Colonel Larkin Smith reported that during the first five months produce valued at approximately $6,000,000 had been received—the main portion consisting of corn, wheat, cured hay, and fodder. The report stated that after September 1 the tithe had been the chief support of the armies in Virginia.[100] By March 1, 1864, the value of the tithe, based on current market prices, approximated $40,000,000.[101] North Carolina, Georgia, and Alabama were the main contributors, with nearly two-thirds of the proceeds being accredited to them. Some states collected nothing, and receipts from the fertile area of others were, in many cases, curtailed by the enemy. Transportation difficulties retarded both the collection and distribution of the produce and gave rise to complaints of inefficient handling of the tax. But management of the receiving, parceling, storage, preservation, and distribution of the tithe proved to be a highly responsible and complicated undertaking, and under the trying circumstances of the time, it is not at all strange that large quantities of the produce were liable to waste and destruction despite the charges of neglect and incompetency.[102] In his report of October 28, 1864, the Commissioner of Taxes stated that the estimated value of the tax-in-kind would probably be equal to the money tax—say $145,527,431.34.[103] This figure was restated November 7 and again on December 15, 1864,[104] but on January 9, 1865, the value of the tithe actually collected was placed at $62,000,000, and it is doubtful whether this amount was increased to any appreciable extent during the last few months of the Confederacy.[105]

The Tax Act of February 17, 1864

Secretary Memminger recognized the inadequacy of the tax act of April 24 at an early date, and in the hope of supplementing the Government's revenue, recommended that an ad valorem tax be placed on the value of all land and Negroes in the Confederate States. Aware of the constitutional objection to be raised by such a tax, the Secretary stated in his report of December 6, 1863, that the necessities of war no longer permitted a strict adherence to the letter of the Constitution which required a census to be taken before direct taxes could be levied in order to establish a basis for apportioning the taxes according to population. Endeavoring to overcome the constitutional objection to an ad valorem tax, Memminger stated that:

The land and Negroes in the Confederate States constitute two-thirds of the taxable values, and if this objection prevailed it would establish the surprising conclusion that all the States which ratified the Constitution, while engaged in a war which put at hazard the lives and fortunes of all their citizens and their own independence, excepted from the contribution to maintain that war the very property for which they were contending. Such a construction is manifestly erroneous, and could never have been intended. The more consistent interpretation is that a principle was established which should operate as soon as the basis for its action was obtained. As soon as the enumeration could be taken there was to be an apportionment; but if an enumeration became impossible, then the tax must be laid according to the other rule of uniformity declared by the Constitution.

There is a general power to lay taxes which becomes subject to a special limitation as soon as an enumeration could be had. That enumeration is ordered to be taken within three years; but it is prevented from being taken by the presence of a public enemy. Under such a state of things the limitation must be considered as in suspense, and the general power may be exercised. It seems to me therefore that the *ad valorem* tax is no infringement of the Constitution.

In the present condition of the country such a tax is more equable and beneficial than any apportioned tax would be. The occupation of large portions of States by the enemy would cast the whole quota of any State upon the unoccupied portions. The States which are in this condition would have the largest quotas to pay on account of their larger representation, and thus the burden of the tax at present would be inverted. The greatest sufferers would be required to bear the heaviest burden. In either view, then, the *ad valorem* tax is greatly to be preferred.[106]

Estimating the Government's needs for 1864 at $400,000,000, the Secretary proposed to raise $100,000,000 by taxation and $300,000,000 by loans. As a means of raising $100,000,000 by taxation, Memminger placed the assessed value of taxable property at $3 billion upon which he recommended an ad valorem tax of 5%. Allowing an abatement of 20% for evasions, failures to make returns, expenses and contingencies, he figured the proceeds at $120,000,000. Half of this amount was to be made available for purchasing supplies; the other half for paying interest on a new billion dollar loan which was planned to absorb the excess currency and furnish the additional $300,000,000 required for supplies. The Secretary asserted that the credit of the bonds of the proposed loan would not be secure unless definitely guaranteed by a tax on real property. This tax he proposed to levy in addition to the existing tax on profits and incomes.[107]

After prolonged discussion concerning the recommendations of Secretary Memminger, Congress approved a new tax law. The 5% rate proposed by Memminger was accepted, and there were various amendments to the act of April 24, 1863, which practically deprived that act of all virility as a tax measure. The new tax law, entitled "An Act to Levy Additional Taxes for the Common Defence and Support of the Government," was approved February 17, 1864, along with the notorious Compulsory Funding Measure. Its chief feature was the system of rebates, whereby the 5% tax on agricultural property was deductible from the value of the tax-in-kind, and the income tax was credited against the ad valorem tax on property. Additional taxes were levied under the law. These included 10% on the value of gold and silver plate and jewelry; 5% on the value of all shares or interests in any corporation; 5% on all solvent credits, on all paper currency exclusive of non-interest-bearing Confederate Treasury notes and not employed in a business already taxed, and on all gold and silver coin, gold dust, gold or silver bullion; 10% in addition to the tax of April 24, 1863, on profits made in business and trade from January 1, 1863, to January 1, 1865; 25% on profits exceeding 25% made by any corporation. Exemptions were similar to those provided under the act of April 24. Taxes on property for the year 1864 were to be assessed as on the day of the passage of the act, and were due and collectible June 1, 1864, or as soon after as practicable, a further extension of 90 days being allowed in states west of the Mississippi River. Real property was assessed at its value in 1861, unless sold after 1863, whereas other taxable items were estimated at prices current at the time of assessment. The tax imposed on bonds of the Confederate States was in no case to exceed their interest, and such bonds when held for minors or lunatics were exempt from the tax when the interest did not exceed $1,000. The tax upon income from property or effects as imposed by the act of April 24 was suspended as was also the 8% tax levied by the former act on agricultural products held on July 1, 1863, and the 1% tax on money, bank notes, and credits held July 1 and not used in a business.[108]

TARIFFS AND TAXES

The tax act of February 17, 1864, like that of its predecessor, met with strong opposition. It was charged that the several rates of assessment had been made in favor of the agricultural interests. Perhaps the most persistent of the objectors were the Southern banks. Their grievances, summarized in the memorial of the South Carolina banks of April 7, 1864, stated that they were taxed twice; first, on their capital and, second, on their deposits and issues which were invested in solvent credits. With the credits exceeding the capital two- and three-fold, the banks claimed they were contributing 15 to 20%, and said that since bank stock was valued at such a high rate the tax frequently exceeded the dividends. The tax on Government securities was denounced as a breach of contract, and it was claimed that while the tax was aimed at speculators, its chief sufferers were trust funds, widows, and those dependent on such incomes.[109] In contrast to the hardship the tax placed on banks, the landed interests bore a valuation admittedly five times less in proportion. Too, the tax on gold and silver coin was objectionable since it was levied in kind—the Government's share of the coin being converted into Treasury notes at the ratio of 18 to 1 by the Treasury order of March 9, 1864. Illustrating the inequality of the measure, it was shown that land worth $10,000 on the basis of 1860 values paid a tax of $500 in Treasury notes, whereas $10,000 in coin paid a tax of $500 in coin or $9,000 in notes.[110]

Perhaps the severest of all defects of the new act was that the tax could be paid with the 4% certificates in which compulsory funding of the redundant notes was proceeding.[111] The superior plan of Secretary Memminger had been to accept merely the interest coupons of the new bond issue along with the new Treasury notes to pay the tax,[112] but the change in plans by Congress precluded the Treasury's receiving any considerable monetary aid from the tax during 1864.

Upon the convening of the Second Congress on May 2, 1864, Secretary Memminger insisted that certain reforms be made in the tax law. The Secretary specifically recommended repeal of the tax-in-kind deduction from the 5% tax on agricultural property, repeal of the ad valorem tax deduction from the income tax, and a correction of the discrimination as to the date of assessment for all taxable items in reference to their values. Memminger also pointed out the inequalities suffered by the banks and corporations. His condemnation of the tax measure affords an estimate of

CONFEDERATE FINANCE

the inadequacy of this presumedly large attempt at taxation. He said the system was marked by inequality amounting to injustice, and was "so cumbrous and intricate, that delay and disappointment will be its inevitable results."[113] But Congress refused to make the specific reforms recommended by the Secretary of the Treasury and hastened its final alienation with that Cabinet member. Moreover, the legislature approved the Soldiers' Tax on June 10, 1864, which added 20% to all assessments then operative.[114]

On June 14, the last day of the session, Congress amended the acts of April 24, 1863, and February 17, 1864, by relieving the banks of the tax on deposits and made another effort to prevent speculation by placing an additional 30% tax on all profits realized on trading and selling between February 17 and July 1, 1864. Congress approved the ruling of the Secretary of the Treasury that the 5% tax on coin or sterling exchange was to be made in specie or in Treasury notes at their current value, thus discrediting its own currency by legislative sanction.[115]

The tax law was found to be ambiguous regarding the year the abatement of the tax-in-kind was to be applied; and since the ad valorem tax on agricultural property fell due June 1, 1864, it would be collected before the value of the tithe could be ascertained.[116] To overcome this obstacle, the collection of the tax was further delayed when on June 14, 1864, Congress suspended collection of the property tax until the value of the tithe was determined.[117] Thus, when Commissioner Allan made his tax report on September 9, 1864, the money collections totaled $109,829,865.08, a comparatively small increase over the report of five months earlier.[118] On October 28, 1864, the Office of the Commissioner of Taxes issued its last report showing tax receipts of $118,845,744.57 on an assessment of $145,527,421.34. The following table shows the amount of money taxes assessed and collected in each state under the Acts of April 24, 1863, February 17, 1864, and June 14, 1864. The total represents the amount of taxes received in the Confederacy during the two years 1863 and 1864 as well as the tax on surplus products for 1862.

TARIFFS AND TAXES

Table Showing the Amount of Taxes Assessed and Collected in the Confederacy Under the Acts of Apr. 24, 1863, Feb. 17, 1864, and June 14, 1864[119]

	Amount of Taxes Assessed	Amount of Taxes Collected
Alabama	$ 18,226,981.55	$ 12,904,516.01
Arkansas	3,103,156.00	1,000,000.00 **
Florida	2,367,835.24	1,262,292.00
Georgia	32,346,554.82	29,394,878.61
Louisiana	11,835,643.96	2,300,000.00 ***
Mississippi	8,289,842.28	3,869,288.38 ****
North Carolina	11,581,391.63	14,575,199.66
South Carolina	18,078,319.86	17,150,458.39
Tennessee*	1,000,000.00	231,551.30
Texas	11,557,696.00	6,500,000.00 *****
Virginia	27,140,000.00	29,657,560.22
Total	$145,527,421.34	$118,845,744.57

    * (no estimate can be made) perhaps
   ** (imperfect returns, say to April 1, 1864)
  *** (to July 1, 1864) say
 **** (to August 17, 1864) say
***** (to June 1, 1864) say

Although the tax legislation on first consideration appeared comprehensive and extremely onerous, it was soon apparent that the deduction of both the tax-in-kind and the income tax from the ad valorem tax on property left comparatively small net proceeds. Had the system of rebates been suspended, it is probable that the total receipts would have been almost trebled. Counting the tax-in-kind at $145,000,000 and the income tax with other credits at a smaller figure, Secretary Trenholm estimated that the total tax devoid of rebates would have been approximately $374,188,414.[120] If it is true that Secretary Memminger, unable to foresee the expanding needs of the Government, had consistently asked for too small an amount from taxation, then it is also true that Congress had been still more reserved in responding. For it was not until the closing months of the Confederacy that the legislative body, after much prodding and long deliberation on the question of continued note issues versus heavy taxation, chose the latter.

CONFEDERATE FINANCE

Tax Legislation During the Last Months of the Confederacy

Convinced that extended taxation was the only salvation for the Government's financial difficulties, Secretary Trenholm used every opportunity to renew the tax recommendations of his predecessor. He proposed that the deduction of the tax-in-kind and income tax from the ad valorem tax on property be suspended, and that banks and corporations be taxed more in line with the agricultural interests. He considered the existing taxes on property and earnings nominal, amounting annually to a mere 1 1/6% of the value of all property, and proposed to increase them greatly.[121] On February 4, 1865, Trenholm stated that:

. . . We have nearly reached the limit of our issues; after that, two courses will be left open to us; one is to break down the barrier and go on printing notes *ad libitum,* the other is to submit to temporary inconvenience and replenish the Treasury by taxation. The first course will destroy the value of the currency and arrest its usefulness; the last will preserve its value and perpetuate its usefulness. To this last policy the support of all wise and patriotic men should be given, and all should unite and bear this temporary inconvenience with cheerfulness.[122]

Despite the repeated recommendations of Secretary Trenholm, it was not until March 11, 1865, that Congress enacted a tax measure imposing rates adequate to meet the needs of the Government. Under the new act, taxes on property for 1865 were to be assessed at once and payment was due on June 1, or as soon thereafter as practicable. Both the tax-in-kind and the tax on incomes and salaries were continued as under former acts, but they could no longer be deducted from the ad valorem tax on property; specie and foreign credits were taxed 20%; other moneys and solvent credits were taxed 5%, except stocks and bonds issued by a state or the Confederate Government in which instance the interest was taxed as income in lieu of taxing the principal; profits made by buying and selling merchandise or property of any description during 1865 were taxed 10% in addition to the tax upon such profits as income; profits exceeding 25% were taxed 25%; all other property, "real, personal, or mixed, of every kind and description," was taxed 8%, but on the basis of the 1860 valuation; and, finally, all the above taxes were increased ⅛ (the tax-in-kind excluded) in order to provide a money revenue for payment of

TARIFFS AND TAXES

the soldiers' increased wages. The tax was payable in Treasury notes of the new issue, or in certificates of indebtedness authorized under the act of February 17, 1864, provided that at least ½ of the tax was paid in Treasury notes. All exemptions enumerated under the former tax laws were reenacted.[123] On March 17, 1865, Congress passed its last tax measure by levying a tax of 25%, payable in kind on April 1, 1865, on all coin, bullion, and foreign exchange in the Confederate States, provided the $3,000,000 specie loan under the same act failed fulfillment.[124] Before the Government could realize revenue from either of these stringent tax laws, the Confederacy collapsed.

It is perhaps fitting and proper that a few words should be said concerning the probable effect adequate taxation would have had on Government finance in the event Congress should have approved Secretary Memminger's often repeated recommendations.

Unquestionably, legislation providing for an adequate tax would certainly have contributed to the reduction of the redundant currency, lowered prices to a limited degree, and somewhat strengthened the Government's credit by supplying the means for paying interest on the funded debt. It should be noted, however, that something other than adequate taxation was required to strengthen and stabilize Confederate finance, the major requirement being continued success by the armed forces.

Until the middle of 1863, the military had given an excellent account of itself, and regardless of an inadequate tax, Confederate finance was not in too bad a condition. True, the currency was already inflated, but Treasury notes continued to be acceptable for debts and circulated freely, a foreign loan was being floated, and Government securities were still attractive to investors at home.

After the disastrous summer of 1863, the situation changed and there started to develop among many of the Government's creditors a growing fear that the South's cause was lost, and that in defeat all Government securities and currency would be worthless. As the Confederate military strengthened or weakened its position, the Government's credit fluctuated—rising and falling with the tide of battle.

Following the surrender, the fear concerning the worthlessness of Government securities in case of defeat became a reality. Under the Fourteenth Amendment to the United States Constitution all Confederate debts, funded and unfunded, were declared illegal and void; that is, all Confederate Treasury notes, stocks, bonds, certificates of indebtedness, and other instruments of credit were adjudged worthless.[125]

It might be concluded, therefore, that an adequate tax, levied throughout the existence of the Confederacy, would doubtlessly have aided to some extent in improving the Government's financial status. The decisive agent, however, in determining the stability or soundness of Confederate finance rested in the success or failure of the military. It was upon the failure of the armed forces to achieve their goal that Confederate finance collapsed despite the late attempt of Congress at extreme taxation.

The following table summarizes the total receipts derived from tariffs and taxes:

TABLE EXHIBITING THE AMOUNT OF TARIFFS AND TAXES COLLECTED IN THE CONFEDERACY[126]

	Amount Collected
Import Duties:	
Acts of Feb. 18, Mar. 15, and May 21, 1861 (payable in Treas. notes, specie, sterling exchange and interest coupons of bonds)	$ 3,424,338.81
Export Duties:	
Act of Feb. 28, 1861 (payable in specie and interest coupons of $15-Million Loan)	30,056.05
Taxes:	
Act of Aug. 19, 1861 (payable in Treas. notes) . .	17,446,736.28
Acts of Apr. 24, 1863, Feb. 17 and June 14, 1864 Tax in Kind (valued at) . . . $ 62,000,000.00 Tax payable in Treas. notes . 118,845,744.57	180,845,744.57
Acts of Mar. 11 and Mar. 17, 1865	————————
Duties and Taxes collected in the Trans-Mississippi Dept. and not shown above	5,768,457.42
Total amount of tariffs and taxes collected	$207,515,333.13

CHAPTER

☆ V ☆

SEIZURES AND DONATIONS

THE PRINCIPAL SOURCES OF REVENUE FOR THE CONFEDERACY WERE loans, paper currency, tariffs, and taxes. As the war expanded, however, the financial needs of the Government became so great that it was necessary to supplement these means by seizures of funds and property and by donations.

Seizures of funds and property by the Confederate Government were of three types: those pertaining to the confiscation of United States specie, bullion, and property located in the South; those dealing with the sequestration of property, real and personal, of alien enemies; and those relating to the impressment of military and naval supplies produced or held by citizens of the Confederacy. Attention is now directed to a discussion of each of these types of seizure as a means of raising revenue and supplies for the Government.

Confiscation of United States Specie and Property Located in the South

On March 5, 1861, Secretary Memminger took the first step towards confiscating Federal funds and property. Issuing a circular letter to the various public officers of the United States still residing in the Confederacy, the Secretary instructed them to make immediate payment into the Confederate Treasury of all sums remaining in their hands as due the United States, with which government the Confederacy would arrange an accounting.[1]

CONFEDERATE FINANCE

Responding to Memminger's letter, the State Convention of Louisiana passed an ordinance on March 7 whereby $389,267.46 in specie and bullion was transferred to the Government of the Confederate States—the amount representing the "Bullion Fund" at the New Orleans Mint.[2]

On May 14, the Confederate Congress officially suspended operation of the Federal mints in the Confederacy and ordered "all moneys and bullion in the hands of mint officers" to be transferred to the Treasurer of the Confederate States. Superintendents of the mints at New Orleans and at Dahlonega, Georgia, were ordered to "take immediate measures for the safety of the tools, implements, and other property at the establishments" and "to sell all perishable articles, and all other small things which could be advantageously disposed of, or for which any price could be obtained."[3] Complying with these orders, the Treasurer of the New Orleans Mint transferred $68,369.92 to the Treasurer of the Confederate States on June 15,[4] and George Kellogg, Superintendent of the Dahlonega Mint, deposited $23,716.01 in specie and bullion with B. C. Pressley, Assistant Treasurer, at Charleston, South Carolina. Following the secession of North Carolina, the Federal mint at Charlotte was seized by the state and on June 27 was transferred to the Confederacy.[5] Included in the transfer were coin and bullion amounting to $26,229.61.[6]

In keeping with the instructions of the Treasury Department, the Mint Superintendents endeavored to sell all articles that could be disposed of advantageously. Crucibles, specie boxes, copper, lead, and other items were sold to Army Ordinance and to manufacturers of military articles.[7] The sum realized from these transactions totaled $2,665.10.[8] Upon "urgent representations" being made by the War Department "all nitric acid at each establishment" was retained, "there being no mode of procuring another supply."[9] Although operation of the mints remained suspended for the duration of the war, "the machinery, implements, and other appendages of the Mint and Assay Office at Charlotte, and the occupation and use of the building were surrendered to the Navy Department" in order to promote the activities of that branch of the Government.[10]

In addition to the mints, the Confederacy confiscated Federal customhouses and depositories of funds located throughout the South. On March 7, 1861, the State of Louisiana ordered Anthony J. Guirot to pay the Confederate Government $147,519.66. This

SEIZURES AND DONATIONS

sum represented the balance of customs collected at New Orleans and received by the State Depositary upon the secession of Louisiana.[11] Guirot also had on hand $37,389.94 credited to United States Disbursing Officers, along with $8,934.53 credited to the Post Office Department and $13,820.82 credited to the United States Department of Revenue. These funds, however, were not to be transferred to the Confederate Treasury but were to be used to pay United States warrants on the above accounts until April 15, 1861.[12] It is apparent that warrants drawn on the funds placed to the account of the United States Disbursing Officers and the Post Office Department were never paid, since on December 31, 1862, Guirot transferred funds totaling $51,210.76 to the Confederate Treasury.[13] Records indicate that Federal funds were also seized at the customhouses and depositories located at New Bern and Wilmington, North Carolina; Fernandina, Florida; and Savannah, Georgia, among others. These funds, however, were nominal—their combined sum being a mere $9,315.66. In all, the Confederate Treasury derived approximately $208,046.08 by confiscating Federal customs and depository funds. Buildings comprising the customhouses and depositories were used for offices by Confederate customs collectors and depositories during the existence of the Confederacy.

In summary, confiscation of the United States mints at New Orleans, Dahlonega, and Charlotte by the Confederacy resulted in the Treasury's early receipt of $510,248.00 in bullion and specie. This amount was increased to $718,249.08 by the confiscation of Federal customs and depository funds. It is impossible at this time to arrive at the property value of the seized mints, customhouses, and depositories. The real worth of the mint establishments to the Confederate cause lay in their ability to furnish nitric acid and other military supplies to Army Ordinance and to provide the Navy with buildings and equipment to carry on certain of its activities. Meanwhile, the customhouses and depositories provided the Confederate customs collectors and depositaries with office accommodations.

Sequestration of the Funds and Property of Alien Enemies

The Confederate Congress was aware of Southern indebtedness to Northern creditors from the very beginning of hostilities,[14] and therefore approved an act on May 21, 1861, authorizing "certain debtors to pay the amounts due by them into the Treasury of the Confederate States."[15]

Under the act, all Southerners indebted to individuals or corporations in the United States were prohibited from paying their Northern creditors during the war.[16] The payment of such indebtedness, however, was to be made to the Confederate Treasury in exchange for Government Certificates which showed "the amount received and on what account, and the rate of interest the account was bearing." The Certificates bore the same interest as the original debt and were redeemable at the end of the war in specie or its equivalent. The act neither confiscated nor repudiated the Southern debt but merely suspended temporarily its payment to Northern creditors, substituting in their stead the Confederate Treasury as receiver during the war.

On August 21, 1861, an act was approved whereby collectors of customs were authorized to take possession of, and sell at public auction, all imported goods, wares, or merchandise which remained unclaimed at the customhouses and which because of their bulky, perishable, or explosive nature were rendered impracticable for deposit in a warehouse.[17] This act along with that of May 21, 1861, laid the foundation for the Confederate sequestration acts, the enactment of which was hastened by the passage of the United States "Act to Confiscate Property used for Insurrectionary Purposes," approved August 6, 1861,[18] and President Lincoln's proclamation of August 16, whereby all goods imported from the Southern States were declared forfeited to the Federal Government, and all Confederate vessels in Northern ports were ordered to leave within fifteen days or be subject to seizure by the United States.[19]

Two weeks later, on August 30, 1861, the Confederate Congress retaliated by approving "An act for the sequestration of the estates, property and effects of alien enemies, and for the indemnity of citizens of the Confederate States, and persons aiding the same in the existing war with the United States." The act stated that:

Whereas the Government and people of the United States have departed from the usages of civilized warfare in confiscating and destroying the property of the people of the Confederate States, of all kinds, whether used for military purposes or not; and whereas, our only protection against such wrongs is found in such measures of retaliation as will ultimately indemnify our own citizens for their losses, and restrain the wanton excesses of our enemies. Therefore—

Be it enacted by the Congress of the Confederate States of America,

SEIZURES AND DONATIONS

That all and every, the lands, tenements and hereditaments, goods and chattels, rights and credits within these Confederate States, and every right and interest therein held, owned, possessed or enjoyed by or for any alien enemy since the twenty-first day of May, one thousand eight hundred and sixty-one . . . are hereby sequestrated by the Confederate States of America, and shall be held for the full indemnity of any true and loyal citizen or resident of these Confederate States, or other persons aiding said Confederate States in the prosecution of the present war . . . for which he may suffer any loss or injury under the act of the United States to which this act is retaliatory.[20]

Certain exemptions from confiscation were provided by the act. Stocks and other public securities of the Confederacy and of the several Southern States, held or owned by alien enemies, were exempt from confiscation as was also any debt, obligation or sum due from the Confederate Government, or any of the states, to an alien enemy. The act also provided for the exemption from confiscation of all property of non-belligerent citizens and residents of the border states—whose adherence to the Confederate cause was still believed possible.

Management of the act was placed under the jurisdiction of the Department of Justice. To aid the Attorney-General in acquiring the property of alien enemies, each judge of the Confederacy was authorized to appoint a Receiver for each section of the state for which he held court. The Receivers were instructed "to take possession, control, and management of the property of alien enemies" in their respective sections of a state. Citizens throughout the South were requested to notify the court of any property to be sequestered and "all attorneys, agents, former partners, trustees, and fiduciaries of alien enemies" were ordered "to give information to the receiver and render an account" of their holdings. Upon failure to comply with the order, agents of alien enemies were subject to arrest and if convicted were either fined, sentenced to jail, or both.[21] Judges were empowered to seize and sell the property of alien enemies in order to preserve it from spoilage or they could leave it in the hands of the debtor or other person provided security was given for its safekeeping. However, in cases where stocks, dividends, rents, interest or profits of property were left in the hands of the debtor or other person by an alien enemy they were to be turned over immediately to the Receiver.[22]

Three commissioners "learned in the law" were appointed by President Davis "to hear and adjudge such claims as may be brought before them by any one aiding the Confederacy and who alleged that he had been put to loss under the Confiscation Act of the United States."[23]

The "Act for the sequestration of the estates, property and effects of alien enemies" was immediately put into operation but not before it was attacked as being unconstitutional. J. L. Pettigru, a distinguished Charleston lawyer and Unionist, bitterly opposed the act as a barbarous and useless measure [24] and with his associate counsels, Nelson Mitchell and William Whaley, brought suit to test its validity. The position of the three lawyers was that of any strict constructionist. They contended that Congress had only those powers which were positively delegated to it by the constitution. These, they held, did not include the power to confiscate the property of enemies, as the exercise of that power had been vested in the individual states since the American Revolution. Despite these contentions, Judge A. G. Magrath of the Confederate Court of South Carolina ruled that power to wage war involved the power to confiscate property, and declared the Sequestration Act of August 30, 1861, constitutional.[25]

With the legal aspects of sequestration settled, the Confederate Courts made every effort to carry out the provisions of the act.[26] Reports from Receivers soon reached the Treasury Department advising Secretary Memminger of the amount and character of the sequestered property. The reports stated that although a large amount of various types of securities and real estate was being sequestered, the amount of currency received was very small; recommendations were made to take steps to sell the seized property and divert the funds to the use of the Treasury. Indicative of the reports was that of Sterling R. Cockrill, Receiver for the Middle Division of Tennessee. He wrote:

> As a receiver, I have about two and one-half million of bank stock in Middle Tennessee, and will have very soon near a million of bonds, such as city bonds, railroad bonds, and county bonds. This three and one-half million will yield very little, however, if the court declines to sell, judging it not to be perishable. I am very much inclined to the opinion that our policy [should be] to divert the interest of "alien enemies" in all the property in the country; close the partnership and let them have no rights in the property [which may] . . . bring them among us when the war is over. As long as the property is not sold, they will claim a right to it. I don't mean to sacrifice it, by any means; but I desire the courts to construe liberally the power to sell. Put the prop-

SEIZURES AND DONATIONS

erty in the Treasury and let the settlement be made in the treaty between the governments. . . . When you have a moment of time, I would be pleased to have your views on this suggestion of settlement with the North by a sale of what we find in the country, and let the governments adjust the money account, if it be ever adjusted.[27]

Memminger answered Cockrill on November 6:

I . . . am glad to see that the amount upon which you can lay your hands amounts to so large a figure. It must be borne in mind, however, that it has not been confiscated, but only set apart as a fund to indemnify our own citizens. If the United States should abandon the policy of confiscation on their side, then an indemnity on ours would not be necessary, and in that event the rights of the alien enemy would revive. I think it is the usage of modern warfare not to confiscate debts, and it would be rather an ungraceful introduction of ourselves into the family of nations to come in with the imputation of sanctioning a repudiated code. At present therefore it seems to me that we should simply sequestrate. In doing this we have not sufficiently noticed the difficulties created by requiring security or payment from our citizens. These difficulties should occupy the attention of Congress as soon as it meets.[28]

The difficulties created by the Sequestration Act as noted by the Receiver and the Secretary of the Treasury occupied the attention of Congress as soon as it met, and on February 15, 1862, the Act of August 30 was amended. The major change provided that "all and every the lands, tenements and hereditaments, goods and chattels, rights and credits, and every right and interest therein" held, owned, assessed or enjoyed by or for any alien enemy since May 21, 1861, *"shall be collected and sold . . . and the proceeds paid into the Treasury of the Confederate States."*[29]

It was further provided:

That all money realized under this act . . . shall be applied to the equal indemnity of all persons, loyal citizens of the Confederate States, or persons aiding the same in the present war, who have suffered, or may hereafter suffer, loss or damage by confiscation . . . or by such acts of the enemy, or other causes incident to the war, as may be described or defined, as affording . . . proper cases for indemnity. And all money realized as aforesaid, shall be paid into the Treasury . . . and the faith of the Confederate States is hereby pledged that the same shall be refunded, as required for the purposes aforesaid.[30]

The amending act also provided that all cases of Southern indebtedness to alien enemies were to be reported to the Confederate Receivers within three months from the date of ratification of the amendment. To ease the financial burden of the debtor, the act provided that, except for the interest which had to be paid to the Receiver at the end of each year, no attempt would be made to collect the debt until twelve months after the declaration of peace, or until otherwise directed by law.

In the hope of curbing the expanding currency, an amendment to this section of the act was recommended February 13, 1863, requiring debtors to pay to the Receivers in Confederate currency both the principal and interest due alien enemies. The recommendation claimed that the indebtedness of citizens of the Confederacy to citizens of the United States amounted to no less than 200 to 300 millions of dollars, and that if these debtors were required to pay the principal at once, the volume of currency would be diminished at least 100 millions by July 1. It was also stated that the debtors were primarily "merchants, trading-men, speculators, and extortioners of the country" who "had doubled and quadrupled sums of money . . . which did not belong to them, but for which they were simply trustees," and that by compelling them to pay their debts "the currency would be reduced, the means of speculation withdrawn, and the Government would reap the benefit of the present use of the funds."[31] The suggested amendment was called to the attention of Duncan F. Kenner, Chairman of the Committee of Ways and Means, but no action was taken by Congress.[32]

Later, Representative Ethelbert Barksdale of Mississippi proposed an amendment aimed, as was the Federal Act of March 12, 1863, at confiscating property abandoned by persons who had gone over to the enemy.[33] He contended that such property was not provided for under the original act, as the Attorney-General had ruled that its owners were not "aliens."[34] Finally, on February 3, 1865, Congress approved a somewhat similar act providing that anyone liable to military service who left the Confederacy without the permission of the President or the General in command west of the Mississippi would be treated as an alien enemy and have his property confiscated.[35]

Although the extent of Southern indebtedness to Northern creditors was believed great, the actual amount of funds received by the Treasury from the sequestration of real and personal property of alien enemies proved relatively small. In the reports of

SEIZURES AND DONATIONS

the Secretary of the Treasury the first mention of receipts from sequestration occurred for the period January 1 to September 30, 1863, during which time $1,862,550.21 was received.[36] For the six months ending April 1, 1864, an additional $3,000,787.37 was placed in the Sequestration Fund,[37] and for the six months ending October 1, 1864, receipts of $1,238,732.75 were reported,[38] making a total of $6,102,070.33. To this figure, however, must be added $1,366,012.95 received from the sale of alien property in the Trans-Mississippi Department [39] and $4,192,998.79 in specie seized from the banks at New Orleans following the surrender of the Crescent City to Federal forces.[40] The grand total received by the Confederate Treasury from the sequestration of the funds and property of alien enemies thus amounted to $11,661,082.07. As a financial measure the policy of sequestration may be termed a failure. It is possible that the small monetary returns resulted from the intangible nature of alien enemy property and the reluctance of many Southerners to pay their Northern indebtedness to the Confederate Government—preferring to continue their debt relation to the North and merely paying the annual interest to the South.

The Impressment of Property Owned by Citizens of the Confederacy

When the Confederate currency began to increase in volume, prices rose correspondingly, and numerous producers, hopeful of receiving still higher prices, withheld goods from market as long as their financial condition permitted or at least until the produce began to spoil. Later, many producers refused to sell their produce, preferring to hold it rather than a mass of depreciating paper. Still later, especially during the last year of the war, producers refrained from selling goods because supply officers were paying for purchases with certificates of indebtedness and it was feared the Government would be unable to pay even in depreciated currency the debts thus made. This refusal of producers to sell goods caused the military authorities to experience increasing difficulty in procuring adequate supplies for the armed forces.[41]

It is quite probable that these circumstances alone would have necessitated the impressment of property. Nevertheless, they were supplemented by the growing feeling shared by both the Government and people that producers and speculators were taking unfair advantage of the general distress by demanding exorbitant prices. As a result of these conditions, Congress was compelled to adopt a policy of impressment, the purpose of which was twofold: first, to compel merchants and producers to release their goods; and, second, to purchase the goods at as low a price as possible.[42]

Up to 1863, Congress had refrained from regulating the impressment of property; hence, when military authorities impressed supplies, they did so according to custom and general principle.[43] Because of the arbitrary methods employed, opposition began to develop.[44] On January 19, 1863, William Simms of Kentucky introduced a resolution in the Senate, claiming:

> The right of the protection of life, liberty, and property is the right inviolate of every citizen of the Confederate States, and . . . all seizures or impressment of any such property are in violation of the plainest provisions of the Constitution . . . and are therefore void.[45]

The resolution, however, failed adoption and on March 26, 1863, as a result of the protests and the growing need for impressments, Congress approved an act authorizing and regulating the impressment of private property for public use. The act stated:

> That whenever the exigencies of an army in the field are such as to make impressment of forage, articles of subsistence or other property absolutely necessary, then such impressments may be made by the officer or officers whose duty it is to furnish such forage, articles of subsistence or other property for such army.

Before supplies could be impressed, officers had to try to buy them from the owner. In cases where the two could not agree on the price, each appointed a local citizen to act as judge. Should the judges disagree regarding the value of the property, they in turn chose an umpire whose decision was final. However, if the impressing officer disagreed on the price set by the umpire on property which had not been raised, grown, or produced by the owner, the officer could appeal to the State Board of Commissioners whose decision would be final. Each state board consisted of two members, one appointed by the President and one by the Governor. In addition to acting as a court of last resort, the board was also responsible for studying the market conditions in the state and fixing the maximum prices which the local impressment agents could pay for supplies.[46] To keep the public informed of any change in prices, schedules were published periodically in newspapers throughout the South. Beginning in May, 1863, the schedules listed 39 basic items; by December, 1864, the number had increased to 93. Originally, the list prices were only slightly less than the market price, but by the end of the war they had dropped far below.[47] Only surplus property was to be impressed, the act specifically stating that any "property necessary for the support of the owner and his family, and to carry on his ordinary agricultural and mechanical business . . . shall not be taken or impressed for public use."[48]

In the event an officer of the commissary or quartermaster department impressed supplies, he left with the owner a certificate showing his branch of service, the time and place of impressment, and the amount paid. When full payment was not made at the time of the impressment, the certificate was bona fide evidence of the amount due and entitled the owner to full payment when presented to a proper disbursing officer. The act of March 26, 1863, was amended on numerous occasions,[49] but its central principle—that of taking property and paying prices fixed by the Government—remained in operation until the last few months of the war.

During 1863 and 1864, reports were heard of large quantities of supplies collected by impressment in various depots,[50] but more frequent were the reports advising of the great difficulty experienced by the military authorities in their attempts to secure subsistence for the armies.[51]

As stated earlier, impressment of property had been objected to prior to the adoption of the act of March 26, 1863, but internal conditions at that time had not yet reached the point where universal impressment was necessary to procure supplies, and the outcry was not too great. But following the disastrous Vicksburg and Gettysburg campaigns of 1863, the Confederate currency depreciated rapidly, making it necessary to place more emphasis on impressments, and as a result of the low prices fixed by various State Boards of Appraisers, a loud cry of opposition and distress arose throughout the South. In order to quell the opposition and alleviate the distress, Governor Brown of Georgia, along with others, recommended that the Government authorize the payment of market prices for subsistence. Brown contended that by paying market prices all need for impressment would cease. Writing to James A. Seddon, Secretary of War, the Governor stated that:

. . . The effect of the present system of low prices and inadequate compensation . . . is to withhold the supplies from the market and cause them to be secreted and concealed from the Government agents. This result has inaugurated the system of supplying the Army by impressment instead of by purchase, which is contrary to the true policy of the Government and against the injunctions in the act of Congress which forbids impressment until after there is a refusal to sell.[52]

Brown stated that the Government's policy of impressment not only added to the difficulty of procuring supplies and increased the suffering in the army for want of food, but it also engendered among the people an "evil spirit, bordering already in many cases upon open disloyalty." He said:

. . . This evil increases and must of necessity continue to increase so long as the Government persists in taking the produce of the people at rates so far below the market price and in distributing the operations of impressing agents so unequally in the different sections of the country. . . .

I therefore urge upon your early consideration the necessity of a change of policy and the propriety of paying the market price for all articles purchased, which will supersede the necessity in most cases of making impressments at all. . . .[53]

In contrast to Brown's recommendations for higher prices were those made by James Oliphant calling for "low prices." Oliphant claimed that "prices should be fixed in everything—even things that are brought in through the blockade." He said further:

In fixing prices, the financial reform should not be lost sight of, but prices should be very low—the lower the better, so they are uniform. Men always value money in proportion to the number of articles they can buy with it. I value the currency much higher when I can buy four bushels of corn with $1 than one that requires $4 to buy one bushel of corn. . . . Some contend for high prices as a stimulus to production, but it has never caused one bushel of corn to be made, or any other production, but it has destroyed confidence in the currency, and made the people indifferent, in view of the enormous debt that was accumulating over them. If there is any doubt of the people accepting such a currency . . . have a law passed placing every man in the Army . . . who refuses to take the currency and the prices. Also, have a penalty for any person offering more than the fixed price: make the property liable to seizure and confiscation when a greater price has been offered or received. By this means, confidence will be restored, and we will have better soldiers, better citizens, better currency, and better prospects before us.[54]

Confronted with these two economic extremes, the Government, mindful of a redundant currency, adhered to its policy of low prices and impressment.

SEIZURES AND DONATIONS

In addition to the opposition to low prices, the policy of impressment was attacked because of its wastefulness. Frequent complaints were made concerning the collection of more goods than there was shelter for and of the heaping up of supplies at inaccessible places. Numerous, too, were the objections regarding stockpiles of provisions being neglected and allowed to rot from exposure. Large quantities of corn, bacon, potatoes, wheat, salt, and hides were destroyed in this manner, while others were reported lost or stolen through carelessness of railroads or other transportation companies.[55]

Because of the shortage of transportation facilities, impressment agents usually took the property of those living nearest the army camps and railroad, causing unequal sharing of the burden—and at times pounced upon supplies on the way to city markets, thus giving rise to grave suffering among the urban population, raising prices still higher, and inciting the bitterest feeling against the military authorities by country and townspeople alike.[56]

The arbitrary manner by which troops in the field seized supplies, leaving only a voucher in payment, inevitably led to numerous outrages being committed under cover of the impressment laws. In the fall of 1863, Governor Brown stated that:

. . . There have been so many outrages committed . . . under the guise of making impressments for the Army by unauthorized persons, who have resorted to it as a convenient mode of stealing and robbing from peaceful and unoffending and in many cases unsuspecting citizens, and so many irregularities and acts of partiality, injustice, and oppression committed by some of those who are authorized to make impressments, stripping some of nearly all their provisions and stock, in violation of the act of Congress, and refusing to grant to the owners the rights provided for them in the act, that I have felt it to be my duty to interpose in behalf of common justice and right, and if possible to force lawless persons to abandon this mode of robbery, and legally authorized impressing agents to discharge their duties in subordination to the laws of the country and the acts of Congress. . . .[57]

Brown's opposition to impressment was echoed by the governors of Texas, Louisiana, Mississippi, Virginia, Alabama, Florida, North Carolina, and South Carolina, and necessarily led to conflicts between the central and state governments.

As a result of the mounting opposition, the system of impressment collapsed during the closing months of the war and military authorities were compelled to pay market prices in specie—the supply of which was very limited and could only be obtained by forced loans or seizure.

Unquestionably, the impressment of property aggravated the burdens of the war, and it is possible that it did "more to shake the confidence of the country . . . than any other cause and all other causes combined."[58] There is probably much truth in Frank Owsley's statement that:

> While impressment was absolutely necessary in order to carry on the war, at the same time it helped to bring the war to a close. Without it the prosecution of the war would have collapsed immediately, and with it the war could not last indefinitely because of the bitterness aroused.[59]

There is, of course, no way of knowing the exact amount of goods impressed, but it is correct to assume that the enormous issues of Treasury notes went largely to making such purchases and, in addition, certificates of indebtedness and unpaid vouchers estimated at $500,000,000 were outstanding as of March 1865.[60]

By way of summary, it may be said that the impressment of property resulted from the increasing volume of currency, the corresponding rises in prices, and the reluctance of producers to sell their commodities. Although the impressment of supplies by the army had been occasionally resorted to early in the war, Congress refrained from adopting "An Act to Regulate Impressments" until March 26, 1863. Numerous amendments were made to the act, but its central principle, that of compelling producers to sell surplus products at a price fixed by Government Appraisers, remained till the end. Following the disastrous campaigns at Vicksburg and Gettysburg in the summer of 1863, the Confederate currency depreciated rapidly, and it became imperative to place more emphasis on impressment as a means of procuring supplies for the armed forces. When carried out legally, impressment proved to be very harsh and unequal in its operation, but when it was not done according to the law, it proved unbearable. Opposition developed universally, and every imaginable obstruction was placed in its way. States' rights advocates played upon the weaknesses of the system in their incessant attacks upon the "military despotism" developing at Richmond, thus destroying the South's unity and weakening her chance for independence. During the closing months of the war, the whole system of impressment collapsed and military authorities were compelled to purchase supplies in the open market. It is impossible to know the exact amount of goods impressed, but it is correct to assume that the enormous issues of Treasury notes went largely to making such purchases and, in addition, unpaid receipts estimated at $500,000,000 were outstanding as of March, 1865.

Donations

Although the Confederate Government had been compelled to adopt a system of impressments in order to procure adequate supplies for the military, it should not be assumed that all Southerners were extortioners or speculators whose hoarding of goods contributed to the evils of the Confederate currency. True, many farmers, merchants, and manufacturers, hopeful of receiving higher prices, did withhold commodities from market as the currency increased in volume and prices rose correspondingly, but it is also true that during the same time there were many loyal and patriotic citizens whose love of independence occasioned them to give freely and gratuitously of their service, time, and worldly possessions in support of a cause which they refused to admit was lost. Throughout the war, donations of specie, Treasury notes, various types of Government securities, jewelry, and military supplies were made to the Confederate Treasury by numerous individuals, institutions, and corporations.

On learning that June 13, 1861, had been proclaimed "a day of fasting and prayer," a clergyman of Georgia proposed through the newspapers that collections be taken that day in aid of the Government.[61] The proposal was immediately acted upon by churches in Georgia, Virginia, North Carolina, South Carolina, Tennessee, Florida, and Alabama, and by July 24, the sum of $5,278.88 had been paid into the Treasury.[62] Writing of these donations, Secretary Memminger said:

. . . When it is considered that the proposal was made so late that it could not be known at all in many of the churches, and in none of them could previous notice have been given, the amount may be regarded as a spontaneous and gratifying indication of the sympathy of the religious community with the government. The source from which the money has come would make it peculiarly appropriate that it should be devoted to some object connected with the sick and wounded. . . . I would therefore respectfully recommend that the amount be set apart as a fund for the use of the sick and wounded, and to that end be paid over to the committee raised by Congress to

CONFEDERATE FINANCE

cooperate with the Mayor of Richmond in taking care of the wounded in the late battle.[63]

Six days later, Congress approved Secretary Memminger's recommendation by resolving that the sum "received into the Treasury from donations by churches, on the last fast day, be appropriated as a fund for the use of the soldiers and officers wounded at the late battle of Manassas." During the course of the war, the fund was supplemented by donations from other churches, schools and orphanages, corporations, and army troops. Frequently, individuals donated Treasury notes and various types of Government securities with the request that the Secretary of the Treasury use them in any manner he thought would best aid the cause of the South. Each donation of this type, like those received from churches, was acknowledged by the Secretary as "a contribution for the sick and wounded of the Army" because he believed "its benign influence would be more highly appreciated in giving comfort to those who share so largely our warmest sympathies in this great conflict. . . ."[64]

Individuals also volunteered to can fruits and vegetables for the army, while others donated their services as tax collectors and commissioners of loans.

Varying quantities of foodstuffs and military supplies were contributed to the Government by individuals and communities. Representative of these donations was one of 250,000 bushels of corn tendered by the citizens of the Valley of the Brazos River.[65] Gifts of tobacco, cotton, potatoes, bacon, salt, and flour were also made.

Southern women figured prominently among the contributors. Ladies Aid Societies sponsored concerts and fairs, and put on state-wide drives to raise funds for the Confederate Treasury. One such drive netted the ladies of South Carolina $30,000 which they donated in partial payment of the iron-clad gunboat "Palmetto State."[66]

In response to an appeal in the *Richmond Dispatch,* many ladies forwarded their gold and silver medals to the Treasury.[67] Each medal, however, was returned, the Secretary of the Treasury stating that:

. . . The pure and elevated spirit of patriotism which prompted this offering itself would be accepted if the necessity existed, which is presumed by the writer in the *Dispatch.* I am happy to inform you that we are not reduced so low in our finances as to ask, at the hands of our daughters, the sacrifice which you have so gracefully made, and I take leave to return the medal with this acknowledgement.[68]

Throughout the war, women offered jewelry and silver plate in order to "sustain and further the efforts of their men in conquering independence."[69] But like the medals, these, too, were refused by the Treasury because it was believed the sacrifice of the women in giving up their plate and jewelry "would not be sufficiently compensated by the amount of money which it would realize," and "if the Government were in possession of the plate, it could not be coined, the Government having no mint and having . . . established no form of coin."[70]

Nevertheless, during the last month of the Confederacy when the utter collapse of the Treasury appeared imminent, Congress was compelled to adopt a "Joint Resolution providing for Donations to the Treasury of the Confederate States." The resolution, approved March 13, 1865, stated that:

Whereas many patriotic citizens have expressed their desire to contribute by donations of money, jewels, gold and silver plate and public securities, to the relief of the Treasury;

Therefore, Resolved by the Congress of the Confederate States of America, that the Secretary of the Treasury be, and he is hereby authorized to receive all such donations, and to publish in the daily papers a list of the donations received and the names of the donors.[71]

Those desirous of making contributions were informed that they would be received by the Treasurer at Richmond, and by the Assistant Treasurers and Pay Depositaries throughout the Confederacy. Officers of the Army, located at posts, were appointed to receive donations from the soldiers. It is impossible to know the amount of these contributions, but it appears to have been rather high, considering the late date of the resolution. The Secretary of the Treasury, George A. Trenholm, alone donated $100,000 in currency and $100,000 in Confederate securities.[72] Listed among the receipts were family plate, jewels, rings, ornaments, and personal effects.[73] During the course of the war, it is probable that donations amounting to more than $2,000,000 were made to the Confederate Treasury.

The following table exhibits the approximate amount of funds realized from the several types of seizures and donations.

CONFEDERATE FINANCE

Table Exhibiting Amount of Funds Raised by Confiscation, Sequestration, Impressment, and Donation[74]

Confiscation of Federal funds and property		
Mints (specie and bullion) . . .	$ 510,248.00	
Customs and Depository funds . .	208,046.08	$718,294.08
Sequestration of the funds and property of alien enemies		
Cis-Mississippi States	$6,102,070.33	
Trans-Mississippi Dept.	1,366,012.95	
New Orleans Banks specie . . .	4,192,998.79	11,661,082.07
Impressment of property of Confederate citizens		
Unpaid Certificates of Indebtedness		500,000,000.00
Donations (approx.)		2,000,000.00
Total		$514,379,376.15

CHAPTER

☆ VI ☆

FINANCIAL OPERATIONS ABROAD

☆ ☆ ☆ ☆ ☆ ☆ ☆ ☆ ☆ ☆

THROUGHOUT THE WAR CONFEDERATE PURCHASING AGENTS, REPREsenting the several bureaus of the War and Navy departments, were sent to Europe to procure essential military supplies.[1] The payment of the debts resulting from these activities proved of vital concern to the Government, and plans were formulated to meet the growing obligations. The plan ultimately adopted by the Confederacy for meeting its financial commitments abroad was developed in four stages:
1. During the first eighteen months of the war, foreign purchases were made almost exclusively with coin, letters of credit, and foreign bills of exchange.
2. From August 1862 to February 1864 the theatre of warfare expanded, and purchases abroad increased in volume. Because of the decreasing availability of foreign bills of exchange in the South and the early effectiveness of the blockade, the Treasury Department endeavored to supply its needs with receipts from the sale abroad of various credit instruments supported by cotton acquired under the Produce Loans.
3. Until adequate funds could be raised abroad from the sale of credit instruments based on cotton, it was necessary for the Government to negotiate contracts with private ship owners for the purchase and delivery of military supplies payable in cotton stored in the Confederacy.

4. Because of the exorbitant cost of supplies under the private contract system and the proven fact that small fast steamers could successfully run the blockade,[2] the Treasury Department decided to procure a fleet of steamers, cancel the contracts made with private ship owners and transport all cotton on Government account. These plans were carried out during the last fifteen months of the war. The cotton was shipped by the Treasury to Fraser, Trenholm & Co., Confederate depositary at Liverpool, England, who sold the cotton and deposited the receipts to the account of the Government. The Treasury Department issued warrants on the account to meet its foreign obligations. This was the last stage in the development of plans for raising funds abroad and it remained in effect until the end of the war.

Although the Government's policy for financing purchases abroad can be traced through these four stages, it should be noted that at no time did any one stage suddenly stop and another immediately start—instead, the transition was gradual. While emphasis on one phase of the financial policy decreased, emphasis on another increased. This gradual changing of policy continued until the fourth and final phase was evolved in the spring of 1864. In order to put the policy into operation, a not too extensive organization was created.

Organization and Personnel for Financing Purchases Abroad

It was soon learned that the most successful manner in getting coin, cotton, and various other forms of credit instruments to Europe was by shipping them through the blockade in small fast steamers to the West Indies where they were reloaded in large steamers and shipped to Europe under a neutral flag. To expedite these operations commercial agents were stationed in the islands.[3] Charles J. Helm was sent to Havana, Cuba; Louis Heyliger to Nassau, New Providence; and Norman S. Walker to Bermuda. In their official capacity the agents supervised blockade-runners, managed problems of finance, and occasionally purchased supplies. Later they were appointed depositaries.[4]

At an early date the commercial house of Fraser, Trenholm & Co., Liverpool, England, was appointed a depositary for Confederate funds and throughout the course of the war acted as a financial clearing house for Confederate agents abroad.[5] To manage

FINANCIAL OPERATIONS ABROAD

better the Government's financial transactions and in general aid in improving its credit abroad, James Spence of Liverpool was appointed a financial agent on August 18, 1862.[6] Following the decision of Congress to float the $15-Million Erlanger Loan, General Colin J. McRae, Confederate Congressman of Mobile, Alabama, was also appointed a financial agent. McRae was to reside at Paris and do everything in his power "to forward and expedite all the details of the loan."[7]

On July 29, 1863, McRae's responsibilities were increased when, in addition to his other duties, he was appointed depositary to receive funds arising from the Erlanger Loan.[8] As Confederate depositary in Paris, McRae managed the financial operations of the War and Navy departments, whereas Fraser, Trenholm & Co. handled those for the other departments of the Government.[9] Following a disagreement between Spence and Emile Erlanger over the administration of the Confederate loan in Europe, Spence's commission was revoked September 15, 1863.[10] In the last year of the war the organization for handling Confederate financial operations abroad was centralized under one head with McRae becoming the Government's sole financial agent and Fraser, Trenholm & Co. its only depositary. Under these arrangements, contracts made for the shipment of Government cotton to Europe or for the procurement of military supplies abroad had to meet the approval of McRae. All coin, bills of exchange, and receipts from cotton were deposited with Fraser, Trenholm & Co. and warrants were issued against the account for payment of any claim duly authorized by McRae.[11]

During the years 1862 and 1863, James M. Mason and John Slidell, Confederate diplomatic commissioners to Great Britain and France, functioned intimately with the officers of the Treasury Department. This was especially true when Treasury agents were negotiating foreign loans or preparing the European market for cotton certificates and cotton bonds.

Purchasing agents representing the various bureaus of the War and Navy departments were also in close contact with the financial representatives of the Confederacy. Notable among these were Caleb Huse and James D. Bulloch, Chief Purchasing Agents for the War and Navy departments, respectively. Others included J. B. Ferguson, James H. North, George T. Sinclair, M. F. Maury, John Wilkinson and John N. Moffitt.

This, in brief, introduces both the organization and policy

adopted by the Confederacy for financing its purchasing operations abroad.

Original Plan for Financing Purchases in Europe

Military supplies purchased abroad during the first eighteen months of the war were paid for almost exclusively with specie, letters of credit, and bills of exchange.[12] Specie and sterling exchange were shipped as frequently as possible to John Fraser & Co., Charleston, South Carolina, and its subsidiary, Fraser, Trenholm & Co., Liverpool, England, and there deposited to the account of the Government. Letters of credit, payable in Europe, were then drawn against the account and placed in the hands of purchasing agents for payment of their foreign obligations.[13] The bills of exchange employed in these operations were purchased with specie and Confederate currency by the Treasury Department from banks and business establishments throughout the South. With the Government's need for sterling exchange increasing, the amount available for purchase decreased. As a result, the premium on exchange mounted rapidly and soon became prohibitive. This led Memminger to explain that "the Government needs all the exchange which can be procured to purchase munitions for the public defence," and he requested the bankers to let the Government "have all in their possession at a moderate rate."[14]

The scarcity of exchange and its high premium also caused Memminger to try to use Government specie stored in the Confederacy as security for credit abroad. Writing to James Spence, financial agent at Liverpool, Memminger said:

> . . . I have on hand gold and silver coin (chiefly the former) two and a half millions of which I desire to apply in payment of articles purchased in England by our agents. . . . We find it impossible to purchase a sufficient quantity of exchange for these purposes, and the small amount to be had is at such high rates that it would be desirable to furnish a substitute. I propose therefore to make payment for purchases by a transfer to the creditor of so much of this coin as may be requisite. I presume that when the coin thus becomes *bona fide* the property of a British subject, that the British Government would, at his instance, permit any of its vessels to bring over the same for him. If this expectation be realized the coin here would be as valuable as exchange, and in England would probably realize its mint value—less freight and insurance.
>
> To enable you to carry out any arrangement you may deem advis-

able, Messrs. Fraser, Trenholm & Co. are authorized to make an absolute transfer of the coin, or to draw bills for the same on E. C. Elmore, esq., treasurer, payable here. . . .[15]

Specie used in these early transactions consisted chiefly of that confiscated from the United States mints and customhouses in the South and from that subscribed to the 15-Million Dollar Loan of February 28, 1861. Banks and commercial houses had subscribed liberally to the loan of February 28, thus sacrificing much of their specie at the beginning of the war.

Up to September 30, 1861, more than $1,400,000 had been shipped to Huse to pay for supplies.[16] By March 7, 1862, an additional $1,261,000 was shipped to Fraser, Trenholm & Co. and placed to the credit of Huse.[17] Additional shipments of specie and exchange were forwarded to Europe throughout the war[18] but emphasis on this means of financing purchasing agents was limited almost entirely to the first eighteen months.[19]

By the fall of 1862, the supply of Confederate funds in Europe, placed at the disposal of the Army and Navy departments, neared exhaustion. Huse had purchased almost twice as much as he could pay for,[20] and Isaac, Campbell & Co. was pressing for payment.[21] Meanwhile, other agents had been compelled to remain inactive for lack of funds. The inability of the Government to ship sufficient funds abroad to pay for its purchases gradually led to a growing desire among Confederate authorities to use cotton as a basis for establishing foreign credit.

Second Plan: The Use of Credit Instruments Based on Cotton Stored in the Confederacy

As early as January 17, 1862, Judah P. Benjamin had been authorized by President Davis to negotiate a $1,000,000 loan with any New Orleans agent of a foreign banking house. Cotton was to be deposited in the agent's hands as collateral for the loan, and the $1,000,000 was to be advanced and placed at the Government's disposal in England.[22] Before the plan could materialize, however, New Orleans was captured by the enemy.

Favoring the use of cotton as a basis for establishing credit abroad, Secretary Memminger induced Congress to approve "An Act to authorize the exchange of bonds for articles in kind, and the shipment, sale, or hypothecation of such articles." This was the third and final form of the Produce Loan. Section 3 of the act authorized the Secretary:

... to accept for the use of the Government in exchange for ... bonds or stock, cotton, tobacco, and other agricultural products in kind, which have been subscribed to the Produce Loan, or which may be subscribed in kind. . . . *Provided,* That in no event shall he receive of cotton or tobacco, a greater value than $35 millions, and the said Secretary is further authorized to deposit the same at such places as he shall deem proper, and to procure advances thereon by hypothecation, or to ship the same abroad, or to sell the same at home or abroad as he may deem best; and, to assist these operations, the said Secretary may issue *PRODUCE CERTIFICATES,* which shall entitle the party to whom issued, or his endorsee, to receive the produce therein set forth, and to ship the same to any neutral port, in conformity with the laws of the Confederate States.[23]

Carrying out the provisions of the act, Secretary Memminger acquired a large amount of cotton.[24] This he offered as security for the various types of cotton certificates and bonds sent to Europe during the second and third stages in the development of the Government's policy for financing its purchases abroad. These stages were developed almost simultaneously. The second stage encompassed the sale abroad of various credit instruments supported by cotton stored in the Confederacy, while the third stage entailed the making of contracts for war materials payable in cotton.

With cotton becoming the basis for establishing Confederate credit abroad, Secretary Memminger decided to see what could be done in the English market with bonds issued under the act of April 21, 1862. Writing to James Spence, the Secretary said:

In conformity with one of your suggestions . . . I propose to offer for sale a small amount of the 8 per cent bonds, with a view to purchase a steamer and a cargo of articles for our Government. It is impracticable to ship cotton or tobacco from our ports at present, and the high rate of exchange makes it not desirable to remit in that form. I have therefore sent over by Lieutenant Wilkinson, of our Navy, five hundred thousand dollars in 8 per cent bonds, to be placed in the hands of our depositaries at Liverpool . . . and I propose to you the agency of selling these and as many more as I may be advised are salable at proper rates. I would be willing to sell one million if no more than 60 per cent could be realized on them in England, and if you could get seventy-five per cent or more the figures may be extended to five millions of dollars. . . . In case you cannot sell for cash you may be able to purchase the steamer or cargo with bonds. . . .[25]

FINANCIAL OPERATIONS ABROAD

On September 20, 1862, Major J. B. Ferguson was dispatched to Liverpool with $1,000,000 of the 8% bonds. The bonds were part of the five millions which Spence had been authorized to sell, and receipts from them were to be applied to Navy contracts made by Captains North and Bulloch. Secretary Memminger wrote that "it is of much importance to the Government that these contracts should be faithfully performed." To effect this he recommended that the price of the bonds be reduced to "fifty cents on the dollar." He said, "The rate of exchange is so very high that we are obliged to submit to this great reduction while our ports are blockaded."[26] By October 24, two millions of the bonds had been sent to Europe and the Treasury Department planned to "send another million in a week or ten days."[27]

About this same time Cotton Certificates based on cotton acquired under the Produce Loans or purchased by Produce Loan agents were being prepared by the Treasury Department for sale in Europe. These Certificates were of two types. One conveyed to the purchaser absolute ownership of a particular lot of cotton (20 bales) with the privilege of shipping the same and was "valued at the expense of purchase plus the fees of agents, plus the amount cotton had appreciated since the date of purchase."[28] The other type was adopted upon the suggestion of James M. Mason, Confederate Commissioner to Great Britain,[29] and with certain modifications became the type preferred by Secretary Memminger.[30] It, too, called for 20 bales of cotton, but also stipulated a specific price (originally 5 pence per pound, later 6 pence per pound). The cotton was "deliverable at certain ports, instead of any port at option of the holder." Since most of the cotton was in the West, "separate certificates for the Gulf and Atlantic ports were issued and in such amounts as could be delivered at each." The certificates were "demandable only after peace, and within six months thereafter," as it was "impossible to deliver cotton in any great amount till then." However, in the event a purchaser desired to run the blockade and was willing to pay a "premium," the following clause was added to the certificates: "The Government further agrees to deliver cotton called for in this certificate at any time during the pending war, at any port within its possession (if practicable to transport the cotton to the port selected) upon the payment by the holder of the cost of transportation." In case a holder failed to make his demand for cotton within the prescribed period, the certificate was not forfeited, but the Government assumed "the option to deliver cotton or return the amount paid . . . with interest at 6 per cent from the [date of] issue of the certificate." For this reason this type of cotton certificate was frequently called a cotton bond. The signature of James M. Mason, Commissioner to Great Britain, was required in order to "guard against capture or loss of the certificates on the way to Europe, and also to give official supervision there."[31]

The Treasury Department prepared 1,500 of this type certificate; 1,000 were for cotton to be delivered at New Orleans or Mobile and 500 were for cotton to be delivered at Charleston or Savannah, each valued at $1,000.[32] The $1,500,000 in cotton certificates was to be delivered by Captain W. G. Crenshaw to Fraser, Trenholm & Co., Confederate depositaries at Liverpool. For security reasons, Commander W. L. Maury was to accompany the certificates to Europe and after their deposit with Fraser, Trenholm & Co., they were to be negotiated by Spence, who had received instructions how to dispose of them.[33]

While these arrangements for utilizing cotton as a means of improving the Government's credit abroad were being carried out in Richmond, John Slidell, Commissioner to France, and Caleb Huse were negotiating with the French banking house of Emile Erlanger & Co. in regard to floating a foreign loan based on Confederate cotton. The ultimate outcome of the negotiations was the 15-Million Dollar Erlanger Loan approved by Congress on January 29, 1863.[34]

As stated previously, the Erlanger Loan called for the issue of £3,000,000 sterling ($15,000,000) in Confederate 20-year 7% coupon bonds with interest payable semi-annually. To make the loan more attractive, each bond was convertible at its face value into cotton at the rate of 6 pence sterling for each pound of cotton; i.e., 4,000 pounds of cotton for each bond of £100, and this at any time not later than six months after the ratification of a treaty of peace. Notice of the intention to convert bonds into cotton had to be given to representatives of the Government in Paris or London, and 60 days after such notice the cotton was to be delivered—if peace, in the ports of Charleston, Savannah, Mobile or New Orleans; if war, at points in the interior of the country, within ten miles of a railroad or stream navigable to the ocean. The delivery of cotton was to be made free of all charges and duties except the existing export duty of 1/8 of 1 cent per pound.[35]

The loan provided for a sinking fund of 5% whereby 2½% or

1/40th of the bonds unredeemed by cotton would be drawn by lot semi-annually, thus liquidating the loan 20 years from date of the first drawing. The loan was sold to Erlanger & Co. at the rate of £77 per £100, with anything over £77 going to Erlanger. The bankers were also allowed a 5% commission on the amount of the loan placed and a 1% commission on the amount they collected.

Upon learning of Erlanger's negotiations for a direct loan, Spence, who had been appointed financial agent to sell Confederate 20-year 8% bonds in England, on finding it impossible to receive more than 60% of their face value, stopped selling immediately because of the harm he felt the "varying rates of Bonds would offer to the success of the Erlanger Loan."[36] Thus with a clear field before it, the Erlanger Loan was placed on the European market. The prospectus of the loan was issued on March 18, and on March 19, books were opened for subscriptions in the principal cities of Europe. Erlanger succeeded in securing the eminent firm of J. Henry Schroeder & Co., and the distinguished brokers, Messrs. Lawrence, Son & Pearce, to conduct the operation in London, while it was managed by Schroeder's agents in Amsterdam, by Fraser, Trenholm & Co. in Liverpool, and by Erlanger & Co. in Paris and Frankfort.[37]

The early success of the loan is undeniable. Although the books were kept open only two and one-half days, the total subscriptions approximated £16,000,000, more than five times the authorized issue.[38] The bonds were offered at 90% and by the end of the first day were selling at a 5% premium. Speculative interest, however, soon declined. Within a week the bonds were quoted at 92, and in less than two weeks had fallen to 85.[39] This sudden drop alarmed the Government's agents abroad, and in the absence of McRae, who had not yet arrived in Europe, Mason, Slidell, Erlanger, and Spence decided upon a plan to sustain the market.[40]

On April 7, 1863, an agreement was signed by Mason authorizing Erlanger to buy back bonds totaling £1,000,000 if necessary.[41] The use of Government funds for buoying the market began on April 8, and within two days approximately £400,000 were spent. During the next several weeks additional purchases were made. The result of these operations proved most desirable—the market value of the bonds again rising above the issue price.[42]

Thus, before McRae had arrived in Europe to manage the loan, the whole £3,000,000 of bonds had been placed and £1,517,000 had already been bought back in an effort to sustain the market.

Of the amount bought back, McRae was able to resell £370,000 by May 23. Fearing that the Government would be unable to place the remaining £1,147,000 of bonds, McRae endeavored to get Erlanger & Co. to take them at the cost price. On June 18, 1863, an agreement was made whereby Erlanger & Co. took £2,296,000 of the loan at 72¢ on the dollar. The remaining £704,000 were held by the French bankers with the privilege of selling the bonds at the same rate within six months. To guarantee sale of the £704,000 of bonds within the allotted time, Erlanger pledged £140,000 caution-money.[43]

When news of the disastrous battle of Vicksburg reached Europe, "the loan, despite the utmost exertion of its friends, fell with accelerating velocity, at first to 80, then to 75, until it touched the unprecedented depth of 36."[44]

Since it was impossible to place the £704,000 of bonds, a new settlement was made on February 22, 1864, whereby £40,000 of the caution-money were returned to Erlanger while the remaining £100,000 plus the £704,000 of bonds were turned over to McRae on behalf of the Government.[45]

McRae and Slidell were of the opinion that the Confederate credit at home and abroad could be improved by canceling the Erlanger bonds as rapidly as possible. They believed such a move would also facilitate negotiation of the £704,000 of bonds still on hand. To promote these objectives, McRae informed Memminger on October 2, 1863, that "Messrs. Erlanger & Co., Messrs. Schroeder & Co., and H. O. Brewer, Esq., are about starting a line of small steamers, to run from Havana to Mobile, in order to bring out cotton under the Loan."[46] At practically the same time a contract was made with the Albion Trading Company of London to carry military supplies from Bermuda and Nassau to the Confederacy and return to the islands with cotton.[47] Under the contract, bonds of the Erlanger Loan were exchanged for cotton certificates which, in turn, were canceled by cotton brought out by the company.[48] The success expected of these operations apparently was not attained, the amount of bonds canceled by cotton and cash being only £256,800.[49]

The final report on the Erlanger Loan shows that £2,491,000 of bonds had been sold, netting the Confederacy $7,675,501.25— a little more than one-half the face value of the loan.

During the months separating the first negotiations for the Erlanger Loan and the actual placing of the bonds on the French

FINANCIAL OPERATIONS ABROAD

Bourse, the Confederacy was without funds in Europe. Meanwhile, the demand for military and naval supplies increased. To provide credit for the purchasing agents until funds could be raised by the Erlanger Loan, Caleb Huse was authorized by Mason to issue a new type of credit instrument called a cotton warrant, and Commander W. L. Maury hypothecated a number of the 1,500 Cotton Certificates which he had been instructed to deposit with Fraser, Trenholm & Co.[50]

The cotton warrants stipulated that the Government would deliver to the holder within a definite period of time (usually 30 to 40 days after presentation of the warrant at the Treasury Department in Richmond) so many pounds of cotton of the quality known as Middling Orleans or its equivalent in value of any other description of cotton at the option of the Government. The cotton was to be in merchantable condition and delivered free of any duty or charges at any shipping port (excepting such ports as were then in possession of the enemy), the port to be designated by the holder of the warrant on its presentation in Richmond. Warrants of this description, calling for 2,300,000 pounds of cotton were issued as collateral for the *Merrimac*.[51] Others, issued to Isaac, Campbell & Co. in payment of supplies already purchased by the company and shipped to the War Department, differed slightly in that they authorized the delivery of 5,000,000 pounds of cotton valued at the specific rate of 5 pence sterling per pound. In the case of Isaac, Campbell & Co., both temporary and permanent warrants were issued. During January 1863, Huse and Mason signed temporary warrants for the company calling for large amounts of cotton. These were "to be exchanged within twenty-one days" for permanent warrants "representing the cotton in parcels of not less than Fifty Bales each Warrant."[52]

While the floating of the Erlanger Loan was taking place, the Government also tried to improve its credit abroad by the use of cotton interest bonds and cotton certificates calling for cotton valued at 6 pence per pound. Neither of these types of credit instruments, however, proved to be of any appreciable financial aid to the Confederacy.

It may be said that any success the Confederacy had in using credit instruments based on cotton to finance its foreign purchases from August 1862 to February 1864 was practically limited to the $7,675,501.25 raised by the Erlanger Loan. The negotiation of 20-year 8% bonds, for which Spence had been appointed, was never successful. Only a few of the bonds were sold because of the low price bid for them and the harm Spence felt the "varying rates of Bonds would offer to the success of the Erlanger Loan."[53] For the same reasons, the cotton certificates and cotton warrants issued by Mason, Huse and others served only as temporary collateral, being taken up as rapidly as possible with funds from the Erlanger Loan, as were also the few cotton interest bonds issued under the act of April 30, 1863. Funds raised by these methods were never sufficient to meet the needs of the Government's purchasing agents and had to be supplemented. Thus, with the Confederacy being unable to secure adequate funds abroad by the use of credit instruments based on cotton, emphasis on this means of acquiring resources decreased, whereas emphasis on the procurement of essential materials through contracts payable in cotton increased. In fact, the development of the second and third stages in the Government's program for financing purchases abroad occurred almost simultaneously and continued from August 1862 until February 1864.

Third Plan: Contracts Made for Supplies Payable in Cotton at Confederate Ports

While the Confederacy was attempting to improve its foreign credit by the use of various cotton securities, numerous proposals were made to the several departments of the Government by individuals who were anxious to make contracts for furnishing supplies to be procured in Europe. With the Government hard pressed for funds, the contractors offered to accept payment in cotton at Confederate ports. Believing such arrangements would facilitate the shipment of essential war materials, increase the number of blockade violations, and relieve the financial embarrassment of purchasing agents in Europe, the Government made a number of private contracts.[54] The results, however, were not the desirable ones expected. Under each contract, an official agent of the War or Navy department stationed in Europe examined the supplies. Numerous difficulties arose. Frequently supplies had to be rejected due to their inferior quality and there were instances of fraudulent bookkeeping.[55] Too, contractors with little or no money occasionally tried to raise funds in Europe by selling bonds and cotton certificates. These activities not only brought them into competition with each other but also with the official agents of the Confederacy, who were authorized to conduct similar operations. As a result, the credit of the Government received additional injury.

Following the large increase in the number of private contracts during 1863, the Government's financial situation in Europe became so acute that Slidell, Mason, Hotze, Spence, McRae, and others hastened to advise the Richmond authorities that such contracts were disrupting the work of the official agents. Hotze wrote:

> It is undeniable that the credit of the Government has suffered most seriously by the clashing interests, the rivalries, and hostilities, sometimes the disgraceful public squabbles of contractors, and of the lax manner in which, in many instances, contracts appear to have been granted. . . .[56]

To improve the situation he recommended the cancellation of all private contracts claiming their terms "are such as to destroy the confidence of prudent merchants, for British commerce however enterprising has no faith in the solvency of a debtor who promises to pay tenfold the value of the goods."[57]

On October 7, 1863, McRae substantiated Hotze's remarks by pointing out "the damage the credit of the Government was sustaining by the multiplicity of agents, contractors, and partners which it has in Europe, none of whom have any credit except what they derive from their connection with the Government and the use of cotton or other means out of which they are making enormous profits, while the country is badly served."[58] After describing the shady practices and enormous profits occurring under certain contracts, McRae stated that:

> There are many other contracts of various shades and hues floating about the London markets, all . . . having but one object, namely, to enrich contractors at the expense of the Government. . . . These men, having neither capital nor credit, begin by hawking their contracts through London, Manchester, and Liverpool markets and sell them to or divide them with the highest bidder. Such exhibitions are vary damaging to our credit, as they create the impression among capitalists and all prudent men that a government which is so reckless of its means is not likely to achieve its independence against such fearful odds.[59]

"To remedy these evils and re-establish the credit of the Government," McRae suggested the following plan:

> First. Revoke or annul all contracts in Europe in which profits or

CONFEDERATE FINANCE

commissions are allowed, whether they be with agents, contractors, or partners.

Second. There should be one contracting or purchasing officer each for the War and Navy Departments in Europe. . . .

Third. There should be one general agent for Europe, who should have the entire control of the credit of the Government abroad, with large discretionary powers for raising money, and to whom the contracting and purchasing officers in Europe should report before making any engagements to pay money or commit the credit of the Government, which should not be done without the consent of the general agent. The same agent should have control of all cotton or other produce sent abroad for sale on account of the Government.

Fourth. The Government should take the exports and imports into its own hands, and no cotton, tobacco, or naval stores should be allowed to leave the country except on Government account or for account of holders of produce bonds, and none but the same parties should be allowed to import, the Government taking the importations of the bondholders on delivery at the Confederate ports, at a price fixed on between them and the agent in Europe, to be paid for at the port of delivery in cotton. . . .

Fifth. Purchase or take possession of all the cotton and tobacco in the country at a price to be fixed by act of Congress. . . .[60]

THE NEW PLAN: COTTON SHIPPED ON GOVERNMENT ACCOUNT AND SUPPLIES PAID FOR WITH PROCEEDS

Before McRae's general plan for re-establishing the Government's credit abroad reached Richmond, a dispatch from Slidell containing recommendations for a centralized agency had already arrived at the capital and was instrumental in moving the Confederate authorities to action.[61] At the instance of Davis, Benjamin proposed an arrangement which was approved by the Treasury, War, and Navy departments in the hope of improving "the future management of the financial disbursements of each abroad." Under the new arrangement, McRae was "made the sole agent for the disposition of securities" in Europe and was empowered to apportion the funds at his command among the different agents of the Government as needed. Thus, the first step in the establishment of a centralized plan for obtaining supplies abroad and for supervising their payment was finally accomplished. The completion of the plan, i.e., the reorganization of foreign finance based on the direct shipment of cotton to Europe and government control of blockade-running, was achieved within the next few months.

FINANCIAL OPERATIONS ABROAD

McRae's plan for the re-establishment of Confederate credit abroad was received with favor. On February 6, 1864, Congress adhered to his recommendations by approving "A bill to impose regulations upon the foreign commerce of the Confederate States to provide for the public defence."[62] The act prohibited "the exportation of cotton, tobacco, military and naval stores, sugar, molasses, and rice . . . except under such uniform regulations as shall be made by the President. . . . *Provided,* That nothing in this act shall be construed to prohibit the Confederate States, or any of them, from exporting any of the articles herein enumerated on their own account." On the same day, legislation was approved forbidding the importation of strong drinks, furs, laces, toys, fireworks, furniture, velvets, jewelry, paintings, and various other articles of luxury. With Congress assuming control over foreign commerce, on February 6, 1864, the second and third stages in the Government's plans for financing its purchases abroad came to an end and the fourth and final stage—that of exporting all cotton on Government account—was well on its way to fruition.

To carry out the provisions of the acts, a list of regulations was formulated in regard to blockade-running. These were summarized by Davis as follows:

First. Every vessel owned by private persons shall be considered on every voyage as chartered to the Confederate Government for one-half of her tonnage, outward and inward.

Second. All private owners of cargo exported from the Confederacy shall bring in return supplies equal to one-half of the proceeds of their exported cargo.

Third. The several States shall remain at liberty to charter the other half of each vessel, and shall be free to carry out or bring back cargo on that half without being subject to the regulations.[63]

On April 18, 1864, Davis approved an agreement made four days earlier by the Treasury, War and Navy departments concerning the purchase, transportation, and sale of cotton, tobacco, and naval stores. The agreement was aimed specifically at cotton. It entrusted purchase and transportation by land to the War Department; the shipment and sale of cotton were entrusted to the Treasury Department together with the purchase of vessels; the planning, building, and sailing of the vessels were entrusted to the Navy.[64] An appropriation of $20,000,000 was made for "purchases of cotton, naval stores and other produce . . . to meet the engagements of the Government," and Lieutenant-Colonel Thomas L. Bayne was appointed to supervise the enterprise.⁶⁵ This was the beginning of a centralized plan for the control of cotton at home, corresponding to the reorganization in Europe under McRae.

Under the new plan all cotton owned by the various departments was transferred to the Treasury Department. This caused some difficulty due to the contracts made by individual departments for supplies payable in cotton at the Confederate ports. To overcome this obstacle, it was decided that no new contracts should be made for the delivery of cotton and the remaining interest in all old contracts was to be brought up or annulled as soon as ships could be procured to take care of the business. Until this could be done, Bayne approved a plan of having "at each port one stock of cotton and one disbursing agent, who would pay [cotton] for such importations and freights as were chargeable to any department of the Government" under the old contracts.⁶⁶ The balance of the cotton was to be shipped as soon as possible via Nassau, Bermuda, or Havana to Liverpool and sold by Fraser, Trenholm & Co., who would hold the proceeds subject to the control of McRae. The several departments in Richmond were to estimate their financial needs abroad; then warrants authorizing payment were to be drawn on the cotton proceeds held by the depositaries and were to be issued in favor of McRae by the Treasury Department. After approving a contract for supplies made by a purchasing agent, McRae was to furnish the required funds from those placed under his control. This new plan for the purchase, transportation, and sale of cotton on Government account, and the sanction and payment of contracts for supplies payable in Europe with proceeds from the sale of cotton by a general agent of the Treasury, was consummated in the summer of 1864.

In order to carry out the new plan for financing Confederate purchases abroad, McRae launched an extensive program for securing vessels to run on Government account. On July 7, 1864, an agreement was made with Fraser, Trenholm & Co. for eight steamers.⁶⁷ Similar arrangements were made with J. K. Gilliat & Co. for six more steamers.⁶⁸

Until the fleet of blockade-runners could be put in operation, a temporary contract was made with Alexander Collie & Co. of London "to provide four large and powerful new steamers."⁶⁹ In addition to these, the Government already owned four steamers, which had been in the service of the Ordnance Bureau, plus three-fourths interest in five steamers operated by W. G. Crenshaw.

Under McRae's program twenty-seven steamers were to be placed at the disposal of the Government by April 1865. Of the fourteen actually bought or built by McRae, however, only six were able to make one or more trips through the blockade before the end of the war.

As the new plan got under way, McRae wrote Seddon on July 4, 1864: "Our credit begins to grow stronger, and by proper management will soon be available for all our wants." He believed that "by the end of the year the Government will have the means in its own hands to obtain all the supplies required abroad without incurring any further foreign debt."[70]

The anticipated results were never realized. The shipping of cotton on Government account had scarcely begun when the operation ran into difficulties. The passage of the act of February 6, 1864, regulating foreign commerce had been immediately greeted with a storm of protest from commercial houses, individual blockade-runners, and especially from the states.

Commercial houses interested in blockade-running attempted "to induce a relaxation of the regulations" by withdrawing their ships from employment, claiming "the terms imposed by the regulations were so onerous as to render impossible the continuance of the business." Davis, however, believed "the withdrawal of the vessels was an experiment by a combination among the owners" to test "the firmness of the Government," and refused to alter the regulations. The results indicate the correctness of his belief for "after various attempts to obtain increased advantages," the vessels not only resumed their voyages but actually increased in number. The President informed Congress that "among the efforts made [by commercial houses] to induce a change of the regulations, was a warning . . . they would transfer their vessels to the Executives of the several States and thus withdraw them from the operations of the regulations."[71]

Unquestionably, the greatest opposition to the trade regulations came from the individual states. As noted earlier, the act of February 6, 1864, imposing regulations upon foreign commerce provided "that nothing in this act shall be construed to prohibit the Confederate States, or any of them, from exporting any of the articles herein enumerated on their own account."[72] Under the regulations summarized by Davis, state-owned vessels were not subject to the restrictions, but state-chartered vessels were. The Confederate authorities contended that the regulations applied to all vessels except those owned outright by the individual states.

The regulations left one-half of each privately-owned vessel free to be chartered by any state, and Davis insisted that this was sufficient. Both James A. Seddon, Secretary of War, and George A. Trenholm, Secretary of the Treasury, agreed with the President.[73] This contention prevented private owners who desired to transport one-half the tonnage on their own account from chartering the balance of their ships to state governors, with whom they could make better bargains than with the Confederate Government. Governors, who had acquired interests for their states in many of the ships, first asked, then demanded, exemption from the regulations. In opposing the regulations, owners of vessels teamed up with the governors. It was argued that if a state should "acquire, by purchase or charter, the use of one-fourth of a steamer the Confederate States should relinquish an equal proportion of the moiety claimed under the regulations and reduce the share reserved for its use to one-fourth."[74] The Executive Department refused to concede the point and a bitter and long-drawn-out controversy developed, but the states and blockade-runners were never able to alter the regulations.[75]

On December 20, 1864, Davis informed Congress that the Government's new plan for paying for its purchases abroad had put an end to a wasteful and ruinous contract system. The President estimated that under the new plan only 100 bales of cotton had to be exported by the Government to purchase the same amount that called for 600 bales under the private contract system.[76]

In his report of December 10, 1864, Seddon stated that 27,299 bales of cotton had been exported under the new plan. These he summarized as follows:

SHIPMENTS OF COTTON SINCE MARCH 1, 1864 [77]

	Bales
For War Department	6,111
For Navy Department	4,861
For Treasury Department, 12,840, and one-half of contract steamers (6,974), 3,487	16,327
Total	27,299

27,299 bales at £40 average = £1,091,960, at $4.85	$	5,296,006
Equal in currency (Treasury notes) at 25 to 1		132,400,150

FINANCIAL OPERATIONS ABROAD

Before the new plan went into operation, vessels had already been required to devote one-third of their tonnage to the use of the Government by authority of the War Department. The principle was the same as that imposed under the act of February 6, 1864, but statistics under the two were not kept separate. The following summary, embracing the period November 1, 1863, to October 25, 1864, indicates the leading articles imported for the Cis-Mississippi Department:

LEADING ARTICLES IMPORTED NOVEMBER 1, 1863, TO OCTOBER 25, 1864 [78]

Lead	pounds	1,490,000
Saltpeter	"	1,850,000
Meat	"	6,200,000
Coffee	"	408,000
Boots and shoes	pairs	420,000
Blankets	"	292,000
Arms (muskets, rifles, and carbines)		136,832

When the Government's new plan for paying for its purchases abroad was first adopted, each department was charged with the duty of managing its own exports and imports, but experience indicated the propriety of consolidating these operations under the Treasury Department. This was done on July 1, 1864, and from that date to the first of December the quantity of cotton exported on Government account was 11,796 bales. Of this quantity, 1,272 bales were lost, and 10,522 bales arrived safely at foreign ports.[79] Most of this cotton was shipped from Wilmington, Charleston, Mobile, and Savannah in small blockade-runners averaging about 200 bales per vessel. The cotton was transported to Nassau, Bermuda, Havana, or Halifax from whence it was reshipped in large steamers to Fraser, Trenholm & Co. at Liverpool.

It is probable that the new arrangements for procuring essential supplies from abroad would have been in full operation by the summer of 1865 had military defeat been postponed. But with the capture of Wilmington, Savannah, and Charleston by Federal forces early in 1865, the new plan received a stunning blow. After February 1865, blockade-running was confined almost entirely to ports on the Gulf of Mexico, with Galveston and other Texas cities thriving on the trade for a brief period.

Although the war ended before the maximum benefits of the new plan could be realized, enough good had resulted to merit its commendation. Through centralized agencies at home and abroad, cotton was purchased, shipped, and sold on Government account and supplies were bought with the proceeds for as little as one-sixth the price paid under private contracts. Upon adoption of the new plan a general improvement was at once apparent in Confederate credit abroad. This was reflected in the improved standing of the Erlanger Loan.

Confederate authorities had been aware of the possibilities of such a plan for many months prior to its adoption.[80] An earlier acceptance of the new plan, however, was precluded by three factors: An effective blockade, a dearth of Confederate vessels, and a belief that foreign recognition or repudiation of the blockade could be hastened by following the course which the Confederacy vainly pursued.

It was only after the Government became convinced that foreign recognition was not forthcoming, and only after commercial houses and private contractors—stimulated by huge profits—proved the inefficacy of the blockade, that the Confederacy decided to adopt its new plan for financing the purchase of military supplies abroad.

From the available records it is impossible to determine the actual amount of Confederate expenditures abroad. In the discussion above, an attempt has been made merely to explain the financial policy adopted by the Government for meeting its foreign expenditures, to identify the organization and personnel responsible for carrying out the policy, and to indicate a few of the obstacles confronting its successful operation.

Appendix A
Customs Collectors[1]

State	Port	Collector
Alabama	Mobile	J. C. Colson, Deputy Collector
		Thaddeus Sanford, Collector of Customs
	Selma	Jonathan Haralson, Surveyor
	Tuxumbia	Jas. W. Rhea, Surveyor
Florida	Chattahooche [Apalachicola]	N. Baker
	Fernandina	Felix Livingston
	Palatka	George Lucas
	Pensacola	Joseph Sierra
	Green Cove Spring	Paul Aman
	Jacksonville	Thomas Ledurth
	Bay Port	A. Jackson Decatur
	Tampa) St. Marks)	A. B. Noyes
	Key West	John P. Baldwin
	St. Johns	Thos. Sedwith
Georgia	Atlanta	F. R. Shackleford
	Augusta	Thomas W. Fleming
	Darien	Woodford Mabry
	Savannah	John Boston
	St. Marys	J. J. Drefour
Louisiana	Tangipohoa) New Orleans)	F. H. Hatch
	Teche	R. N. McWilliams
	Shreveport	P. H. Risson
North Carolina	Beaufort	Josiah F. Bell
	Elizabeth City	W. C. Davis
	Edenton	E. Wright
	New Bern	Singleton
	Plymouth	Joseph Ramsey

1. The list was compiled from the following: Index Book of the Confederate Treasury Records (Treas. Dept., National Archives); R. G. 109. Chap. X—Vol. 164. Letters and Telegrams of the Secretary's Office, Treasury Department, to Collector of Customs, March 21, 1861, to January 24, 1862, 27-32; Thian, *Corresp. of Treas. CSA.*, IV, 129-130.

CONFEDERATE FINANCE

State	Port	Collector
North Carolina	Wilmington	James T. Miller—succeeded by Ed. Savage, Dec. 1861 — Ed. Savage succeeded by Henry Savage, Apr. 1862.
	Ocracoke	O. H. Dewey
South Carolina	Charleston	William F. Colcock
	Georgetown	W. L. Croft
Tennessee	Memphis	T. H. Trice
	Nashville	Jesse Thomas
Texas	Brazos de Santiago)	
	Brownsville)	Francis W. Latham
	Point Isabel)	
	Eagle Pass	Lorenzo Castro
	Galveston	James Sorley
	Sabine	B. F. McDonough
	LaSalle [Saluria]	D. M. Stapp
	Pass del Norte	L. G. Jones
Virginia	Norfolk	J. J. Simkins
	Richmond	(W. M. Harrison, Sept. 1, (1861-Apr. 8, 1862 (R. H. Lorton, Apr. 8, (1862—end of C. S. A.
	Staunton	A. F. Kinney
Mississippi	Pearl River	R. Eager
	Natchez	John Hunter
	Vicksburg	John Bobb
Arkansas	(None listed)	

Appendix B

Showing the average values of certain kinds of property as assessed and returned in the several States under the war-tax act of August 19, 1861.[1]

States	Real Estate	Slaves	Horses, Cattle &c.	Gold Watches	Pianos	Pleasure Carriages
Alabama						
Arkansas						
Florida	*$ 4.98	$437.08	$ 5.54	$72.68	$187.36	$96.11
Georgia						
Louisiana						
Mississippi						
North Carolina	3.45	326.83		82.68	197.74	74.17
South Carolina	6.69	452.79	28.87	70.80	173.79	79.64
Tennessee						
Texas	2.09	515.13	10.85	76.84	217.56	123.64
Virginia	10.12	350.00	25.50	57.60	133.67	73.33
General Average	*$ 5.46	**$416.56	$17.69	$72.12	$182.02	$89.37

*Per acre.
**Per capita.

1. Thompson Allan to C. G. Memminger, Jan. 6, 1863 (enclosure). *Confed. Treas. Reports*, III, 127.

Appendix C

TABLE SHOWING AVERAGE VALUE OF ONE DOLLAR IN GOLD IN NEW YORK AS COMPARED WITH UNITED STATES CURRENCY DURING EACH MONTH OF THE WAR, FROM JANUARY 1862 TO APRIL 1865.[1]

	1862	1863	1864	1865
January	$1.03	$1.45	$1.55	$2.15
February	1.03	1.61	1.55	2.06
March	1.01	1.54	1.63	1.79
April	1.01	1.51	1.74	1.46
May	1.03	1.49	1.79	
June	1.06	1.45	2.06	
July	1.15	1.30	2.59	
August	1.14	1.25	2.59	
September	1.18	1.34	2.25	
October	1.29	1.47	2.08	
November	1.31	1.48	2.33	
December	1.32	1.51	2.32	

TABLE SHOWING AVERAGE VALUE OF ONE DOLLAR IN GOLD IN RICHMOND AS COMPARED WITH CONFEDERATE TREASURY NOTES DURING EACH MONTH OF THE WAR, FROM MAY 1861 TO APRIL 1, 1865.[1]

	1861	1862	1863	1864	1865
January		$1.25	$3.00	$20.00 to 20.50	$45 to 60
February		1.25	4.00	22.50 to 25.00	45 to 65
March		1.30	5.00	23.00 to 24.50	70 to 60
April		1.40	5.50	22.00 to 23.00	60.00
May	$1.10	1.50	5.50	18.00 to 21.00	
June	1.10	1.50	7 to 8	17.00 to 19.00	
July	1.10	1.50	9.00	20.00 to 23.00	
August	1.10	1.50	12 to 13	22.50 to 25.00	
September	1.10	2.50	12 to 13	22.50 to 27.50	
October	1.15	2.50	14.00	26.00 to 27.00	
November	1.15	3.00	15 to 17	27.50 to 33.50	
December	1.20	3.00	18 to 20	34.00 to 49.00	

1. From tables compiled by Wm. B. Isaacs & Co., Bankers, Richmond, Va., found in James H. Hammond Papers.

Appendix D

TABLE SHOWING ASSESSED VALUE OF TAXABLE PROPERTY AS OF JULY 24, 1861.[1]

States	Value of all real estate including town lots	Value of Town Lots alone	Number of Negroes	Value of Negroes	Capital invested in Trade, Merchandise, etc.
Alabama	143,765,708**		435,473	261,283,800	41,362,517
Arkansas	68,662,395	5,227,689	109,065	65,439,000	2,864,059
Florida	18,592,933**		63,809	38,285,400	2,002,568
Georgia	196,904,370	35,139,415	467,461	280,476,600	15,577,193
Louisiana	210,356,327**		312,186	187,311,600	36,657,729
Mississippi	143,000,000**		479,607	287,764,200	19,253,370
North Carolina	97,772,975	12,050,373	328,377	197,026,200*	20,000,000
South Carolina	121,333,873	31,333,873	407,185	244,311,000	26,388,861
Tennessee	242,591,851	29,770,858	287,112	172,267,200*	25,000,000
Texas	140,267,740	17,982,980	184,956	110,973,600	19,256,500
Virginia	374,989,888	59,563,667	495,826	297,495,600	48,489,131
	1,758,238,060	191,068,855	3,571,057	2,142,634,200	256,851,928

	Bank Capital	Railroad and other Stocks	Money at Interest	Total
Alabama	5,000,000	20,975,639	22,578,370	494,966,034
Arkansas		142,000	1,334,631	138,442,085
Florida	381,263	6,368,699	2,121,069	67,751,932
Georgia	9,028,078	24,000,000	107,336,258	633,322,499
Louisiana	24,496,866	16,073,270	5,701,493	480,597,285
Mississippi	436,344	9,024,444	12,198,954	471,677,312
North Carolina	6,626,478	13,698,469*	8,000,000	343,124,122
South Carolina	14,000,000	19,000,000*	15,000,000	440,033,734
Tennessee	8,131,762	27,348,141*	10,000,000	485,338,954
Texas		7,578,943	4,000,000	282,076,783
Virginia	16,707,775	47,000,000	10,147,367	794,829,761
	84,808,566	191,209,605	198,418,142	4,632,160,501

*Estimated.
**No means of separating the value of town lots from the aggregate value of "Real Estate and Town Lots."

1. Table included in report of Memminger to Howell Cobb, July 24, 1861. *Confed. Treas. Reports*, III, 19-23.

NOTES

CHAPTER I

1. On December 20, 1860, six weeks after Lincoln's election, South Carolina seceded from the Union; Mississippi, Alabama, Florida, Georgia, and Louisiana followed in January 1861; Texas on February 1, 1861. Arkansas, Tennessee, North Carolina, and Virginia held back until later.
2. Ernest A. Smith, *The History of the Confederate Treasury* (hereafter cited, *Hist. of Confed. Treas.*), 1.
3. Christopher Gustavus Memminger was born at Nayhingen, Wurtemberg, Jan. 9, 1803; died Mar. 7, 1888, Charleston, S. C. At the age of four, following the death of his father, he migrated to America with his mother who died shortly after reaching Charleston. Placed in an orphanage till eleven years old, he was then removed by Thomas Bennett (later Governor of South Carolina), who offered him all the advantages of a wealthy home. Memminger graduated from South Carolina College in 1819. In 1838, as a member of the South Carolina State House of Representatives, he began a long struggle to disassociate the State from banking corporations and to force the banks to maintain specie payments on pain of forfeiture of their charters. In these contests he won considerable reputation as a sound financier. Henry D. Capers, *The Life and Times of C. G. Memminger* (hereafter cited, *Memminger*), 7-370.
4. Robert U. Johnson and Clarence C. Buel, eds., *Battles and Leaders of the Civil War* (hereafter cited, *Battles and Leaders*), I, 104.
5. Jefferson Davis, *The Rise and Fall of the Confederate Government*, I, 242-243.
6. Capers, *Memminger*, 347-348.
7. Edward A. Pollard, *Life of Jefferson Davis* (hereafter cited, *Davis*), 181.
8. J. C. Schwab, *The Confederate States of America, 1861-65; A Financial and Industrial History of the South During the Civil War* (hereafter cited, *Confed. Sts. of Am.*), 4.
9. R. W. Barnwell, Robt. Toombs, and R. B. Rhett were mentioned as available for the Treasury portfolio.
10. Lewis Cruger to Jefferson Davis, May 25, 1878. Jefferson Davis Papers.
11. While at Montgomery, Ala., the Treas. Dept. was located in a suite of offices in the Commerce Bldg., corner of Commerce and Market Streets. Upon removal from Montgomery to Richmond, on May 26, 1861, the several offices were housed in various quarters in the city. The Bureau of the Comptroller occupied a house "on the corner of 6th and Main Streets"; the Bureaus of the Commissioner of Taxes and the Produce Loan were located in the Richmond House. John W. Hall, Chief Clerk, to F. M. McMullen, Chm., Com. on Public Bldgs., C. S., H. of R., Feb. 12, 1865. James M. Matthews, ed., *The Statutes at Large of the Provisional Government of the Confederate States of America from the institution of the government, February 8, 1861, to its termination, February 18, 1862, inclusive* (hereafter cited, *Stats. at Large*), 295; Wm. W. Crump, Asst. Sec. of

Treas., to A. L. Edwards, Supt. of Richmond House, Feb. 20, 1865. Vol. 115F. Record Book of Copies of Letters of Secretary of Treasury from October 17, 1864 to March 31, 1865 [MS vol. in R. G. 56. Confed. Treas. Dept. Archives (hereafter cited, Vol. 115F. Record of Letters of Treas.)], 267.

12. "An Act to Establish the Treasury Department," approved Feb. 21, 1861, *Provisional and Permanent Constitutions Together with the Acts and Resolutions of the First Session of the Provisional Congress of the Confederate States, 1861* (hereafter cited, *Prov. and Perm. Consts.*), 13-16.

13. *Stats. at Large*, sec. 6, p. 14.

14. *Ibid.*, sec. 7, p. 14. On Mar. 6, 1865, an act was approved "to authorize the First Auditor to receive and keep the accounts of the Navy Department." Charles W. Ramsdell, *Laws and Joint Resolutions of the Last Session of the Confederate Congress (November 7, 1864-March 18, 1865) Together with the Secret Acts of Previous Congresses* (hereafter cited, *Laws*), 85.

15. The Treas. Dept. personnel was classified and paid annual salaries as follows: Sec. of the Treas. $6000 payable quarterly in advance; Asst. Sec. of Treas., Comptroller, Auditor, Register, and Treasurer $3000; Chief Clerks $1500; Clerks $1200; Messengers $500. "An Act to Create the Clerical Force of the Several Executive Departments. . . ," approved Mar. 7, 1861. *Prov. and Perm. Consts.*, secs. 1-2, pp. 47-48; "An Act to Determine the Salaries of Vice President and the Heads of the Departments," approved Feb. 21, 1861. *Ibid.*, 11.

16. "An Act to Appoint a Second Auditor of the Treasury," approved Mar. 15, 1861. *Stats. at Large*, 66. A bureau of the Third Auditor was created Jan. 8, 1864 to take charge of all duties connected with the Post Office Dept. which the First Auditor had been required to perform. James M. Matthews, ed., *Public and Private Laws of the Confederate States of America, Passed at the First and Second Congresses, 1862-'64* (hereafter cited, *Public Laws of CSA.*), 173. I. W. M. Harris was appointed Third Auditor.

17. Capers, *Memminger*, 319.

18. Smith, *Hist. of Confed. Treas.*, 3-4.

19. The complete roster for each of the several bureaus is given in the "Salary List for Personnel of the Treasury Department, C.S.A." Vol. 79. Record of Certificates of Stock (MS. vol. in R.G. 56. Confed. Treas. Dept. Archives), 8-10.

20. *Stats. at Large*, 177-183. Thompson Allan was appointed Chief Clerk Oct. 1, 1861 to superintend the duties of the office. Memminger to Allan, Sept. 28, 1861. Vol. 111B. Record Book of Copies of Letters of Secretary of Treasury from March 1, 1861 to October 12, 1861 [MS. vol. in R.G. 56. Confed. Treas. Dept. Archives (hereafter cited, Vol. 111B. Record of Letters of Treas.)], 598.

21. Memminger to Robt. Tyler, Register, May 6, 1863. Raphael P. Thian, comp., *Correspondence of the Treasury Department of the Confederate States of America, 1861-'65* (hereafter cited, *Corresp. of Treas. CSA.*), IV, 449.

22. "An act for the assessment and collection of taxes," approved May 1, 1863. *Public Laws of CSA.*, 140. Under the act of Feb. 17, 1864, the bureau was continued and its clerical force increased. *Ibid.*, 227-229.

23. Memminger to Robt. Tyler, Jan. 3, 1862. *Corresp. of Treas. CSA.*, IV, 247-248.

24. Memminger to Thos. S. Bocock, Speaker, H. of R., Oct. 3, 1862. Raphael P. Thian, comp., *Reports of the Secretary of the Treasury of the Confederate States of America, 1861-'65* (hereafter cited, *Confed. Treas. Reports*), III, 91-92.

25. "An act to authorize the issue of Treasury Notes . . . ," approved

NOTES

Mar. 9, 1861. *Prov. and Perm. Consts.,* 51-54.

26. Joseph Daniel Pope to Gov. Pickens, Columbia, S. C., Sept. 8, 1862. Raphael P. Thian, comp., *Correspondence with the Treasury Department of the Confederate States of America, 1861-'65* (hereafter cited, *Corresp. with Treas. CSA.*), V, 644.

27. Memminger to S. G. Jamison, Mar. 1, 1862. *Corresp. of Treas. CSA,* IV, 268.

28. Memminger to B. F. Slocum, May 10, 1862. Telegram Messages, Treasury Department: Telegrams of the Confederate Treasury Department from February 27, 1861 to July 30, 1864. MS. vol. in R. G. 56. Confed. Treas. Dept. Archives (hereafter cited, Tel. Messages, Treas. Dept.), 230.

29. Memminger to Jefferson Davis, Feb. 10, 1864. *Corresp. of Treas. CSA.,* IV, 581.

30. *Ibid.*

31. "An Act to amend 'An act to organize the clerical force of the Treasury Department,'" approved May 1, 1863. *Public Laws of CSA.,* 135.

32. *Ibid.,* 135, 191-192, 276; Ramsdell, *Laws,* 57-58; *Journal of the Confederate States of America Congress* (hereafter cited, *Jour. C o n f e d. Cong.),* VII, 529-530.

33. A. Moise, Chief Clerk of the First Auditor and Agent for the Clerks of that bureau, was furnished transportation for approximately 5,000 lbs.; William W. Charlton, Agent for the Clerks in the Bureau of the Commissioner of Taxes, was furnished transportation for approximately 15,000 lbs.; and J. W. Robertson, Chief Clerk of the First Auditor's Bureau, acting as "Agent of the Clerks in that and other Bureaux" was furnished transportation for approximately 6,000 lbs. Vol. 115F. Record of Letters of Treas., 96, 100, 119.

34. For a copy of the "Regulations," see Capers, *Memminger,* 323-324.

35. *Ibid.,* 325-328. Following the resignation of Philip Clayton, William W. Crump became Asst. Sec. to the Treas., CSA.

36. Act of Mar. 7, 1861. *Prov. and Perm. Consts.,* 41.

37. Lewis Cruger to Memminger, Aug. 6, 1861. Vol. 121A. Comptroller's Office: Letters Addressed by Lewis Cruger, Comptroller of the Treasury, March 23, 1861 to December 16, 1861 [MS. vol. in R. G. 56. Confed. Treas. Dept. Archives (hereafter cited, Vol. 121A. Letters of Comptroller)], 256-257.

38. Memminger to Cruger, Aug. 10, 1861. *Ibid.,* 270.

39. Cruger to Memminger, Aug. 11, 1861. *Ibid.,* 272.

40. "Report of the Operations and Conditions, etc., of the Comptroller's Office," Cruger to Memminger, Dec. 6, 1861. *Ibid.,* 497-499.

41. Memminger to Lewis Cruger, June 3, 1863. Letters from Secretaries, from January 10, 1862 to June 11, 1863, to the Comptroller's Office [MS. vol. in R. G. 56. Confed. Treas. Dept. Archives (hereafter cited, Letters from Sec. to Comptroller's Office)].

42. *Corresp. of Treas. CSA,* IV, 533. Dec. 8, 1863. *Ibid.,* IV, 552.

43. Memminger to head of each bureau, Dec. 8, 1863. *Ibid.,* IV, 552.

44. Memminger to Gen. G. W. C. Lee, Commanding Forces for Local Defense, Jan. 5, 1864. *Ibid.,* IV, 563.

45. *Ibid.*

46. Trenholm to Gov. Z. B. Vance, Nov. 5, 1864. Vol. 115F. Record of Letters of Treas., 42.

47. John W. Hall, Chief Clerk, to Lewis Cruger, Dec. 29, 1864. *Ibid.,* 180.

48. William W. Crump to Trenholm, Jan. 31, 1865. *Ibid.,* 260-261.

49. *Ibid.*

50. Trenholm to W. Porcher Miles, Feb. 1, 1865. *Ibid.,* 264.

51. Trenholm to S. C. Hayes, Nov. 26, 1864. *Ibid.,* 97.

52. The mints had been created under the Act of Congress of the United

States passed Mar. 3, 1835, entitled "An Act to Establish Branches of the Mint of the United States." William A. Elmore, Supt., Mint at N. O., La., to Memminger, Apr. 19, 1861. *Corresp. with Treas. CSA.,* V, 68-71. Holding a similar position to that of Elmore were George Kellogg, Supt., Mint at Dahlonega, Ga., and G. W. Caldwell, Supt., Mint at Charlotte, N. C. The officers comprising the personnel of each mint were: Superintendent, Treasurer, Coiner, Assayer, Melter, and Refiner, all deriving appointments from the President. *Ibid.*

53. "A Resolution to Continue the Mints at New Orleans and Dahlonega," approved Mar. 4, 1861. *Prov. and Perm. Consts. CSA.,* 50.
54. William A. Elmore, Supt., Mint at N. O., to Memminger, Apr. 19, 1861. *Corresp. with Treas. CSA.,* V, 68.
55. W. M. Johnston to W. W. Avery, July 23, 1861. *Ibid.,* V, 240.
56. The "Act to suspend the operations of the Mints," approved May 14, 1861, pertained only to the mints of N. O., La., and Dahlonega, Ga. *Stats. at Large,* 110. North Carolina did not secede from the Union until May 20, 1861, and it was not until June 27, 1861, that the mint at Charlotte "was formally transferred to the Confederate States by an Ordinance of Convention." G. W. Caldwell, Supt., Mint at Charlotte, N. C., to Memminger, Oct. 9, 1861. *Corresp. with Treas. CSA.,* V, 371-372.
57. Elmore to Memminger, Mar. 6, 1861. *Corresp. with Treas. CSA.,* V, 7.
58. Memminger to Elmore, Apr. 2, 1861. *Corresp. of Treas. CSA.,* IV, 42.
59. James D. Dénégré to Memminger, Apr. 17, 1861. *Corresp. with Treas. CSA.,* V, 65.
60. Elmore to Memminger, Apr. 22, 1861. *Ibid.,* V, 74.
61. Gallier & Easterbrook, Architects, to Elmore, Apr. 27, 1861. *Ibid.,* V, 83.
62. William Lee, *The Currency of the Confederate States of America. A Description of the Various Notes, Their Dates of Issue, Varieties, Series, Subseries, Letters, Numbers, etc.; Accompanied with Photographs of the Distinct Varieties of Each Issue* (hereafter cited, *Currency of CSA.*), 27.
63. Memminger to W. A. Elmore, Apr. 12, 1861. *Corresp. of Treas. CSA.,* IV, 60.
64. Memminger to George Kellogg, Supt. of Mint, Dahlonega, Ga., June 25, 1861. *Ibid.,* 241; W. M. Johnston to W. W. Avery, July 23, 1861; William Johnston and J. W. Osborne to Memminger, July 24, 1861. *Corresp. with Treas. CSA.,* V, 240, 241.
65. Memminger to R. W. Barnwell, Ch., Com. of Finance, Aug. 6, 1861. *Corresp. of Treas. CSA.,* IV, 171-172.
66. Letters from Memminger to James W. Osborne and W. Johnston, Raleigh, June 21, 1861, quoted in report of Trenholm to A. H. Stephens, Dec. 19, 1864. *Confed. Treas. Reports,* III, 403-405.
67. Memminger to George Kellogg, Dahlonega, Ga., June 25, 1861. Vol. 111B. Record of Letters of Treas., 241.
68. Memminger to R. W. Barnwell, Aug. 6, 1861. *Corresp. of Treas. CSA.,* IV, 171-172.
69. "An Act to establish Assay Offices at Charlotte and Dahlonega," approved Aug. 24, 1861. *Stats. at Large,* 192. Dr. J. H. Gibbon received appointment as Assayer at Charlotte, and Lewis W. Quillian was appointed to fill the similar office at Dahlonega. Memminger to Lewis W. Quillian, Oct. 1, 1861. Vol. 111B. Record of Letters of Treas., 602.
70. "An Act to establish an assay office at New Orleans," approved Jan. 27, 1862. *Stats. at Large,* 253.
71. Trenholm to A. H. Stephens, Dec. 19, 1864. *Confed. Treas. Reports,* III, 403-405.
72. Memminger to J. H. Gibbon, May 28, 1862. R. G. 109. Vol. 163, p. 338.
73. Trenholm to A. H. Stephens, Dec.

NOTES

19, 1864. Resolution is quoted in *Confed. Treas. Reports*, III, 403-405.
74. *Ibid.*
75. Act of Feb. 14, 1861. *Prov. and Perm. Consts.*, 6-7.
76. "A Resolution for the Enforcement of the Revenue Laws," approved Feb. 16, 1861. *Ibid.*, 8.
77. Memminger to F. R. Shackelford, Collector, Atlanta, Ga., May 17, 1861. *Corresp. of Treas. CSA.*, IV, 83.
78. *Idem* to all Collectors of Customs, June 26, 1861. *Ibid.*, IV, 129-130.
79. The customhouse at New Orleans was closed in the spring of 1862 upon the fall of that seaport to the enemy. Prior to April 1865, practically every major customhouse east of the Mississippi had been closed, and it was recommended that "their effects be turned over to the nearest principal Depositaries." Trenholm to The President, Mar. 31, 1865. Vol. 115F. Record of Letters of Treas., 363.
80. Memminger to Col. M. C. Rogers, Huntville, Tex., Aug. 12, 1862. R. G. 109, Chap. X—Vol. 163, p. 627.
81. *Idem* to Lewis Cruger, Apr. 29, 1863. Letters from Sec. to Comptroller's Office, 122; *idem* to W. Y. Leitch, June 9, 1864. *Corresp. of Treas. CSA.*, IV, 672.
82. *Idem* to A. H. Stephens, Mar. 17, 1862. *Confed. Treas. Reports*, III, 67.
83. *Ibid.*
84. Under "An Act to increase the compensation of certain officers of the Treasury," approved Feb. 16, 1864, the depositaries were divided into three classes with compensation depending on the amount of money handled regardless of their being a Pay Depository or Funding Depository. *Public Laws of CSA.*, 191-192.
85. Trenholm to O. R. Singleton, Nov. 30, 1864. Vol. 115F. Record of Letters of Treas., 104.
86. Trenholm to Capt. John H. Jarmagin, A. Q. M., Griffin, Ga., Mar. 11, 1865. Vol. 115F. Record of Letters of Treas., 323.
87. *Idem* to John N. Hendren, Mar. 14, 1865. *Ibid.*, 325.
88. Memminger to W. H. N. Smith, H. of R., May 18, 1864. *Corresp. of Treas. CSA.*, IV, 654; Trenholm to C. J. McRae, Treas. Agt., Dec. 10, 1864. Vol. 115F. Record of Letters of Treas., 128-129.
89. Wm. Murdock to Jefferson Davis, Apr. 18, 1861. *Corresp. with Treas. CSA.*, V, 66; Schwab, *Confed. Sts. of Am.*, 138.
90. L. G. Bowers, Agent, Emile De Erlanger & Co., to Memminger, June 13, 1864. *Corresp. with Treas. CSA.*, V, 419.
91. *Ibid.*
92. "An act to authorize the establishment of an Office of Deposit in connection with the Treasury," approved Feb. 23, 1865. Ramsdell, *Laws*, 54-55.
93. *Ibid.*
94. For the use of the Bank notes, the Confederate Government paid 6% interest. Memminger to John D. Williams, Pres., Bank Clarendon, Fayetteville, N. C. Vol. 111B, Record of Letters of Treas., 263.
95. Trenholm to J. A. Seddon (in behalf of the Banks of Charleston, as to the inconvenience caused by General Order No. 77A & I. G. O.), Oct. 20, 1864. Vol. 115F. Record of Letters of Treas., 9.
96. Jno. Fraser & Co. to Memminger, Jan. 13, 1862; *idem* to Fraser, Trenholm & Co., Jan. 24, 1862. *Corresp. with Treas. CSA.*, V, 467-468, 478-479.
97. Memminger to James Spence, Feb. 9, 1863. *Corresp. of Treas. CSA.*, IV, 416.
98. Memminger to Gen. C. J. McRae, Agt., Confed. Govt., Paris, France, July 19, 1863; *idem* to E. C. Elmore, Sept. 15, 1863. *Ibid.*, 492-493, 520.
99. Col. J. Gorgas to Memminger, Mar. 30, 1863. *Corresp. with Treas. CSA.*, V, 69; Memminger to Lewis Cruger, June 1, 1864. *Ibid.*, 661-662.
100. James Spence's commission had been

CONFEDERATE FINANCE

revoked during the summer of 1863, shortly after McRae's appointment as Treasury Agent.

101. Memminger to Fraser, Trenholm & Co., May 24, 1864. *Corresp. of Treas. CSA.*, 658-659; Samuel B. Thompson, *Confederate Purchasing Operations Abroad*, 91.

102. Memminger to Davis, Feb. 23, 1864. *Corresp. of Treas. CSA.*, IV, 593.

103. "An Act to authorize the appointment of an agent of the Treasury Department west of the Mississippi," approved Jan. 27, 1864. *Public Laws of CSA.*, 176.

104. "An Act to establish and organize two bureaus in connection with the agency of the Treasury, for the trans-Mississippi department, one of which is to be known as the bureau of the Auditor and the other as the bureau of the Comptroller for the trans-Mississippi Department," approved Feb. 17, 1864. *Ibid.*, 231-232. "Regulations for the Transmississippi Agency of the Treasury," Memminger to P. W. Gray, Mar. 1, 1864. *Corresp. of Treas. CSA.*, IV, 595-596. D. F. Shall was appointed Auditor and T. H. Kennedy received appointment as Comptroller.

105. Trenholm to Thos. S. Bocock, Dec. 27, 1864. *Confed. Treas. Reports*, III, 409; *idem* to *idem*, Dec. 26, 1864; *idem* to A. H. Stephens, Dec. 26, 1864. Vol. 115F. Record of Letters of Treas., 177.

106. Trenholm to P. W. Gray, Feb. 15, 1865. *Ibid.*, 290.

107. "An Act to authorize the appointment of certain tax officers for the Trans-Mississippi Department," approved Mar. 13, 1865. Ramsdell, *Laws*, 132-133.

108. Carl Russel Fish, *The American Civil War*, 433.

CHAPTER II

1. Thian, *Extracts from Jour. of Prov. Cong.*, 7-8.

2. Memminger to Samuel Smith, Mar. 8, 1861. *Corresp. of Treas. CSA.*, IV, 14. The paper of the bonds was to be "watered and look like Bank note paper, and the plate handsome and difficult to counterfeit." *Idem* to Richard James, Engraver, New Orleans, Feb. 27, 1861. R. G. 109. Chap. X—Vol. 163, p. 38.

3. "Loan for the Defense of the Confederate States," an advertisement prepared Mar. 16, 1861, and published in numerous Southern newspapers. *Corresp. of Treas. CSA.*, IV, 25.

4. Memminger to G. B. Lamar, Bank of the Republic, N. Y., Mar. 1, 1861. Vol. 111B. Record of Letters of Treas., 1-2.

5. *Corresp. of Treas. CSA.*, IV, 27.

6. Memminger to R. R. Cuyler, Savannah, Ga., Mar. 27, 1861. *Ibid.*, IV, 36.

7. A Treas. Dept. circular to the banks suspending specie payments, entitled "To the President and Directors of the ....," Mar. 27, 1861. *Ibid.*, IV, 36-38.

8. On Mar. 18, 1861, the Sec. of the Treas. appointed Central Boards of Commissioners for the Loan for Miss., Ga., S. C., La., Fla. (except Pensacola), Tex., Ala., and Pensacola, Fla. These same Boards of Commissioners acted in a similar capacity taking Treas. Note subscriptions for 8% 20-yr. bonds under the 100-Million Dollar Loan of Aug. 19, 1861, and for 6% certificates under the Act of Dec. 24, 1861. *Corresp. of Treas. CSA.*, IV, 26, 79, 211, 234-235, 245.

9. Memminger to Byrd Douglas, Chm. of Central Board of Com., Nashville, Tenn., May 20, 1861. Vol. 111B. Record of Letters of Treas., 128.

10. Alex. B. Clitherall, Register of Treasury, to Messrs. C. B. Baldwin, Eli Abbott, T. N. Martin, Houston, Chicasaw County, Miss., May 1, 1861. *Corresp. of Treas. CSA.*, IV, 71.

11. Memminger to Jefferson Davis, Apr. 20, 1861. *Ibid.*, IV, 65.

12. "Instructions to the Commissioners

NOTES

appointed to receive subscriptions to the Loan for Defence of the Confederate States, April 22, 1861." Vol. 111B. Record of Letters of Treas., 65.

13. Memminger to Jefferson Davis, May 2, 1861. Vol. 111B. Record of Letters of Treas., 82.
14. Memminger to the Central Board of Commissioners for the Loan for each State, May 7, 1861. *Ibid*, 91-92.
15. J. W. Garrott and James L. Price to Memminger, Apr. 28, 1861. *Corresp. with Treas. CSA.*, V, 82.
16. Memminger to Charles T. Haskell, Abbeville, S. C., July 23, 1861. Vol. 111B. Record of Letters of Treas., 372.
17. The Central Board of Commissioners for the Loan for Va. was appointed May 21, 1861; for Tenn., June 6, 1861; and for N. C., July 1, 1861. *Ibid.*, 129, 157, 187-188.
18. Memminger to Commissioners appointed for receiving subscriptions to the Confederate Loan, Nov. 25, 1861. *Corresp. of Treas. CSA.*, IV, 234-235.
19. Schwab, *Confed. Sts. of Am.*, 7.
20. "An act to authorize a loan and the issue of Treasury Notes; and to prescribe the punishment for forging the same, and for forging Certificates of Stock, and Bonds," approved May 16, 1861. Lt. Col. Robert N. Scott, comp., *War of the Rebellion: A Compilation of the Official Records of the Union and Confederate Armies* [(hereafter cited, *Off. Rec. Rebellion*). The italics in quote are those of the writer], 4th S., I, 328-329.
21. Memminger to E. Starnes, Mar. 24, 1861; *idem* to Robert M. Patton, Mar. 24, 1861; *idem* to F. S. Lyon, Mar. 24, 1861. *Corresp. of Treas. CSA.*, IV, 89-90.
22. Memminger to E. Starnes, May 24, 1861. *Ibid.*, IV, 89-90.
23. Memminger to Trenholm, June 6, 1861. *Ibid.*, IV, 95.
24. Pollard, *Davis*, 175; James D. Richardson, comp., *A Compilation of the Messages and Papers of the Confederacy: Including the Diplomatic Correspondence, 1861-1865* (hereafter cited, *Messages and Papers of the Confederacy*), I, 123.
25. The resolution was introduced by Walker Brooke, in Secret Session of the Prov. Cong., Monday, May 6, 1861. In this case Brooke would be responsible for the origin of the Produce Loan, having tendered the resolution. *Jour. Confed. Cong.*, I, 186.
26. Capers, *Memminger*, 342.
27. Wm. T. Sanford to Howell Cobb, June 19, 1861; W. H. Jones to Memminger, July 11, 1861; Chas. G. Johnson to Pres. Davis, July 19, 1861; copy of letter to editor of *Weekly News*, Enterprise, Miss., July 25, 1861, from "An Old Merchant"; James L. Jones to Memminger, July 31, 1861. *Corresp. with Treas. CSA.*, V, 143-145, 207, 230, 246-247, 256.
28. DeBow to G. A. Trenholm, Aug. 5, 1864. J. D. B. DeBow Papers (hereafter cited, DeBow Papers). Although there was a hearty response to the Loan, many sections of the country remained unsolicited. To remedy this, DeBow, statistician and editor of the famous *DeBow's Review*, was appointed Aug. 3, 1861, "to organize the entire country" and "develop more completely the details of the [Produce Loan] plans." Memminger to DeBow, Aug. 3, 1861. Vol. 111B. Record of Letters of Treas., 426.
29. Pollard, *Davis*, 176.
30. Vice President Stephens "addressed the people of his old district in Georgia" at several rallies on the subject of the loan and each time experienced the "happiest results." In Wilkes County alone, cotton amounting to $100,000 was subscribed at the conclusion of his speech. At another rally 2,800 bales of cotton were subscribed. An excerpt from the *Feliciana Democrat*,

July 4, 1861. *Corresp. with Treas. CSA.*, V, 283-284.
31. Memminger to E. A. Nisbet and W. B. Johnston, June 17, 1861. *Corresp. of Treas. CSA.*, IV, 104.
32. Memminger to John A. Jordan, Little Rock, Ark., July 23, 1861. *Ibid.*, IV, 164.
33. Richardson, *Messages and Papers of the Confederacy*, I, 123.
34. "An act to authorize the issue of Treasury notes, and to provide a war tax for their redemption," approved Aug. 19, 1861. *Acts and Resolutions, 3d Sess., Prov. Cong.*, 20-30.
35. The loan of Aug. 19, 1861, unlike the previous Confederate loans, was directed at the banking and commercial interests as well as the agricultural interests. It was hoped that the former would take a large amount of the bonds in exchange for Treasury notes, while the latter would continue to subscribe proceeds from a portion of their crops.
36. DeBow's Report, Jan. 16, 1862. *Confed. Treas. Reports*, III, 48.
37. V. P. Reed to Memminger, July 13, 1861. *Corresp. with Treas. CSA.*, V, 210-211.
38. Wm. T. Sanford to Howell Cobb, June 19, 1861. *Ibid.*, V, 143-145; Memminger to A. M. Dantzler, July 11, 1861; Memminger to R. Moorman, Sept. 2, 1861. *Corresp. of Treas. CSA.*, IV, 150, 182.
39. Memminger to James H. Brigham, July 17, 1861; Memminger to John D. Williams, July 23, 1861. *Ibid.*, IV, 158, 163.
40. Memminger to Gen. W. W. Harllee, July 9, 1861. *Ibid.*, IV, 147-148.
41. J. H. Hammond to Memminger, July 11, 1861. James H. Hammond Papers, XXIX. During the agitation for Government ownership of the entire cotton crop, there was also some opposition to the idea. Ed. DeLony to Memminger, Aug. 17, 1861, said the government will become "a great commercial machine . . . an immense cotton brokerage, with hundreds of agents like leeches, fastened upon and drawing out the substance of the Government. . . ." It would fix rates, perhaps 1/3 below cost and "it would be a step towards the assumption of central power that Lincoln's Congress would hardly dare to exercise." *Corresp. with Treas. CSA.*, V, 280-281.
42. Herschel V. Johnson to Hammond, Aug. 29, 1861. Hammond Papers, XXIV.
43. Memminger to C. L. Dubuisson, Oct. 3, 1861. *Corresp. of Treas. CSA.*, IV, 196; Pollard, *Davis*, 178-179.
44. *Debow's Review*, Oct.-Nov., 1861, p. 462 (Convention, Macon, Ga., Oct. 1861); *Charleston Courier*, Mar. 3, 1862 (Cotton and Tobacco Planters Convention, Richmond, Va.).
45. Memminger to Messrs. O'Hear, Roper, Stoney, Charleston, S. C., July 23, 1861. *Corresp. of Treas. CSA.*, IV, 163.
46. Memminger to J. G. Wright, Paris, Texas, Sept. 6, 1861. *Ibid.*, IV, 185.
47. Memminger to Gen. W. W. Harllee, Marion, S. C., July 9, 1861. *Ibid.*, IV, 147-148.
48. Memminger to Robert Tyler, Register of the Treasury, CSA., Jan. 3, 1862. *Corresp. of Treas. CSA.*, IV, 247-248. Explaining the necessity for "receipts" Memminger wrote B. C. Pressley, Asst. Treas., Charleston, S. C., Jan. 28, 1862, saying, "You are doubtless aware that our greatest embarrassment is from the difficulty of preparing the bonds or certificates [due to scarcity of bond paper and engravers]. That difficulty compels the intermediate receipts, which I would be glad to dispense with by placing bonds or certificates in your hands." *Ibid.*, IV, 260-261.
49. Memminger to DeBow, Jan. 13, 1862. DeBow Papers.
50. Robert Tyler, son of President John Tyler, became a member of the Philadelphia Bar, 1844. From 1853-1861 he was Prothonotary of the Supreme Court of Pa. With the start of the Civil War he moved to Va., and was appointed Register of the

NOTES

Treasury, CSA., 1861-1864. Wilson and Fiske, eds., *Appleton's Cyclopaedia of American Biography* (hereafter cited, *Appleton's Cyclo. of Am. Biog.*), VI, 199.

51. Memminger to Robt. Tyler, Jan. 3, 1862. *Corresp. of Treas. CSA.*, IV, 247-248; Memminger to Howell Cobb. Pres. of Cong., Jan, 20, 1862. *Confed. Treas. Reports*, III, 47.
52. Robt. Tyler to Memminger, Jan. 16, 1862. *Corresp. of Treas. CSA.*, IV, 255.
53. Memminger to Archibald Roane, Jan. 21, 1862. *Ibid.*, IV, 259.
54. "Instructions for the Agents Collecting Subscriptions to the Produce Loan, Jan. 3, 1862." *Confed. Treas. Reports*, III, 53-54.
55. Memminger to L. W. Lawler, Gen. Agt., Feb. 17, 1862. *Corresp. of Treas. CSA.*, IV, 265.
56. Memminger to Messrs. John Fraser & Co., Gen. Agts., Mar. 24, 1862; idem to idem, Apr. 9, 1862. *Ibid.*, IV, 272-273, 282-283.
57. *Richmond Enquirer*, editorial "Cotton and the Blockade," Mar. 8, 1862.
58. Treas. Report, Mar. 14, 1862. *Confed. Treas. Reports*, III, 59-66.
59. Act of Apr. 18, 1862; Act of Apr. 21, 1862. *Public Laws of CSA.*, 28-29, 47. Of the $250,000,000 authorized under the act of Apr. 18, 1862, a minimum of $165,000,000 was to be issued in the form of stocks and bonds; $50,000,000 in Treasury notes to be issued without reserve; and $10,000,000 in Treasury notes to be issued as a reserve fund. *Ibid.*, 28-29.
60. *Ibid.* In addition to the $35-million in bonds, Congress also placed $2-million in Treasury notes in the depositories to be drawn on by agents for the purchase of produce. "An Act making appropriations to carry into effect 'An act authorizing the exchange of bonds for articles in kind, and the shipment, sale or hypothecation of such articles,'" approved Apr. 21, 1862. *Ibid.*, 50.
61. "Produce Loan—Instructions," July 24, 1862. DeBow to Subordinate Agents. DeBow Papers.
62. Memminger to Messrs. Phinizy and Clayton, Oct. 8, 1862. *Corresp. of Treas. CSA.*, IV, 362.
63. *Charleston Courier,* July 1, 1862; Memminger to DeBow, June 23, 1862. DeBow Papers.
64. Circular, Memminger to Subscribers to the Produce Loan, Aug. 1, 1862. *Ibid.*
65. Memminger to DeBow, July 11, 1862. *Ibid.*
66. Memminger to DeBow, Oct. 8, 1862. *Ibid.*
67. Memminger to Pres. Davis, Sept. 13, 1862. *Corresp. of Treas. CSA.*, IV, 352.
68. DeBow to Robt. Tyler (no date); acknowledged Tyler to DeBow, Sept. 19, 1862. DeBow Papers.
69. Memminger to J. S. K. Bennett, Oct. 4, 1862; idem to James Sorley, Oct. 17, 1862; idem to Dr. S. P. Moore, Nov. 11, 1862. *Corresp. of Treas. CSA.*, IV, 360-361, 366, 384.
70. Memminger to James Spence, Nov. 26, 1862. *Ibid.*, IV, 388-389.
71. "Cotton Certificate Instructions," Memminger to James M. Mason, Oct. 24, 1862. *Ibid.*, IV, 372-374.
72. Memminger to Robt. Tyler, Oct. 27, 1862; Memminger to G. A. Trenholm, Nov. 11, 1862. *Ibid.*, IV, 375, 384-385. A Cotton Certificate called for 20 bales of cotton, each valued at $50 per bale (5 pence Sterling or 10c per lb. x 500 lbs. to the bale); thus its face value of $1,000.
73. Memminger to S. R. Mallory, Sec. of Navy, Nov. 7, 1862. *Ibid.*, IV, 382.
74. Robt. Tyler to DeBow, Nov. 21, 1862. DeBow Papers.
75. Memminger to DeBow, Dec. 5, 1862. *Ibid.*
76. Memminger to Messrs. J. T. Doswell & Co., Dec. 5, 1862. *Ibid.*
77. Memminger to DeBow, Dec. 5, 1862. *Ibid.*
78. Major A. A. Burleson was appointed a Special Agent by the Quartermaster General to fill Army contracts payable in cotton, one of the con-

tracts being with Messrs. Barriere and Brothers for 10,000 bales of cotton and another with Messrs. Walker, Harris, and Fowlkes for cotton valued at $1,000,000. Memminger to DeBow, Dec. 22, 1862. *Ibid.*
79. "Annual Report of the Produce-Loan Office," Jan. 9, 1863, Archibald Roane, Principal Clerk in charge of the Produce-Loan Office, to Memminger; "Report of Condition of Treasury Department," Memminger to T. S. Bocock, Jan. 10, 1863. *Confed. Treas. Reports,* III, 129-132, 99-115.
80. DeBow to Memminger, Jan. 1, 1863. DeBow Papers.
81. Robt. Tyler to DeBow, Jan. 15, 1863. *Ibid.*
82. Schwab, *Confed. Sts. of Am.,* 16.
83. Erlanger Contract, Oct. 28, 1862. Pickett Papers, II (May 13, 1862-July 5, 1867).
84. "An Act to authorize a Foreign Loan," approved Jan. 29, 1863. Ramsdell, *Laws,* 164-165.
85. "Erlanger Contract," Jan. 9, 1863. *Confed. Treas. Reports,* III, 98a-98c.
86. On Sept. 24, 1863, a second contract for a loan was agreed to between the Sec. of Treas. and Erlanger and Co. The two loans were similar differing only in the second being for £5-million Sterling (25 million dollars), and the Government, although again selling the loan to Erlanger at the rate of £77 per £100, was to share equally anything over £77. "Erlanger Agreement," Sept. 24, 1863. *Confed. Treas. Reports,* III, 231-233. The contract for a second Erlanger Loan was approved in secret by Cong., Feb. 17, 1864. "An act to authorize a further Foreign Loan," approved Feb. 17, 1864. Ramsdell, *Laws,* 171-172. The second Erlanger Loan, however, was never carried out.
87. James Spence to Memminger, Dec. 19, 1862. Pickett Papers, II.
88. Henry Hotze (commercial agent) to J. P. Benjamin, Mar. 21, 1863. Pickett Papers, "Confederate State Department," I, No. 20; L. Q. C. Lamar to J. P. Benjamin, Mar. 20, 1863. *Ibid.,* H.
89. James Ford Rhodes, *History of the United States from the Compromise of 1850,* IV, 367, footnote 1.
90. Henry Hotze to J. P. Benjamin, Aug. 17, 1863. Pickett Papers, "Confederate State Department," J, No. 38b.
91. "Report on the Erlanger Loan, Feb. 11, 1865," showing proceeds from loan as of Oct. 1, 1864. *Confed. Treas. Reports,* III, 435-436.
92. Memminger to S. R. Mallory, Aug. 5, 1863. *Corresp. of Treas. CSA.,* IV, 499-500.
93. Telegram verified by letters, Memminger to DeBow, Feb. 5, 1863. DeBow Papers. Following the suspension of purchases of cotton, the Secs. of War, Navy, and the Treasury agreed to have only agents of the Produce-Loan Office make the purchases for the three Depts., hoping to keep prices down, by ending competition of double sets of agents, each Dept. supplying funds for its specific purchases. A. Roane to DeBow, May 20, 1863; Memminger to DeBow, June 4, 1863. *Ibid.*
94. Chas. Baskerville (Sub-Agt.) to DeBow, Feb. 11, 1863. *Ibid.*
95. Circular letter, Memminger to all agents, Mar. 6, 1863. *Ibid.*
96. "Treasury Circular No. 12," Memminger to all agents, Apr. 21, 1863. *Ibid.*
97. "An Act to Authorize the Issue of Bonds for Funding Treasury Notes," approved Feb. 20, 1863. *Public Laws of CSA.,* 97-98. This act was an attempt to get cotton for the Government by limiting the date to receive 8% bonds for subscriptions. Many planters, however, refused to comply with their subscriptions thinking that the increase in prices would more than compensate for the little difference (2% decrease) in the interest rate of the bonds. According to circular instructions issued Feb. 25, 1863, all subscriptions taken after Feb. 20, and paid before Aug 1,

NOTES

merited 7% Bonds. *Corresp. of Treas. CSA.,* IV, 420-421.

98. "Regulations for Produce Loan Agents" pertaining to Tithe cotton, Memminger to Agts., Nov. 16, 1863. *Confed. Treas. Reports,* III, 220-221.

99. Archibald Roane, Clerk in Charge of the Produce Loan Office, was advanced to the grade of Chief Clerk, with the "duty of superintending and conducting the business" of the Bureau. Roane to Memminger, "Report of Produce Loan Office," Nov. 30, 1863. *Ibid.,* III, 215-219.

100. Memminger to Robt. Tyler, Register, May 6, 1863. *Corresp. of Treas. CSA.,* IV, 449.

101. Ramsdell, *Laws,* 166-167.

102. *Ibid.* The 250-Million Dollar Loan of Apr. 30, 1863, was floated in lieu of one hundred millions of dollars in bonds, which the Sec. of the Treas. had been authorized to issue Mar. 23, 1863, at a rate of interest of 6% per year, "payable at the pleasure of the owner in the currency in which interest was paid on the other bonds of the Confederate States or in cotton of the quality of New Orleans middling, valued at eight pence sterling per pound." *Ibid.;* editorial on the act, June 25, 1863. *Corresp. of Treas. CSA.,* IV, 474.

103. A. Roane to DeBow, June 23, 1863. DeBow Papers.

104. Memminger to S. R. Mallory, June 6, 1863. *Corresp. of Treas. CSA.,* IV, 467-468.

105. *Ibid.*

106. Editorial on Cotton Bond Act, sent by John M. Strother (Chief Clerk) to *Lynchburg Republic, Jackson Mississipian, Knoxville Register, Montgomery Advertiser, Mobile Tribune, Atlanta Confederacy, Savannah Republican, Charleston Courier, Columbia Carolinian, Raleigh Register, Wilmington Journal,* and *Augusta Constitutionalist,* June 26, 1863. *Ibid.,* IV, 474.

107. *Charleston Mercury,* July 18, 1863.

108. The *Mercury* figured the exchange value of Treasury notes for specie, July 1863, as being 3 to 1. This appears to be quite an underestimate, as most reliable tables show exchange value for July 1863 as being 9 to 1. This would have made the interest in specie an even higher rate. See Appendix C.

109. "Instructions for Bids for Cotton Bonds," June 25, 1863. *Corresp. of Treas. CSA.,* IV, 475.

110. Memminger to J. P. Benjamin, July 20, 1863. *Ibid.,* IV, 484.

111. Numerous bids were made at "par value." Memminger from Geo. Thackrah, F. A. Smeltz, John L. Peck, July 18, 1863; also others. *Corresp. with Treas. CSA.,* V, 116.

112. P. V. Daniel, Jr. (Pres., Richmond, Fredericksburg, and Potomac R. R. Co.) to Memminger, July 24, 1863. *Ibid.,* V, 120-121.

113. John M. Strother to Editors of *Richmond Examiner* and *Richmond Sentinel,* July 21, 1863. *Corresp. of Treas. CSA.,* IV, 485.

114. Memminger to Robt. Tyler, Aug. 19, 1863. *Ibid.,* IV, 505.

115. John Strother to Editors, *Richmond Examiner* and *Richmond Sentinel,* 18, 1863. *Ibid.,* IV, 504.

116. Memminger to W. Y. Leitch, Asst. Treas., Charleston, S. C., Dec. 10, 1863; same to all Pay Depositaries. Tel. Messages Treas. Dept., 396. On Feb. 6, 1864, the act of Apr. 30, 1863, authorizing the 250-Million Dollar Loan, was repealed, the total amount of 6% Cotton Bonds issued under the act being $8,372,000. Thian, *Register of the Debt, Funded and Unfunded, of CSA.,* 187.

117. DeBow to Memminger, June 3, 1863. DeBow Papers.

118. DeBow to Gen. Joe. E. Johnston, Oct. 27, 1863. *Ibid.* To private parties hauling Govt. cotton, agents were prepared to pay freight at the rate of "25c in money or ¼ lb. of salt per bale, for every mile of wagon transportation." Circular from

Produce Loan Office, Oct. 27, 1863. *Ibid.*
119. DeBow to Gen. Johnston, Oct. 21, 1863. *Ibid.*
120. T. Sanford (Depositary) to Memminger, Sept. 12, 1863. *Corresp. with Treas. CSA.*, V, 140-141.
121. Newspaper clipping, "Cotton Agency for Mississippi and Louisiana," Oct. 14, 1863. DeBow Papers.
122. *Off. Rec. Rebellion*, 1st S., LII, pt. 2, pp. 568-570. Also see, Frank L. Owsley, *King Cotton Diplomacy: Foreign Relations of the Confederate States of America*, 47.
123. A. Roane to DeBow, Jan. 29, 1864. DeBow Papers.
124. Roane to DeBow, Jan. 22, 1864. *Ibid.*
125. Instructions from DeBow to Henry V. McCall (Special Traveling Agt.), Feb. 4, 1864. *Ibid.*
126. DeBow to J. C. Bridgeforth, Apr. 20, 1864; Dr. Jno. Ambrose (telegram) to DeBow, Apr. 20, 1864; DeBow to Gen. Wirt Adams, Apr. 29, 1864; *idem* to Memminger, Apr. 30, 1864; *idem* to Gen. Polk, Apr. 6, 1864; and others. *Ibid.*
127. Unknown Miss. newspaper clipping, Apr. 12, 1864. *Ibid.*
128. T. J. Wharton to President Davis, Apr. 16, 1864. Jefferson Davis Papers.
129. Report on the Condition of Government Cotton Contiguous to the Mississippi and its Tributaries, DeBow to Memminger, Apr. 4, 1864. *Confed. Treas. Reports*, III, 341-345.
130. Roane to DeBow, Apr. 5, 1864. DeBow Papers. It was stated that much of the cotton in the exposed areas could be sold to buyers operating for France, England, and Belgium. R. G. Latting to Memminger, May 23, 1864; John Duncan to Memminger, May 7, 1864. *Corresp. of Treas. CSA.*, IV, 656, 650.
131. B. M. Bond to Memminger, May 2, 1864. *Ibid.*, IV, 645.
132. The agreement entered into by the War, Navy, and Treas. Depts. took place Apr. 17, 1864. Geo. A. Trenholm, Sec. of the Treas., to Maj. J. M. Seixas, Aug. 12, 1864. *Ibid.*, IV, 725.
133. Roane to DeBow, Apr. 5, 1864. DeBow Papers.
134. G. A. Trenholm, Sec. of the Treas., to P. W. Gray, July 5, 1864; Trenholm to Lt. Col. Thos. L. Bayne, July 28, 1864. *Corresp. of Treas. CSA.*, IV, 686-688, 701-702.
135. *Jour. Confed. Cong.*, VII, 13. Frank L. Owsley, *State Rights in the Confederacy*, 130-131, gives an excellent account of the combines created between the states and steamship owners, in opposition to the Confed. Govt.'s attempt to get stowage.
136. Geo. A. Trenholm to C. J. McRae, July 17, 1864; Memminger to James A. Seddon, Sec. of War, Apr. 30, 1864. *Corresp. of Treas. CSA.*, IV, 693, 644-645.
137. George A. Trenholm, born in S. C., 1806; died in Charleston, S. C., Dec. 10, 1876. He was a merchant many years in Charleston. Prior to the Civil War, his firm transacted a large business in cotton, and enjoyed almost unlimited credit abroad. During the war the firm engaged extensively in blockade-running. Trenholm was a strong adherent of the Confederacy, and was appointed Sec. of the Treas. June 18, 1864—3 days after C. G. Memminger resigned. He held his new office until the close of the war when he was taken prisoner by the National troops and held until Oct. 1865, when pardoned by Pres. Johnson. *Appleton's Cyclo. of Am. Biog.*, VI, 59.
138. Trenholm to James A. Seddon, Sec. of War, Aug. 13, 1864. *Corresp. of Treas. CSA.*, IV, 725-727.
139. Trenholm to Roane, Aug. 24, 1864. *Corresp. of Treas. CSA.*, IV, 742-743.
140. "Annual Report of the Produce Loan Office, Nov. 10, 1864" *Confed. Treas. Reports*, III, 385-388.
141. "Annual Report of the Produce-Loan Bureau," Nov. 10, 1864. *Confed. Treas. Reports*, III, 385-388.
142. Frequently the Federal Agents took

NOTES

cotton whose ownership raised a question of doubt. In these cases private parties were compelled to contest their claim before the U. S. Treas. Dept. C. Baskerville to DeBow, Aug. 15, 1865. DeBow Papers.
143. Hugh McCulloch to Harrison Johnston, Asst. Special Agt., June 24, 1865. Press Copies of Letters, Restricted Commercial Intercourse, June 1 to 30, 1865, Treasury Dept. (R. G. 56, Confed. Treas. Dept. Archives), 287.
144. Baskerville to DeBow, Oct. 12, 1866. DeBow Papers.
145. Statement written and signed by J. T. Pickett, Sept. 11, 1865. Pickett Papers, II.
146. A booklet by J. Barr Robertson, *The Confederate Debt and Private Southern Debts*, 8.
147. *Ibid.*
148. Memminger to Howell Cobb, Nov. 20, 1861. *Confed. Treas. Reports*, III, 33-37.
149. In addition to the loans already discussed for the voluntary funding of Treasury notes, the Sec. of the Treas. was authorized on Dec. 24, 1861, to issue an additional $30,000,000 in 20-year 6% bonds, with interest payable semi-annually. The bonds—typical call certificates—aimed at preventing a redundant currency. They were to be exchanged for Treasury notes and could be re-converted into Treasury notes.
150. Memminger to Jefferson Davis, Oct. 6, 1862. *Confed. Treas. Reports*, III, 93-94.
151. *Ibid.*
152. "An Act to reduce the rate of interest on the funded debt of the Confederate States," approved Oct. 13, 1862. *Public Laws of CSA.*, 87.
153. Memminger to Jefferson Davis, Oct. 6, 1862. *Confed. Treas. Reports*, III, 93-94.
154. *Charleston Courier*, Oct. 31, 1862; Nov. 18, 1862.
155. "An Act to authorize the issue of Bonds for funding Treas. Notes," approved Feb. 20, 1863. *Public Laws of CSA.*, 97-98.
156. Thian, *Register of the Debt, Funded and Unfunded, of CSA.*, 185-186.
157. Memminger to Thos. S. Bocock, Jan. 10, 1863. *Confed. Treas. Reports*, III, 99-115.
158. *Ibid.*
159. John Gill Shorter, Gov. of Ala., to Memminger, Dec. 4, 1862. *Corresp. with Treas. CSA.*, V, 677-678.
160. Memminger to L. H. Anderson, Aiken, S. C., Dec. 13, 1862. *Corresp. of Treas. CSA.*, IV, 395.
161. Schwab, *Confed. Sts. of Am.*, 50-51.
162. "An Act to provide for the funding and further issue of Treasury Notes," approved Mar. 23, 1863. *Public Laws of CSA.*, 99-102.
163. Memminger to James P. Boyce, Mar. 24, 1863. *Corresp. of Treas. CSA.*, IV, 430-431.
164. Thian, *Register of the Debt, Funded and Unfunded, of CSA.*, 186.
165. Memminger to R. M. T. Hunter, Jan. 23, 1864. *Confed. Treas. Reports*, III, 243-245.
166. Memminger to T. S. Bocock, Dec. 7, 1863. *Ibid.*, III, 177-194.
167. Bonds issued in exchange for notes funded in January were to be exempt from the 5% tax for one year; whereas, bonds issued for notes funded in Feb. were to be exempt from only one-half the tax, while those issued for notes funded in Mar. were to be exempt from only one-fourth the tax. Officers, soldiers, and seamen, in service, were to be entitled to exemption from the whole tax for sums funded at any time prior to Apr. 1, 1864. *Ibid.*
168. Memminger to T. S. Bocock, Dec. 7, 1863. *Ibid.*, III, 177-194.
169. *Lynchburg Republican*, Jan. 27, 1864; *Petersburg Express*, Nov. 29, Dec. 12, 1863; Jan 5, 1864; *Richmond Enquirer*, Oct. 30, Nov. 6, 1863; Jan. 8, 1864.
170. *North Carolina Standard*, Oct. 9, 1863; *Raleigh Progress*, Jan. 8, 1864.
171. "An Act to reduce the currency and to authorize a new issue of notes

and bonds," approved Feb. 17, 1864. *Public Laws of CSA.*, 205-208; *Richmond Sentinel*, Apr. 2, 1864; *Washington Herald*, Feb. 18, 1914.
172. J. B. Jones, *A Rebel War Clerk's Diary at the Confederates States Capital* (hereafter cited, *Diary*), II, 154 (Feb. 21, 1864).
173. Memminger to T. S. Bocock, May 2, 1864. *Confed. Treas. Reports*, III, 257-267.
174. "An Act to reduce the currency and to authorize a new issue of notes and bonds," approved Feb. 17, 1864. *Public Laws of CSA.*, 205-208.
175. John M. Strother, Chief Clerk to Editor, *Floridian Journal*, Tallahassee, Fla., Apr. 19, 1864. *Corresp. of Treas. CSA.*, IV, 632.
176. For a list of newspapers carrying notices of the loan see *Corresp. of Treas. CSA.*, IV, 632.
177. Memminger to W. Y. Leitch, Asst. Treas., Columbia, S. C., June 6, 1864. *Ibid.*, IV, 668.
178. Memminger to Editor, *Raleigh Confederate*, June 6, 1864. Tel. Messages, Treas. Dept., 456.
179. The auction was held in the townhall of Columbia, S. C., with T. W. Mordecai of J. G. Gibbes & Co. as auctioneer. The bonds, totaling $2,-900,000, had been brought from Richmond, Va., in a mail car under the care of R. A. Lancaster. W. Y. Leitch to Memminger, June 14, 1864. *Corresp. with Treas. CSA.*, V, 419-420; Memminger to J. H. Reagan, Postmaster General, CSA., June 6, 1864. *Corresp. of Treas. CSA.*, IV, 668. For a graphic account of the auction, see *Columbia Carolinian*, June 22, 1864.
180. To secure the services of capable businessmen as agents and to induce their earnest attention in promoting the loan, each was to receive a commission on all sales at the rate of ¼ of 1% on the first $2,000,000 sold in one year, ⅛ of 1% on the next $8,000,000, and 1/16 of 1% upon the excess over $10,000,000. *Corresp. of Treas. CSA.*, IV, 652-653.
181. G. A. Trenholm to T. S. Bocock, Feb. 1, 1865. *Confed. Treas. Reports*, III, 431.
182. Thian, *Register of the Debt, Funded and Unfunded, of CSA.*, 187-189.
183. G. A. Trenholm to R. M. T. Hunter, Pres. pro tem. of Sen., Nov. 7, 1864. *Confed. Treas. Reports*, III, 353-368.
184. Thian, *Register of the Debt, Funded and Unfunded, of CSA.*, 187-189.
185. *Richmond Examiner*, Feb. 28, Mar. 1, 15, 1864; *Charleston Courier*, Mar. 4, 1864.
186. "An Act to amend an act entitled 'An Act to reduce the currency and to authorize a new issue of notes and bonds,' approved February 17, 1864," approved June 14, 1864. *Public Laws of CSA.*, 272.
187. Thian, *Register of the Debt, Funded and Unfunded, of CSA.*, 187-189.
188. To compare Sec. Memminger's plan for improving the finances with that approved by Congress, see "Report of the Condition of the Treasury Department, December 7, 1863," *Confed. Treas. Reports*, III, 177-194, and "An Act to reduce the currency and to authorize a new issue of notes and bonds," approved Feb. 17, 1864. *Public Laws of CSA.*, 205-208.
189. Jefferson Davis to Memminger, June 21, 1864. Capers, *Memminger*, 367-368.
190. *Jour. Confed. Cong.*, VII, 109-110.
191. *Ibid.*
192. Jones, *Diary*, II, 222 (May 30, 1864).
193. Memminger to Davis, June 15, 1864. *Corresp. of Treas. CSA.*, IV, 676-677; Capers, *Memminger*, 365-367.
194. *Ibid.*
195. Trenholm, although appointed Sec. of the Treas. on June 18, 1864, did not assume full responsibility for the Treas. Dept. until July 20, 1864, at which time the correspondence of the Dept. first bore his signature.
196. G. A. Trenholm to R. M. T. Hunter, Nov. 7, 1864. *Confed. Treas. Reports*, III, 353-368.
197. "An Act to raise coin for the purpose of furnishing necessary supplies

NOTES

for the army," approved Mar. 17, 1865. Ramsdell, *Laws*, 147-149.

198. The full story of the "The Richmond Banks Loan" may be gleaned from *Misc. Doc. No. 5, H. R. 45 Cong., 2d Sess.*, 1-94.

199. Micajah H. Clark, "The Last Days of the Confederate Treasury and What Became of Its Specie," *Southern Historical Society Papers*, IX (1881), 542-556. On May 4, 1865, at Washington, Ga., Clark had been "appointed Acting Treasurer of the Confederate States" by Pres. Davis and was "authorized to act as such during the absence of the Treasurer." Varina Howell Davis, *Jefferson Davis, Ex-President of the Confederate States. A Memoir by His Wife*, 868.

200. Table compiled from data found in Thian, *Register of the Debt, Funded and Unfunded, of CSA.*, 179-190; Thian, comp., *Confederate Notes with Description of Emblems, 1861-1864*, pp. 10-16.

CHAPTER III

1. Memminger to S. G. Jamison, Mar. 1, 1862. *Corresp. of Treas. CSA.*, IV, 268.
2. Memminger to John Fisher, Pres., Branch Bank of St. of S. C., and J. A. Crawford, Pres., Commercial Bank, Columbia, Apr. 22, 1862. *Ibid.*, IV, 290-291.
3. Pope had just finished his job as Chief Collector of War Tax at Columbia when he received the new appointment. A year later he was promoted to the rank of chief clerk. Three weeks after his promotion, Pope resigned, and the position of Chief Clerk of the Treasury-Note Division at Columbia was filled by Charles F. Hanckel of Pocataligo, S. C. Memminger to Pope, May 1, 1863; *idem* to C. F. Hanckel, May 23, 1863; *idem* to Bolling Baker, First Auditor, June 11, 1863. *Ibid.*, IV, 446, 462, 469.
4. Memminger's report to Thos. S. Bocock, Dec. 7, 1863. *Confed. Treas. Reports*, III, 177-194. Memminger had previously recommended the establishment of a Treasury-Note Bureau in his reports of Aug. 18, 1862, and Jan. 10, 1863. *Ibid.*, 74-77, 99-115.
5. *Public Laws of CSA.*, 178-179.
6. *Ibid.*, Sec. 2.
7. Memminger recommended Jamison to Pres. Davis, saying: "Mr. Jamison has had charge of the Treasury notes and coupons and of the engraving and issuing thereof from the commencement, and is thoroughly conversant with its details and management. . . . Memminger to Pres. Davis, Feb. 10, 1864. *Corresp. of Treas. CSA.*, IV, 581.
8. Jamison to W. W. Crump, Mar. 25, 1864. *Corresp. with Treas. CSA.*, V, 340-341.
9. Jamison to Trenholm, Oct. 31, 1864. *Confed. Treas. Reports*, III, 388-390.
10. The three stanzas are from a seven-stanza poem found in an undated newspaper clipping in the DeBow Papers. It is probably from a Richmond newspaper and should bear the date for sometime around Apr. 26, 1864, the day the Treasury-Note Bureau moved to Columbia, S. C.
11. Memminger to W. Y. Leitch, Asst. Treas., Charleston, S. C., May 7, 1864. *Corresp. of Treas. CSA.*, IV, 649-650.
12. *Idem to* Jamison and Leitch, June 13, 1864. *Ibid.*, IV, 675.
13. Jamison to Trenholm, Oct. 31, 1864. *Confed. Treas. Reports*, III, 388-390.
14. *Ibid.* At the peak of its operations, Aug. 2, 1864, the Treasury-Note Bureau employed 249 ladies to trim and number notes and bonds, and sign for the Treasurer and Register. Jamison to Trenholm, Aug. 2, 1864. *Corresp. with Treas. CSA.*, V, 448-449. The total number of male and female signers for the Treasurer was 190; for the Register, 198. A list of all the signers of Treasury notes is found in Thian, *Register of the*

CONFEDERATE FINANCE

Debt, Funded and Unfunded, of CSA., 3-4.
15. Trenholm to Jamison, Jan. 16, 1865, cited in letter from Jamison to Trenholm, Jan. 24, 1865. *Corresp. with Treas. CSA.,* V, 544-545.
16. The total amount of Treasury notes issued under the act of Feb. 17, 1864, including fifty-cent notes, was $456,-142,990.50. Thian, *Register of the Debt, Funded and Unfunded, of CSA.,* 178.
17. Telegram from Jamison at Charlotte, N. C., to Trenholm, Feb. 20, 1865. *Corresp. with Treas. CSA.,* V, 555.
18. The advance of the enemy upon Columbia having interrupted the issue of Treasury notes, Produce-Loan agents were directed to make every effort to sell Government cotton (with the privilege of exportation) for specie—the specie to be used to purchase Treasury notes. Trenholm to T. Sanford, Depositary, Montgomery, Ala., Mar. 3, 1865. *Corresp. of Treas. CSA.,* IV, 861; Trenholm to J. C. Breckinridge, Sec. of War, Mar. 22, 1865. Vol. 115F. Record of Letters of Treas., 342.
19. Jamison to Trenholm, Feb. 21, 1865. *Corresp. with Treas. CSA.,* V, 556.
20. Telegram from Jamison at Greensboro, N. C., to Trenholm, Mar. 4, 1865. *Ibid.,* V, 556.
21. Jamison to Trenholm, Mar. 16, 1865. *Ibid.,* V, 558; Trenholm to W. F. Miller, Mar. 30, 1865; *idem* to Stephen Duncan, Mar. 30, 1865. *Corresp. of Treas. CSA.,* IV, 887-888.
22. John W. Hall, Chief Clerk, Treas. Dept., to Maj. D. H. Wood, Quartermaster, Mar. 30, 1865. Vol. 115F. Record of Letters of Treas., 358.
23. Memminger to G. B. Lamar, Bank of the Republic, N. Y., Mar. 13, 1861. R. G. 109. Chap. X—Vol. 163, p. 64½. Lamar, a loyal friend of the South who held an office in the Bank of the Republic, N. Y., was a native of Savannah, Ga. Upon the outbreak of war, he returned to Savannah, became associated with the Bank of Commerce there, and remained a constant correspondent of the Treas. Dept.
24. *Idem* to *idem,* Apr. 2, 1861. *Corresp. of Treas. CSA.,* IV, 41. This first issue of Confed. Treas. Notes produced by the National Bank Note Co., along with the succeeding issue under the same act of Mar. 9, 1861, produced by the Southern Bank Note Co., were perhaps the most handsome of all Confed. issues, being steel-plate engravings on an excellent grade of bank-note paper. Notes issued under act of Mar. 9, 1861, were the only notes to bear the autograph signatures of the Treasurer and Register, all other issues of general currency being signed for the two Treasury officials by clerks, appointed for that purpose under the act of July 24, 1861. Fractional currency; that is, 50c notes, bore engraved signatures of the Treasurer and Register.
25. *Ibid.*
26. *Idem* to *idem,* Apr. 11, 1861. *Ibid.,* IV, 58.
27. *Idem* to Joel White, May 4, 1861. *Ibid.,* IV, 77.
28. *Idem* to Clitherall, May 7, 1861. *Ibid.,* IV, 78.
29. Clitherall to Memminger, May 14, 1861. *Corresp. with Treas. CSA.,* V, 105. Samuel Schmidt was managing partner of the New Orleans branch of the American Bank Note Company, which company had other branches in N. Y. and Boston. At the outbreak of hostilities, Schmidt named his establishment the Southern Bank Note Company.
30. Dénégré to Memminger, May 18, 1861. *Corresp. with Treas. CSA.,* V, 107.
31. Memminger to Geo. A. Trenholm, May 28, 1861. *Corresp. of Treas. CSA.,* IV, 94.
32. *Ibid.,* IV, 106-107.
33. Wm. P. Reyburn to Memminger, July 24, 1861. *Corresp. with Treas. CSA.,* V, 242-243.

NOTES

34. Memminger to Dénégré, July 15, 1861. *Corresp. of Treas. CSA.*, IV, 154.
35. *Ibid.*, IV, 317, 319, 320, 528.
36. Philip H. Chase, *Confederate Treasury Notes: The Paper Money of the Confederate States of America, 1861-1865*, 127.
37. M. J. Wicks to Memminger, Aug. 8, 1861; Daniel Ravenel, Chm. of Bank Comm., Charleston, S. C., to Memminger, Aug. 23, 1861; James D. Dénégré to Memminger, Aug. 26, 1861; Thomas Layton, Cashier, Southern Bank, N. O., La., to Memminger, Sept. 2, 1861. *Corresp. with Treas. CSA.*, V, 270, 293, 295-296, 306.
38. C. M. Furman, J. K. Sass, S. T. Robinson, Comm. from Banks of S. C., to Memminger, Aug. 27, 1861. *Ibid.*, V, 296-297.
39. Memminger to C. M. Furman, J. K. Sass, S. T. Robinson, Charleston, S. C., Oct. 10, 1861. Vol. 111B. Record of Letters of Treas., 639. The total amount received from the banks was $10,602,132.24.
40. Memminger to Evans & Cogswell, Charleston, S. C., Oct. 19, 31, 1861. Vol. 111B. Record of Letters of Treas., 170, 175.
41. Memminger to John Fisher, Pres., Branch Bank of St. of S. C., and J. A. Crawford, Pres., Commercial Bank, Columbia, Apr. 22, 1862. *Corresp. of Treas. CSA.*, IV, 290.
42. S. Schmidt to Memminger, Aug. 26, 1861. *Corresp. with Treas. CSA.*, V, 295.
43. Memminger to Dénégré, Aug. 28, 1861. Vol. 111B. Record of Letters of Treas., 496.
44. Telegrams, Memminger to Gov. Moore, N. O., Oct. 4, 1861; *idem* to *idem*, Oct. 5, 1861; *idem* to E. Keatinge, Oct. 8, 1861. Tel. Messages Treas. Dept., 159, 160, 162.
45. Memminger to Dénégré, Oct. 14, 1861; *idem* to *idem*, Oct. 15, 1861. *Corresp. of Treas. CSA.*, IV, 211, 216.
46. Memminger to Dénégré, Nov. 14, 1861; *idem* to *idem*, Nov. 16, 1861. Tel. Messages Treas. Dept., 181, 183.
47. Schmidt had produced some 2,000 sheets of notes, bearing $5 and $10 as approved under act of May 16, 1861, which he turned over to the Government. Dénégré to Memminger, Oct. 5, 1861; *idem* to *idem*, Nov. 1, 1861. *Corresp. with Treas. CSA*, V, 361, 415.
48. Thomas Layton, Cashier, Southern Bank, N. O., La., to Memminger, Sept. 12, 1861. *Corresp. with Treas. CSA.*, V, 325-326; Philipp Amendt to Mrs. Mary Amendt, N. O., La., Oct. 12, 1861. *Corresp. with Treas. CSA.*, V, 387. Only Manouvrier notes of one denomination were ever issued by the Treasury. These were $5 notes of the F, G, H, and I series which indicates that 4,000 of the notes were in circulation, a thousand being the usual number printed under each series letter. These notes had been issued before the theft had been discovered.
49. Memminger to Leggett, Keatinge & Ball, Mar. 12, 1862. *Corresp. of Treas. CSA.*, IV, 270.
50. Paterson to Memminger, Apr. 28, 1862. *Corresp. with Treas. CSA.*, V, 534.
51. "History of Confederate Stamps," *Confederate Veteran*, II, Mar., 1894, pp. 77-78. The Government issued the first Confederate postage stamp on Oct. 18, 1861, a 5-cent green stamp. This was soon followed by a 10-cent blue, and a 2-cent green stamp. The green ink being exhausted, the 5-cent green stamp was printed in blue and the 10-cent blue in red. All these were prepared by Hoyer and Ludwig. Later De La Rue & Co. prepared plates and furnished stamps of the 5-cent blue and a 1-cent orange which was never issued. Plates of the 5-cent blue were afterward used by Archer & Daly in printing the regular supply. Archer & Daly also furnished the 10-cent blue in three varieties and a 20-cent green. *Ibid.*
52. Evans & Cogswell to Memminger,

CONFEDERATE FINANCE

July 3, 1862. *Corresp. with Treas. CSA.,* V, 580-581.

53. Memminger to B. F. Evans, Oct. 8, 1862. *Corresp. of Treas. CSA.,* IV, 362.

54. Evans & Cogswell to J. D. Pope, Supt., Treas.-Note Div., Apr. 1, 1863. *Corresp. with Treas. CSA.,* V, 69-70.

55. Memminger to Evans & Cogswell, Apr. 7, 1863; *idem* to J. T. Paterson & Co., Apr. 7, 1863; *idem* to Blanton Duncan, Apr. 6, 1863. *Corresp. of Treas. CSA.,* IV, 437, 438.

56. Memminger to Jos. D. Pope, Aug. 4, 1862; *idem* to *idem,* Aug. 13, 1862. *Corresp. of Treas. CSA.,* IV, 333, 336; Keatinge & Ball to Memminger, Aug. 16, 1862. *Corresp. with Treas. CSA.,* V, 595.

57. Pope to Memminger, Aug. 18, 1862. *Ibid.,* V, 596-598.

58. Blanton Duncan to Memminger, Apr. 8, 1862. *Ibid.,* V, 511; Memminger to Gen. Winder, Provost Marshall, Apr. 11, 1862; Memminger to Jos. D. Pope, Sept. 29, 1862. *Corresp. of Treas. CSA.,* IV, 285, 359-360.

59. For rates at which the Southern Express Co. transported Govt. funds, see *Ibid.,* IV, 400-401.

60. For legislation prohibiting the forging and counterfeiting of Confederate Treasury notes, stock, bonds, etc., see Act of Mar. 9, 1861. *Prov. and Perm. Consts.,* 51-54; Acts of May 16, 1861, and Aug. 19, 1861. *Stats. at Large,* 117-118, 177-183; Acts of Sept. 26, 1862, Oct. 13, 1862, Apr. 30, 1863. *Public Laws of CSA.,* 61, 80-81, 133-134.

61. Memminger to Col. G. W. Lee, Commanding Post, Atlanta, Ga., Nov. 6, 1862. *Corresp. of Treas. CSA.,* IV, 381. As of Apr. 23, 1863, the following detectives were working under Lee's supervision: R. A. McGiboney, operating in Miss. and Ala.; W. H. Gilbert, in middle and northern Ga.; James A. Burton, in Tex. and La.; A. A. Burton, in Ark; Col. F. Alex Ramsey, in northern Miss., and western Tenn.; W. H. Grider, in Ala. and Tenn., and W. P. Hughey, in Fla. and southern Ga.; making a total of seven. G. W. Lee to Memminger, Apr. 23, 1863. *Corresp. with Treas. CSA.,* V, 82-83. F. H. Lafon, W. J. Goodrich, and Messrs. Shivers and Conway were appointed for temporary duty.

62. Geo. P. Beirne to Memminger, Apr. 2, 1863. *Ibid.,* V, 71-72.

63. W. H. Gilbert to Col. G. W. Lee, Apr. 22, 1863. *Ibid.,* V, 83-84.

64. Act of July 24, 1861. *Stats. at Large,* 167.

65. Memminger to A. H. Stephens, V. Pres., CSA., Aug. 26, 1862. *Confed. Treas. Reports,* III, 81-82.

66. W. B. Johnston to Memminger, Nov. 8, 1861. *Corresp. with Treas. CSA.,* V, 423. Memminger to Maj. Gen. Whiting, Wilmington, N. C., Jan. 21, 1864, containing an extract from the *New York World* of Jan. 10, 1864. *Corresp. of Treas. CSA.,* IV, 570-571.

67. R. A. McGiboney, Detective, to John W. Hall, Ch. Clerk, Treas. Dept., Sept. 5, 1864; *idem* to *idem,* Sept. 16, 1864. *Corresp. with Treas. CSA.,* V, 487-488, 496; G. A. Trenholm to P. W. Gray, Treas. Agt., Trans-Miss. Dept., Sept. 26, 1864. *Corresp. of Treas. CSA.,* IV, 772-773.

68. The border bearing the advertisement was cut off by the purchaser, the lithographed note thus becoming a well-executed counterfeit.

69. Samuel C. Upham to Wm. Lee, Oct. 12, 1874. Lee, *Currency of CSA.,* 24-25.

70. Memminger to Thos. S. Bocock, Aug. 18, 1862. *Confed. Treas. Reports,* III, 73-77.

71. Act of Oct. 13, 1862. *Public Laws of CSA.,* 80-81.

72. S. G. Jamison to Memminger, Jan. 19, 1864. *Corresp. with Treas. CSA.,* V, 298-299.

73. For an explanation of the technique employed in producing Chemico-

NOTES

graph plates, see Chase, *Confed. Treas. Notes*, 123-127.
74. Specimens of the Chemicograph notes may be found in the Raphael P. Thian Collection. See the Thian album entitled "Confederate States of America Treasury Department: Notes and Bonds, 1861-1865."
75. Act of May 1, 1863. *Public Laws of CSA.*, 160.
76. Act of Jan. 30, 1864. *Ibid.*, 177; Act of Feb. 23, 1865. Ramsdell, *Laws*, 55.
77. *Stats. at Large*, 55.
78. *Ibid.*, 171.
79. Thian, *Register of the Debt, Funded and Unfunded, of CSA.*, 5.
80. *Stats. at Large*, 117-118.
81. "Statement exhibiting the Receipts and Expenditures of the Government from its organization to and including November 16, 1861." *Confed. Treas. Reports*, III, 38.
82. Memminger to Howell Cobb, Pres. of Cong., July 29, 1861. *Ibid.*, III, 29-32.
83. Memminger to Howell Cobb, July 20, 1861. *Ibid.*, III, 13-17.
84. Memminger to Howell Cobb, July 29, 1861. *Ibid.*, III, 29-32.
85. Act of Aug. 19, 1861. *Stats. at Large*, 177-183.
86. Act of Dec. 24, 1861. *Ibid.*, 231.
87. Memminger to Howell Cobb, July 20, 1861; *idem* to *idem*, Nov. 20, 1861. *Confed. Treas. Reports*, III, 13-17, 33-37.
88. Memminger to Thos. S. Bocock, Mar. 14, 1862. *Ibid.*, III, 59-66.
89. *Ibid.*
90. Act of Apr. 18, 1862. *Public Laws of CSA.*, 28-29.
91. Act of Sept. 23, 1862. *Ibid.*, 59.
92. Memminger to Thos. S. Bocock, Aug. 18, 1862. *Confed. Treas. Reports*, III, 73-77.
93. Memminger to Thos. S. Bocock, Jan. 10, 1863. *Ibid.*, III, 99-115.
94. G. A. Trenholm to R. M. T. Hunter, Pres. pro tem. of Sen., Nov. 7, 1864. *Ibid.*, III, 353-368.
95. Act of Apr. 17, 1862. *Public Laws of CSA.*, 34.
96. Memminger to Geo. A. Trenholm, May 10, 1862; *idem* to Thos. Metcalf, May 12, 1862. *Corresp. of Treas. CSA.*, IV, 293-294.
97. Advertisement titled "Interest-Bearing Treasury Notes," June 4, 1862. *Ibid.*, IV, 307.
98. Memminger to Thos. S. Bocock, Aug. 18, 1862. *Confed. Treas. Reports*, III, 73-77.
99. Memminger to Thos. S. Bocock, Jan. 10, 1863. *Ibid.*, III, 99-115.
100. Memminger to Thos. S. Bocock, Aug. 18, 1862. *Ibid.*, III, 73-77.
101. Memminger to Thos. S. Bocock, Sept. 15, 1862. *Ibid.*, III, 89-90.
102. Act of Sept. 23, 1862. *Public Laws of CSA*, 59.
103. Thian, *Register of the Debt, Funded and Unfunded, of CSA.*, 175-176.
104. Memminger to Thos. S. Bocock, Oct. 3, 1862. *Confed. Treas. Reports*, III, 91-92.
105. Memminger to Davis, Oct. 6, 1862. *Ibid.*, III, 93-94.
106. Memminger to Thos. S. Bocock, Jan. 10, 1863. *Ibid.*, III, 99-115.
107. *Ibid.*
108. Memminger to Thos. S. Bocock, Jan. 10, 1863. *Ibid.*, III, 99-115.
109. Act of Mar. 23, 1863. *Public Laws of CSA.*, 99-102.
110. Thian, *Register of the Debt, Funded and Unfunded, of CSA.*, 186.
111. Memminger to Thos. S. Bocock, Jan. 10, 1863. *Confed. Treas. Reports*, III, 99-115.
112. Memminger to Thos. S. Bocock, Dec. 7, 1863. *Ibid.*, III, 177-194.
113. Memminger to R. M. T. Hunter, Jan. 23, 1864. *Ibid.*, III, 243-245.
114. Thian, *Register of the Debt, Funded and Unfunded, of CSA.*, 176-177.
115. Memminger to Thos. S. Bocock, Dec. 7, 1863. *Confed. Treas. Reports*, III, 177-194.
116. Act of Feb. 17, 1864. *Public Laws of CSA.*, 205-208; "Instructions for carrying into effect the act of February 17, 1864." *Corresp. of Treas. CSA.*, IV, 589-592.
117. Memminger to Thos. S. Bocock, May 2, 1864. *Confed. Treas. Reports*, III, 257-267.

CONFEDERATE FINANCE

118. Tyler to Memminger, Apr. 30, 1864. *Ibid.*, III, 288-290.
119. Trenholm to Gov. M. L. Bonham, S. C., Aug. 5, 1864. *Corresp. of Treas. CSA.*, IV, 712-713.
120. Trenholm to R. M. T. Hunter, Pres. pro tem. of Sen., Nov. 7, 1864. *Confed. Treas. Reports*, III, 353-368. Cp. Schwab, *Confed. Sts. of Am.*, 76.
121. Trenholm to R. M. T. Hunter, Nov. 7, 1864. *Confed. Treas. Reports*, III, 353-368.
122. *Richmond Examiner*, Nov. 8, 1864.
123. *Charleston Courier*, Dec. 3, 10, 1864; Jan. 4, 1865; *Richmond Examiner*, Dec. 13, 19, 22, 1864; *Charleston Mercury*, Feb. 4, 1865; *Raleigh Progress*, Mar. 6, 1865.
124. *Raleigh Progress*, Feb. 20, 1865.
125. *Jour. Confed. Cong.*, Mar. 1865.
126. William West Bradbeer, *Confederate and Southern State Currency. Historical and Financial Data. Descriptions with Illustrations* (hereafter cited, *Confed. and Southern St. Currency*), 107-155. Bradbeer lists ten Southern States, and Missouri, as having issued State Treasury notes, Tennessee being the only exception.
127. Memminger to Thos. S. Bocock, Jan. 10, 1863. *Confed. Treas. Reports*, III, 99-115.
128. Bradbeer cites all the acts and amounts of State Treasury notes approved by each State. Bradbeer, *Confed. and Southern St. Currency*, 107-155.
129. *Richmond Examiner*, Dec. 8, 11, 23-25, 1863.
130. Act of Feb. 6, 1864. *Public Laws of CSA.*, 183.
131. The poem has been printed under various titles, i.e., "The Confederate Note," "The Lost Cause," "In Memorium; Respectfully dedicated to the holders of Confederate Treasury Notes," etc. Major A. L. Jonas of Mississippi was accorded official recognition as the author by the United Daughters of the Confederacy at their Convention in Norfolk, Va., 1907.
132. Memminger to L. J. Gartrell, Chm. Judiciary Com., Mar. 13, 1862. *Corresp. of Treas. CSA.*, IV, 270-271.
133. Anonymous communication to Memminger, July 19, 1861. *Corresp. with Treas. CSA.*, V, 231-232.
134. Table compiled from data found in Thian, *Register of the Debt, Funded and Unfunded, of CSA.*, 173-180; Thian, "Confederate Notes with Descriptions of Emblems," 1-9.

CHAPTER IV

1. "An act to continue in force certain laws of the United States of America," approved Feb. 9, 1861. *Treasury Circular No. 5. Acts and Regulations of the Congress of the Confederate States, in relation to the customs and the officers thereof*, 3.
2. Act of Feb. 14, 1861. *Ibid.*, 10-11; *Prov. and Perm. Consts.*, 6-7.
3. Memminger to Pres. Davis, Mar. 25, 1861. *Corresp. of Treas. CSA.*, IV, 33-34. For a list of Customs Officers see *Ibid.*
4. Memminger to C. C. Walden, Mar. 18, 1861. *Ibid.*, IV, 27.
5. "A resolution for the enforcement of the Revenue Laws," approved Feb. 16, 1861. *Prov. and Perm. Consts.*, 8. The exemption of Texas from the revenue laws was apparently a means of inducing that State to enter the Confederacy. Texas entered the Confederacy two weeks later, Mar. 2, 1861.
6. Wm. Johnston to Memminger, Mar. 11, 1861. *Corresp. with Treas. CSA.*, V, 10-11.
7. Memminger to C. P. Cooper, Apr. 4, 1861. *Corresp. of Treas. CSA.*, IV, 44. Revenue Depots on the "interior border" were located at Florence and Chester, S. C.; Augusta and Atlanta, Ga.; Athens and Stevenson, Ala.; and Hernando, C o r i n t h, Holly Springs, East Port, and Norfolk, Miss. *Ibid.*
8. Telegrams, Memminger to C. P. Polk, Collector, Corinth, Miss., Apr. 23, 1861; Memminger to C. P. Cooper, Apr. 25, 1861. *Ibid.*, IV, 67, 68.
9. Memminger to F. R. Shackelford, Collector, Atlanta, Ga., and others,

NOTES

May 1/, 1861. *Ibid.*, IV, 83. For list of the discontinued customhouses, see *Confed. Treas. Reports*, III, 13.
10. Act of Feb. 14, 1861. *Prov. and Perm. Consts.*, 7. After the union of Va., N. C., and Tenn. with the Confederacy, customhouses were established at Richmond and Norfolk, Va.; Wilmington, Beaufort, and Ocracoke, N. C.; and Nashville, Tenn. Memminger to Wm. M. Harrison, Collector, Richmond, Va., and others, June 26, 1861. *Ibid.*, IV, 129-130.
11. Trenholm to Davis, Mar. 31, 1865. Vol. 115F. Record of Letters of Treas., 363.
12. Thian, *Extracts from Jour. of Prov. Cong.*, 9.
13. Acts of Feb. 18, 1861; Feb. 26, 1861. *Prov. and Perm. Consts.*, 9-10, 29.
14. Act of Mar. 15, 1861. *Stats. at Large*, 69.
15. Act of Mar. 16, 1861. *Prov. and Perm. Consts.*, 79.
16. Memminger to Howell Cobb, Pres. of Cong., May 10, 1861. *Confed. Treas. Reports*, III, 7-11.
17. *Confed. Prov. Const.*, I, 6, 1; *Confed. Perm. Const.*, I, 8, 1.
18. Act of May 21, 1861. *Stats. at Large*, 127-135.
19. It was believed that with the revenue tariff of 1857 in operation in the South and the protective Morrill tariff in the North, the latter would drive a large portion of the imports into Southern ports to be transported North and West. Wm. Johnston to Memminger, Mar. 11, 1861; A. Porter, Pres., St. Bank of Ga., to *idem*, Mar. 19, 1861. *Corresp. with Treas. CSA.*, V, 10-11, 12.
20. A. B. Noyes, Collector, to Memminger, Oct. 18, 1861. *Corresp. with Treas. CSA.*, V, 389.
21. James T. Miller, Collector, Wilmington, N. C., to Memminger, Oct. 19, 1861; T. Sanford, Collector, Mobile, Ala., to *idem*, Oct. 21, 1861; W. F. Colcock, Collector, Charleston, S. C., to *idem*, Oct. 22, 1861. *Ibid.*, V, 390-391, 395-396, 399.
22. The table was compiled from the following reports of the Sec. of the Treas. to Cong.; Memminger to Thos. S. Bocock, Mar. 14, 1862; *idem* to *idem*, Jan. 10, 1863; *idem* to *idem*, Dec. 7, 1863; *idem* to *idem*, May 2, 1864; Trenholm to R. M. T. Hunter, Nov. 7, 1864; P. W. Gray, Agt. of the Treasury, Marshall, Tex., to Trenholm, Dec. 26, 1864. *Confed. Treas. Reports*, III, 59-66, 99-115, 177-194, 257-267, 353-368, 445-450.
23. *U. S. Const.*, I, 9, 6; *Confed. Prov. Const.*, I, 7, 5; *Confed. Perm. Const.*, I, 9, 6.
24. *Charleston Courier*, Mar. 25, 1861.
25. Memminger to Howell Cobb, May 1, 1861. *Confed. Treas. Reports*, III, 3-6.
26. Memminger to R. M. T. Hunter, Apr. 7, 1863. *Ibid.*, III, 159-163.
27. Act of Feb. 17, 1864. *Public Laws of CSA.*, 205-208.
28. Trenholm to R. M. T. Hunter, Nov. 7, 1864. *Confed. Treas. Reports*, III, 353-368.
29. The table was compiled from data found in *Ibid.*, III, 39-40, 177-194, 257-267, 353-368, 445-450.
30. *Charleston Courier*, Oct. 17, Nov. 14-15, 1861.
31. *Richmond Examiner*, Dec. 6, 14, 30, 1861.
32. *Jour. Confed. Cong.*, (secret sess.), Nov. 28, Dec. 9, 1861; Feb. 19, 1862.
33. *Charleston Courier*, Apr. 4, 5, 1862; *Richmond Examiner*, Apr. 5, 23, 1862.
34. *Vicksburg Evening Citizen*, Aug. 20, 1861.
35. *Richmond Enquirer*, Nov. 25, 1861; Jones, *Diary*, I, 102 (Dec. 25, 1861); *Charleston Mercury*, Apr. 29, 1862; *Charleston Courier*, Nov. 5, 1862.
36. *Richmond Dispatch*, Dec. 7, 1861; *Richmond Examiner*, Jan. 17, 1862.
37. Pollard, *Davis*, 115.
38. *Richmond Dispatch*, Apr. 19, 1862; *Petersburg Express*, Aug. 27, Nov. 5, 1862.
39. Memminger to Howell Cobb, May 1, 1861. *Confed. Treas. Reports*, III, 3-6.
40. Dénégré to Memminger, May 4, 1861. *Corresp. with Treas. CSA.*, V, 86-90.
41. E. J. Forstall to D. F. Kenner, Feb.

21, 1861. R. G. 56. Confed. Treas. Dept. Archives.
42. Memminger to Howell Cobb, May 10, 1861. *Confed. Treas. Reports,* III, 7-11.
43. Act of May 16, 1861. *Stats. at Large,* 117-118.
44. *Ibid.*
45. Memminger to Ed. Robertson, Auditor of the state, Baton Rouge, La., May 21, 1861. Similar letter sent to each State Auditor, a list of which is appended to the above letter. *Corresp. of Treas. CSA.,* IV, 87-88.
46. Memminger to Howell Cobb, July 24, 1861. *Confed. Treas. Reports,* III, 19-22.
47. Act of Aug. 19, 1861. *Stats. at Large,* 177-183.
48. Chief Collectors for the War Tax were: Adam C. Felder, Ala.; Wm. H. Haliburton, Ark.; E. E. Blackburn, Fla.; E. Starnes, Ga.; Robt. M. Lusher, La.; John H. Handy, Miss.; Wm. K. Lane, N. C.; Joseph D. Pope, S. C.; Dr. J. G. M. Ramsey, Tenn.; Geo. J. Durham, Tex.; and Henry T. Garnett, Va. *Corresp. of Treas. CSA.,* IV, 189-190, 229, 238. R. G. 109. Chap. X—Vol. 163, p. 484.
49. Memminger to Thompson Allan, Sept. 28, 1861. Vol. 111B. Record of Letters of Treas., 598.
50. Memminger to Robt. M. Lusher, Chief Collector, N. O., La., Oct. 15, 1861. R. G. 109. Chap. X—Vol. 189, pp. 14-15.
51. Memminger to Howell Cobb, Nov. 20, 1861. *Confed. Treas. Reports,* III, 33-37.
52. Thompson Allan to Memminger, Jan. 6, 1863. *Ibid.,* III, 115-123.
53. Henry Sparnick, Acting Chief Clerk War-Tax Bureau, to Memminger, July 15, 1862. *Corresp. of Treas. CSA.,* IV, 323-326.
54. *Idem to idem,* Nov. 1863. *Ibid.,* III, 212-213; *Richmond Examiner,* Dec. 30, 1863.
55. Acts of Apr. 19, Sept. 30, Oct. 13, 1862. *Public Laws of CSA.,* 42, 65, 80.
56. Memminger to Thos. S. Bocock, Aug. 18, 1862. *Confed. Treas. Reports,* III, 73-77.
57. *Idem to idem,* Jan. 10, 1863. *Ibid.,* III, 99-115.
58. T. Allan to Memminger, Nov. 1863. *Ibid.,* III, 212-213.
59. *Idem to idem,* Jan. 6, 1863. *Ibid.,* III, 115-123.
60. The sum of $70,000 was returned to Louisiana and $111,174.69 was returned to North Carolina. *Public Laws of CSA,* 70.
61. Joseph D. Pope to Memminger, Apr. 10, 1862. *Corresp. with Treas. CSA.,* V, 513-517.
62. Taken from the Report of the Commissioner of Taxes, Nov. 1863. *Confed. Treas. Reports,* III, 212-213.
63. Stephens' speech of July 11, 1861. *Appleton's Annual Cyclopaedia for 1861,* 143.
64. Memminger to Thos. S. Bocock, Mar. 14, 1862; *idem* to Jeff. Davis, Oct. 6, 1862; *idem* to Thos S. Bocock, Jan. 10, 1863. *Confed. Treas. Reports,* III, 59-66, 93-94, 99-115.
65. *Richmond Examiner,* Sept. 23, 1862.
66. *Richmond Whig,* Oct. 1862.
67. Memminger to Thos. S. Bocock, Jan. 10, 1863. *Confed. Treas. Reports,* III, 99-115.
68. *Charleston Courier,* Jan. 20, Mar. 14, 1863; *Charleston Mercury,* Mar. 26, Apr. 1, 1863; *Richmond Examiner,* Mar. 9, 16, 17, 21, 26, Apr. 15, 1863; *Raleigh Progress,* Mar. 16, 26, 1863.
69. *Richmond Enquirer,* Feb. 17, 1863.
70. Memminger to Thos. S. Bocock, Jan. 10, 1863. *Confed. Treas. Reports,* III, 99-115.
71. The earliest suggestion of a Confederate tax-in-kind is perhaps that found in a letter from W. W. Harris, Silver Hill, N. C., to Jefferson Davis, Jan. 6, 1863. The letter enclosing the plan was endorsed by Davis, called to the attention of the Sec. of the Treas., and appears to be the basis for Memminger's recommendation. *Corresp. with Treas. CSA.,* V, 5.
72. Memminger to R. M. T. Hunter,

NOTES

Apr. 7, 1863. *Confed. Treas. Reports*, III, 159-163.
73. Act of Apr. 24, 1863. *Public Laws of CSA.*, sec. 1, pp. 115-126.
74. *Richmond Sentinel*, Apr. 27, 1863.
75. *North Carolina Standard*, Aug. 25, 26, Sept. 1, 1863.
76. John T. Donald, Thomastown, Miss., to Memminger, Oct. 30, 1863. *Corresp. with Treas. CSA.*, V, 191.
77. Thompson Allan, Comm. of Taxes, to Memminger, Nov. 1863. *Confed. Treas. Reports*, III, 195-211.
78. *Richmond Enquirer*, Mar. 8, 1863.
79. *Confed. Perm. Const.*, I, 2, 3; *U. S. Const.*, I, 2, 3.
80. Pres. Davis' message of Dec. 8, 1863. *Appleton's Annual Cyclopaedia for 1863*, p. 794.
81. Act of May 1, 1863. *Public Laws of CSA.*, 140-153.
82. *Ibid.*
83. The new collectors were T. C. Green, Va.; E. G. Cabaniss, Ga.; G. F. Neill, Miss.; D. N. Kennedy, Tenn.; and A. B. Greenwood, Ark.
84. "Instructions for Officers Engaged in the Collection of Taxes for the Confederate States," May 15, 1863. *Corresp. of Treas. CSA.*, IV, 450-460.
85. Thompson Allan to Memminger, Nov. 1863. *Confed. Treas. Reports*, III, 194-211.
86. Thompson Allan to Memminger, Feb. 1, 1864. *Ibid.*, III, 249-254; idem to idem, Feb. 15, 1864. *Corresp. with Treas. CSA.*, V, 315.
87. Idem to idem April 29, 1864. *Confed. Treas. Reports*, III, 281-284.
88. *Ibid.*
89. For a complete list (numbering in the hundreds) of officers, agents, and men detailed for duty in the Q. M. Dept. to handle the tax-in-kind, see "Register of Officers and Agents of Tax in Kind" in R. G. 109. Chap. V—Vol. 199.
90. When a district or locality was declared impracticable, the Controlling Quartermaster immediately directed the Post Quartermaster to transfer the assessor's estimate of the tax-in-kind to the district tax collector to be collected in its money value only. *Instructions to be Observed by Officers and Agents Receiving the Tax in Kind*, sec. 24, p. 6.
91. *Ibid.*, secs. 15, 18, 39, 80, pp. 4-5, 7, 12.
92. Agents appointed to take charge of the depots were to be non-conscripts, or persons disabled in service. *Ibid.*, sec. 16, p. 4.
93. After Mar. 1864, the Tax Bureau of the Treas. Dept. transferred the entire management of the tax-in-kind to the War Dept. This included the appointment of tithe assessors as well as the receiving, protecting, preserving, and distributing of the tithe. Thompson Allan to Col. Larkin Smith, Asst. Q. M. Gen. in charge of Tithe, Mar. 4, 1864. R. G. 109. Chap. X—Vol. 191. Record Book B, Office of Commissioner of Taxes, 535.
94. The 50% penalty was added to the assessed money value of the unpaid portion of the tax and the assessor's estimate was turned over to the District Collector of the money tax for collection in currency. *Instructions to be Observed by Officers and Agents Receiving the Tax in kind*, secs. 22-23, pp. 5-6.
95. *Ibid.*, secs. 27, 31, pp. 6-7. For the tobacco and cotton tithe received under the Act of April 24, 1863, see *Ibid.*, secs. 77-78, p. 12.
96. Larkin Smith, Asst. Q. M. Gen., to Thompson Allan, Feb. 11, 1864; idem to idem, Feb. 15, 1864. *Corresp. with Treas. CSA.*, V, 567, 567-568.
97. *Instructions to be Observed by Officers and Agents Receiving the Tax in Kind*, sec. 53, p. 9.
98. Act of Feb. 17, 1864. *Public Laws of CSA.*, 208-211.
99. "An Act to Amend the Laws Relating to the Tax in Kind," approved June 10, 1864. *Ibid.*, 264.
100. Report of Col. Larkin Smith, Nov. 30, 1863. R. G. 56. Confed. Treas. Dept. Archives.
101. *Richmond Enquirer*, Mar. 8, 1864.
102. *Richmond Enquirer*, Dec. 21, 1864; Alexander Stephens, *A Constitutional View of the Late War Between the States*, II, 572.

CONFEDERATE FINANCE

103. Thompson Allan to Geo. A. Trenholm, Oct. 28, 1864. *Confed. Treas. Reports*, III, 368-373.
104. Trenholm to R. M. T. Hunter, Pres. pro tem. of Sen., Nov. 7, 1864; *idem* to F. S. Lyon, Chm. of Comm. of Ways and Means, Dec. 15, 1864. *Ibid*, III, 353-368, 414-414a.
105. Trenholm to T. S. Bocock, Jan. 9, 1865. *Ibid.*, III, 423-425. The reports of the Sec. of the Treas. for the period Feb. to Apr. 1865 failed to mention the value of the tithe collected.
106. Memminger to T. S. Bocock, Dec. 7, 1863.. *Ibid.*, III, 177-194.
107. *Ibid.*
108. "An Act to Levy Additional Taxes for the Common Defence and Support of the Government," approved Feb. 17, 1864. *Public Laws of CSA.*, 208-211.
109. Memorial of the South Carolina Banks to Memminger, Apr. 7, 1864. *Confed. Treas. Reports*, III, 277-281.
110. Memminger to T. S. Bocock, May 2, 1864. *Ibid.*, III, 257-267.
111. "An Act to Reduce the Currency and to Authorize a new Issue of Notes and Bonds," approved Feb. 17, 1864. *Public Laws of CSA.*, 205.
112. Memminger to T. S. Bocock, Dec. 7, 1863. *Confed. Treas. Reports*, III, 177-194.
113. Memminger to T. S. Bocock, May 6, 1864. *Ibid.*, III, 257-267.
114. "An Act to Raise Money to Increase the Pay of Soldiers," approved June 10, 1864. *Public Laws of CSA.*, 265.
115. "An Act to Amend the Tax Laws," approved June 14, 1864. *Ibid.*, 273-275.
116. Memminger to T. S. Bocock, May 2, 1864. *Confed. Treas. Reports*, III, 257-267.
117. "An Act to Amend the Tax Laws," approved June 14, 1864. *Public Laws of CSA.*, 273-275.
118. Thompson Allan to G. A. Trenholm, Sept. 9, 1864. *Corresp. of Treas. CSA.*, IV, 758-763.
119. *Idem* to *idem*, Oct. 28, 1864. *Confed. Treas. Reports*, III, 384.
120. Trenholm to R. M. T. Hunter, Nov. 7, 1864. *Ibid.*, III, 353-368.
121. Trenholm to R. M. T. Hunter, Nov. 7, 1864; *idem* to F. S. Lyon, Chm. Comm. of Ways and Means, Dec. 15, 1864; *idem* to T. S. Bocock, Jan. 9, 1865. *Ibid.*, III, 353-368, 414-414a, 423-425.
122. Trenholm to W. Y. Leitch, Asst. Treas., Feb. 4, 1865. Vol. 115F. Record of Letters of Treas., 274.
123. "An Act to Levy Additional Taxes for the Year 1865 for the Support of the Government," approved Mar. 11, 1865. Ramsdell, *Laws*, 101-107.
124. "An Act to Raise Coin for the Purpose of Furnishing Necessary Supplies for the Army," approved Mar. 17, 1865. *Ibid.*, 147-149.
125. For a legal interpretation of the Fourteenth Amendment to the U. S. Const. in regards to Confed. debts, see J. Barr Robertson, *The Confederate Debt and Private Southern Debts*, 8.
126. Table compiled from data found in *Confed. Treas. Reports*, III, 39-40, 59-66, 99-115, 177-194, 212-213, 257-267, 353-368, 384, 445-450.

CHAPTER V

1. Circular letter from Memminger to the U. S. public officers residing in the Confederacy, Mar. 5, 1861. *Corresp. of Treas. CSA.*, IV, 5.
2. R. G. 56. Vol. 62B. Confederate Treasurer at New Orleans. Following the secession of La. on Jan. 26, 1861, State authorities seized the Federal Mint and Sub-Treasury at N. O. Anthony J. Guirot, former U. S. Treasurer of the Mint, was placed in charge of the funds as State Depositary and later as Asst. Treas. of the Confed. Sts. "Report of W. E. Myers, 1st Comptroller's Office, U. S. Treas. Dept., May 15, 1861." *Ibid.* Under the U. S. act of May 23, 1850, the "Bullion Fund" was a deposit of public money placed at a Mint for the purpose of making immediate payments to depositors of gold and silver bullion. Guirot to Memminger, May 20, 1861. *Ibid.*

NOTES

3. Memminger to Geo. Kellogg, Supt. Mint, Dahlonega, Ga., May 16, 1861; *idem* to W. A. Elmore, Supt. Mint, N. O., May 16, 1861. *Corresp. of Treas. CSA.,* IV, 81-82.
4. This sum was in addition to the "Bullion Fund" and consisted of coined and uncoined profits of the mint, gold and silver coins reserved for assay, incidental and contingent fund, wages of workmen, etc. Guirot to Memminger, June 20, 1861. R. G. 56. Vol. 62B; R. G. 56. Vol. 103. Record of Misc. Covering Warrants, 6, 11.
5. G. W. Caldwell, Mint Supt., Charlotte, N. C., to Memminger, Oct. 9, 1861. *Corresp. with Treas. CSA.,* V, 371-372.
6. *Idem* to *idem,* Nov. 26, 1861. *Ibid.,* V., 435.
7. Memminger to Lt. Col. J. Gorgas, Chief of Ordnance, Sept. 30, 1861; *idem* to Chas. Loeffler, Mfr. of Mil. Articles, N. O., Oct. 3, 1861; *idem* to W. A. Elmore, Mint Supt., N. O., Oct. 3, 1861. Vol. 111B. Record of Letters Treas. Dept., 599, 606, 609.
8. R. G. 56. Vol. 103. Record of Misc. Covering Warrants, 31.
9. Trenholm to Alex. H. Stephens, Dec. 19, 1864. *Confed. Treas. Reports,* III, 403-405.
10. *Ibid.;* J. Thomas Scharf, *History of the Confederate States Navy from its Organization to the Surrender of its Last Vessel* (hereafter cited *Confed. Navy),* 50, 138, 373 (note 1), 554 (note 1); *Off. Rec. Union and Confed. Navies,* 1st S., VIII, 861; *Ibid.,* IX, 795, 806-807.
11. "An ordnance to transfer certain funds to the Government of the Confederate States of America," approved by the State Convention of Louisiana, Mar. 7, 1861. R. G. 56. Vol. 62B.
12. Guirot to Memminger, May 6, 1861. *Ibid.*
13. R. G. 56. Vol. 103. Record of Misc. Covering Warrants, 30.
14. At the beginning of the war, E. A. Pollard placed the extent of Southern indebtedness to the North at $400,000,000 while the *New York Tribune* estimated it at approximately $200,000,000. Perhaps the most conservative of all estimates was the $40,000,000 quoted by the *New Orleans Price Current.* Pollard, *Davis,* 183-184, 209, 211, 213; *New York Tribune,* Sept. 18, 1861; *New Orleans Price Current,* May 1, 1861.
15. Act of May 21, 1861. *Stats. at Large,* 151.
16. The act did permit Confed. citizens to pay debts owed to creditors residing in the border states of Delaware, Maryland, Kentucky, Missouri, and the District of Columbia. *Ibid.* This was done in the hope of preventing the border states from actively participating in the war on the side of the North.
17. Act of Aug. 21, 1861. *Stats. at Large,* 187.
18. Act of Aug. 6, 1861. Geo. P. Sanger, ed., *The Statutes at Large, Treaties, and Proclamations, of the United States of America, from December 5, 1859 to March 3, 1863* (hereafter cited, *U. S. Stats. at Large),* XII, 319.
19. Presidential Proclamation, Aug. 16, 1861. *Ibid.,* XII, 1262.
20. Act of Aug. 30, 1861. *Stats. at Large,* 201-207.
21. *Ibid.*
22. *Ibid.* Each Receiver rendered an account to his District Court every six months and forwarded a copy to the Treasurer of the CSA.
23. Geo. P. Scarburgh, Walker Brooke, and Thomas C. Reynolds were appointed to the Board of Commissioners, Dec. 13, 1861. *Jour. Confed. Cong.,* I, 564. The Commissioners were to "hold at the seat of Government two terms each year" and were to remain in session "so long as the business before them shall require." Act of Aug. 30, 1861. *Stats. at Large,* 204.
24. Pollard, *Davis,* 184.
25. "Rebel Sequestration Act," Judge Magrath's Opinion, Oct. 24, 1861, in Moore, *Rebellion Record,* III, 243-244; *Charleston Courier,* Oct. 21-25, 1861 (arguments), Nov. 9, 1861 (full text of decision).

26. *Charleston Courier*, Aug. 12, 1862; Rhodes, *Hist. of U. S.*, III, 465.
27. S. R. Cockrill to Memminger, Oct. 29, 1861. *Corresp. with Treas. CSA.*, V, 412-413.
28. Memminger to S. R. Cockrill, Nov. 6, 1861. *Corresp. of Treas. CSA.*, IV, 230.
29. Act of Feb. 15, 1862. *Stats. at Large*, 260-266. The italics are those of the writer.
30. *Ibid.*
31. T. J. Campbell, Receiver, Eastern Division of Tenn., to Dr. J. G. M. Ramsey, Depositary, Feb. 13, 1863; J. G. M. Ramsey to Memminger, Feb. 14, 1863. *Corresp. of Treas. CSA.*, IV, 417.
32. Memminger to D. F. Kenner, Feb. 18, 1863. *Ibid.*, IV, 417.
33. Barksdale's amendment was proposed Nov. 9, 1864. *Jour. Confed. Cong.*, 265.
34. Schwab, *Confed. Sts. of Am.*, 119.
35. Act of Feb. 3, 1865. Ramsdell, *Laws*, 34-35.
36. Memminger to T. S. Bocock, Speaker, H. of R., Dec. 7, 1863. *Confed. Treas. Reports*, III, 177-194.
37. *Idem* to *idem*, May 2, 1864. *Ibid.*, III, 257-267.
38. G. A. Trenholm to R. M. T. Hunter, Pres. pro tem. of Sen., Nov. 7, 1864. *Ibid.*, III, 353-368. This was the last complete report on the condition of the Treasury.
39. P. W. Gray, Agt. of the Treasury, Marshall, Texas, to Trenholm, Dec. 26, 1864. *Ibid.*, III, 445-450.
40. The complete story of the seizure of $4,192,998.79 of the New Orleans banks specie may be gleaned from the correspondence and reports of the Confed. Sec. of the Treas., as found in: *Corresp. of Treas. CSA.*, IV, 302-303, 361, 362-363, 365-367, 377, 476, 576-577, 639, 653, 654, 679; *Corresp. with Treas. CSA.*, V, 135-136, 403-404; *Confed. Treas. Reports*, III, 133-134, 153-155, 427; Tel. Messages Treas. Dept., 222, 231-233, 238, 240-241.
41. Jones, *Diary*, I, 194 (Nov. 21, 1862); L. B. Northrop, Commissary-General of Subsistence, to Maj.-Gen. Samuel Jones, Nov. 11, 1863. *Off. Rec. Rebellion*, 1st S., XXIX, pt. 2, p. 912; R. E. Lee to James A. Seddon, Sec. of War, Jan. 21, 1864. *Ibid.*, XXXIII, 1113-1114; E. K. Smith to *idem*, Feb. 11, 1865. *Ibid.*, XLVIII, pt. 1, pp. 1381-1382.
42. Herschel V. Johnson to Trenholm, Aug. 16, 1864. *Corresp. with Treas. CSA.*, V, 459-463; *Off. Rec. Rebellion*, 4th S., III, 594-597.
43. For impressments during the American Revolution, and also the French Revolution, see Sumner, *Financier of Am. Rev.*, I, 141-142, 154, 239-245; White, *Money and Banking*, 143-144; Thiers, *French Revolution*, III, 126; Montgaillard, *Etat de la France au mois de Mai, 1794*, pp. 35-41.
44. Jones, *Diary*, I, 194, 198; *Jour. Confed. Cong.*, I, 761; *ibid.*, III, 37; *Off. Rec. Rebellion*, 4th S., I, 646, 666; *ibid.*, III, 26, 39, 235, 441.
45. *Jour. Confed. Cong.*, III, 21.
46. *Ibid.*
47. Price schedules were made every two months. Specimens appear in the *Charleston Courier*, July 9, Oct. 3, 1863; Oct. 25, Dec. 27, 1864; *Richmond Examiner*, May 29, 1863, Aug. 4, Nov. 1, 1864; *Off. Rec. Rebellion*, 1st S., XXVI, pt. 2, pp. 206-207 (Sept. 4, 1864); *ibid.*, XXXIV, pt. 2, pp. 811-812 (Jan. 1, 1864); *ibid.*, XL, pt. 3, pp. 766-768 (July 8, 1864); *ibid.*, XLII, pt. 2, pp. 1152-1153 (Aug. 1, 1864); *ibid.*, XLII, pt. 3, pp. 1350-1351 (Dec. 30, 1864).
48. Act of Mar. 26, 1863. *Stats. at Large*, 102-104.
49. Acts of Apr. 27, 30, 1863; Feb. 16, 17, June 14, 1864; Mar. 18, 1865. *Stats. at Large*, 127-128, 131, 192-193, 196-197, 278-279; Ramsdell, *Laws*, 151-153.
50. Maj. W. E. Moore, Asst. Chf. of Subsistence, to Maj. A. D. Banks, Chf. of Subsistence, Morton, Miss., Aug. 12, 1863. *Off. Rec. Rebellion*, 1st S., XXX, pt. 4, pp. 491-492; Maj. Giles M. Hillyer, Chf. of Subsistence, to Gen. Braxton Bragg, Aug. 25, 1863. *Ibid.*, 547-549; "Subsist-

NOTES

ence stores at depots on the line of Mobile and Ohio Railroad, Aug. 1, 1864." *Ibid.*, XXXIX, pt. 2, pp. 742-743; "Subsistence stores in Mississippi and East Louisiana, Dec. 15, 1864." *Ibid.*, XLV, pt. 2, pp. 737-738.

1. L. B. Northrop, Commissary-General of Subsistence, to J. A. Seddon, Sec. of War, Sept. 4, 1863. *Off. Rec. Rebellion*, 1st S., XXX, pt. 4, p. 550; Robert E. Lee to A. R. Lawton, Quartermaster-General, Jan. 18, 1864; *idem* to *idem*, Jan. 19, 1864; *idem* to J. A. Seddon, Jan. 21, 1864; *idem* to *idem*, Jan. 23, 1864; "General Orders. No. 7, Hdqrs. Army of Northern Virginia, Jan. 22, 1864." *Ibid.*, XXXIII, 1094-1095, 1098-1099, 1113-1114, 1114-1115, 1117; L. B. Northrop to J. A. Seddon, Jan. 12, 1865; Northrop to John C. Breckinridge, Sec. of War, Feb. 9, 1865. *Ibid.*, XLVI, pt. 2, pp. 1040, 1211.
2. Brown to Seddon, Nov. 9, 1863. *Off. Rec. Rebellion*, 4th S., II, 943-944.
3. *Ibid.*
4. James Oliphant, Judesville, N. C., to Pres. Davis, May 9, 1864. *Corresp. with Treas. CSA.*, V, 402-403.
5. R. E. Lee to Jeff. Davis, Jan. 11 1864. *Off. Rec. Rebellion*, 1st S., XXXIII, 1076-1077.
6. Jones, *Diary*, I, 301 (Apr. 29, 1863); II, 56 (Sept. 29, 1863); II, 103 (Nov. 23, 1863); *Richmond Examiner*, Jan. 16, Nov. 3, 1863; *Charleston Courier*, Sept. 24, Oct. 2, 1863; *Richmond Whig*, July 21, 1864.
7. Brown to Seddon, Nov. 9, 1863. *Off. Rec. Rebellion*, 4th S., II, 943-944.
8. *Annual Cyclopaedia* (1863), p. 207; quoted in Owsley, *State Rights*, 225.
9. *Ibid.*, 225.
0. On Feb. 18, 1865, CSA. Sec. of War Breckinridge stated requisitions of the War Dept. on the Treasury since commencement of the war totaled $1,737,746,121.83 of which he estimated $430,923,996.03 remained unpaid. "This estimate," he said, "is under rather than over the deficiency." Comparing expenditures of Confed. War Dept. with those of U. S. War Dept., Breckinridge showed expenditures of U. S. War Dept. up to Jan. 1, 1865, to be $2,-101,910,728.39. Breckinridge to Davis, Feb. 18, 1865. *Off. Rec. Rebellion*, 4th S., III, 1094.
61. Memminger to W. C. Rives, June 28, 1861. *Corresp. of Treas. CSA.*, IV, 134.
62. A list of churches and the amount of their donations is found in a letter from Memminger to Howell Cobb, Pres., Cong. CSA., July 24, 1861. *Confed. Treas. Reports*, III, 25-27.
63. *Ibid.*
64. Memminger to Pike Powers, Clover, Va., Nov. 21, 1861. *Corresp. of Treas. CSA.*, IV, 233.
65. Memminger to A. H. Moss, Cameron, Tex., July 26, 1861. *Corresp. of Treas. CSA.*, IV, 165-166.
66. Childs, *Ravenel Journal* (Oct. 13, 1862), 160. Later the ladies of S. C. collected an additional $30,000 which they contributed for the construction of iron-clads. Memminger to S. R. Mallory, Sec. of Navy, Apr. 28, 1864. *Corresp. of Treas. CSA*, IV, 640.
67. Memminger to Ann E. Beckham, Culpepper, Va., July 10, 1861; *idem* to Fannie B. Epes and Sarah W. Bouldin, Nottoway Court-House, Va., July 17, 1861; *idem* to Anna Talley, Clarkesville, Va., Aug. 2, 1861. *Corresp. of Treas. CSA.*, IV, 149, 158, 169.
68. Memminger to M. S. Mayo, Richmond, Va., July 6, 1861. *Ibid.*, IV, 145.
69. Sarah E. Cochran, Camden, Ala., to Pres. Davis, May 10, 1862. *Corresp. with Treas., CSA.*, V, 551-552; Memminger to Mrs. Doctor Moore, Athens, Ga., Mar. 15, 1864. *Corresp. of Treas. CSA.*, IV, 604.
70. Memminger to Davis, Jan. 29, 1864. *Ibid.*, IV, 576.
71. The resolution is quoted in an advertisement titled "Donations to the

Treasury" enclosed in a letter from John W. Hall, Chf. Clk. Treas., to Editor of the *Richmond Sentinel*, Mar. 15, 1865. *Corresp. of Treas. CSA.*, IV, 871-872.
72. Trenholm to W. G. Leitch, Asst. Treas., Chester, S. C., Mar. 21, 1865. *Ibid.*, IV, 878.
73. For contributions under the resolution of Mar. 13, 1865, see Vol. 115F. Record of Letters of Treas., 325, 336, 337, 353, 363; *Corresp. of Treas. CSA.*, IV, 871, 876, 885, 890; *Corresp. with Treas. CSA.*, V, 557-558, 559-561.
74. The table was compiled from data found in R. G. 56, Vol. 62B.; Vol. 103. Record of Misc. Covering Warrants, 6, 11, 30, 31; *Corresp. with Treas. CSA.*, V, 371-372, 435; *Confed. Treas. Reports*, III, 177-194, 257-267, 353-368, 445-450; *Off. Rec. Rebellion*, 4th S., III, 1094; *Corresp. of Treas. CSA.*, IV, 302-303, 361-363, 365-367, 576-577, 653-654, 679, 871, 876, 885, 890.

CHAPTER VI

1. For an admirable study concerning activities of Confederate purchasing agents abroad, see Samuel B. Thompson, *Confederate Purchasing Operations Abroad*. Chapters III and IV treat the financial aspect of these purchases.
2. Of the vessels operating out of Nassau from Jan. 1863 to Apr. 1864, only one out of every six was reported captured. It is therefore possible that 80% of all supplies shipped by the agents reached the Confederacy. Owsley, *King Cotton Diplomacy*, chap. VIII. These figures, however, may be somewhat misleading due to the fact that there were too few ships and had all the ships reached their destination the needs of the Confederacy would still not have been met.
3. James D. Bulloch, *The Secret Service of the Confederate States in Europe*, II, 233.
4. J. Gorgas, Chf. of Ordnance, to Memminger, Mar. 30, 1863; Seddon to *idem*, Mar. 30, 1863. *Corresp. with Treas. CSA.*, V, 69; Memminger to C. J. Helm, Havana, Cuba, June 23, 1864. *Corresp. of Treas. CSA.*, IV, 680.
5. Memminger to Fraser, Trenholm & Co., Liverpool, Apr. 13, 1861. Vol. 111B. Record of Letters Treas. Dept., 50; Jno. Fraser and Co., Charleston, S. C., to Fraser, Trenholm & Co., Jan. 24, 1862. *Corresp. with Treas. CSA.*, V, 478-479.
6. Spence's appointment was made on the recommendation of James M. Mason, Confed. Commissioner to England. Memminger to James Spence, Liverpool, Aug. 18, 1862; *idem* to Mason, Oct. 24, 1862. *Corresp. of Treas. CSA.*, IV, 337, 372-373.
7. Memminger to Gen. C. J. McRae, Feb. 3, 1863. *Ibid.*, IV, 412-413.
8. Memminger to McRae, July 29, 1863; *idem* to E. C. Elmore, Treasurer, CSA., Sept. 15, 1863. *Ibid.*, IV, 492-493, 520.
9. Memminger to McRae, Feb. 16, 1864. *Ibid.*, IV, 583-585.
10. Memminger to McRae, Sept. 15, 1863; *idem* to F. T. & Co., Sept. 15, 1863; *idem* to Spence, Sept. 15, 1863. *Ibid.*, IV, 520-521, 522-523, 524. Spence was allowed a commission of $15,000 in specie for his services. Trenholm to McRae, Aug. 12, 1864. *Ibid.*, IV, 722-723.
11. Memminger to McRae, May 24, 1864; *idem* to F. T. & Co., May 24, 1864. *Ibid.*, IV, 656-657, 658-659.
12. Confederate currency, i.e., Treasury notes, was never accepted abroad as a medium of exchange.
13. Memminger to F. T. & Co., Apr. 13, 1861; *idem* to John Fraser & Co., Apr. 15, 1861; *idem* to F. T. & Co., May 18, 1861. Vol. 111B. Record of Letters Treas. Dept., 50, 50-51, 179-180.
14. Memminger to John Boston, Depositary, Savannah, Ga., May 26,

NOTES

1862; *idem* to B. C. Pressley, Depositary, Charleston, S. C., May 26, 1862. Vol. Tel. Messages, 239.
15. Memminger to Spence, Liverpool, Oct. 21, 1862. *Corresp. of Treas. CSA.*, IV, 368-369.
16. Leroy P. Walker, Sec. of War, to Huse and Anderson, Aug. 17, 1861; Jno. Fraser & Co. to Benjamin, Sept. 30, 1861. *Off. Rec. Rebellion*, 4th S., I, 564-565, 633.
17. Benjamin to Huse, Mar. 10, 1862; *idem* to Isaac, Campbell & Co., Mar. 17, 1862. *Ibid.*, 985, 1007.
18. *Corresp. of Treas. CSA.*, IV, 483-484, 522-523, 656-658; Vol. 115F. Record of Letters Treas. Dept., 167.
19. Thompson, *Confederate Purchasing Operations Abroad*, 50.
20. Up to Dec. 5, 1862, Huse had paid out $3,095,139.18 but still held unpaid requisitions for £444,850, a sum equivalent to $5,925,402 in Confed. currency. J. Gorgas to J. A. Seddon, Sec. of War, Dec. 5, 1862. *Off. Rec. Rebellion*, 4th S., II, 227-228.
21. Benj. W. Hart to Geo. W. Randolph, Sec. of War, Nov. 17, 1862. *Ibid.*, 4th S., II, 190-191.
22. J. P. Benjamin, Sec. of War, to E. J. Forstall, N. O., La., Jan. 17, 1862. *Ibid.*, 4th S., I, 845-846.
23. Act of Apr. 21, 1862. *Public Laws of CSA.*, 47.
24. Memminger to James M. Mason, Comm. CSA., London, Oct. 24, 1862. *Corresp. of Treas. CSA.*, IV, 372-374.
25. Memminger to James Spence, Liverpool, Aug. 18, 1862; *idem* to F. T. & Co., Aug. 18, 1862. *Ibid.*, IV, 337-338.
26. Memminger to Spence, Sept. 20, 1862. *Ibid.*, IV, 355-356.
27. Memminger to James M. Mason, Comm., CSA., London, Oct. 24, 1862. *Ibid.*, IV, 372-374. On Dec. 19, 1862, Bernard Avegno was appointed a Confed. Commercial Agent to Vera Cruz to try $50,000 of the bonds in the Mexican market. He was instructed to "sell them for coin or sterling bills at as high a rate as possible, not less however than 50 per cent." The proceeds were to be shipped to F. T. & Co., Liverpool. In case the bonds could not be sold within six months, they were to be delivered to the CSA. depositary at Brownsville or San Antonio, Tex. Memminger to Bernard Avegno, Dec. 19, 1862. *Ibid.*, IV, 398.
28. Memminger to Messrs. J. T. Doswell and Co., Dec. 5, 1862; *idem* to DeBow, Dec. 5, 1862. DeBow Papers.
29. Memminger to James Spence, Nov. 26, 1862. *Corresp. of Treas. CSA.*, IV, 388-389.
30. Memminger to James M. Mason, Oct. 24, 1862. *Ibid.*, IV, 372-374.
31. *Ibid.*
32. Memminger to Robt. Tyler, Register, Oct. 27, 1862; *idem* to G. A. Trenholm, Nov. 11, 1862. *Ibid.*, IV, 375, 384-385.
33. Memminger to Robt. Tyler, Dec. 16, 1862; *idem* to Capt. W. G. Crenshaw, Dec. 18, 1862; *idem* to James Spence, CSA. Financial Agt., Liverpool, July 21, 1863. *Ibid.*, IV, 397, 487.
34. "An Act to authorize a Foreign Loan," approved Jan. 29, 1863. Ramsdell, *Laws*, 164-165.
35. "Erlanger Contract," Jan. 9, 1863. *Confed. Treas. Reports*, III, 98a-98c.
36. James Spence to Memminger, Dec. 19, 1862. Pickett Papers, II.
37. Memminger to C. J. McRae, Agent for the Loan, Paris, July 29, 1863. *Corresp. of Treas. CSA.*, IV, 493.
38. J. M. Mason to J. P. Benjamin, No. 32, Mar. 30, 1863. Pickett Papers.
39. Henry Hotze to Benjamin, No. 20, Mar. 21, 1863; Mason to *idem*, No. 31, Mar. 20, 1863; *idem* to *idem*, No. 32, Mar. 30, 1863; *idem* to *idem*, No. 33, Apr. 9, 1863. *Ibid.*
40. Mason to Benjamin, No. 33, Apr. 9, 1863. *Ibid.*
41. Copy of Agreement enclosed in letter from Mason to Benjamin, No. 33, Apr. 9, 1863. *Ibid.*

CONFEDERATE FINANCE

42. Mason to Benjamin, Apr. 27, 1863. *Ibid.* On Apr. 24 Erlanger was authorized to use an additional £500,000 to support the market if it became necessary to do so. *Ibid.*
43. McRae to Memminger, No. 3, July 9, 1863. R. G. 56 Confed. Papers Box No. 96. Caution-money was a sum of money deposited by a party to a contract as a guarantee that he would adhere to the terms of the contract or forfeit the sum to the other party.
44. Henry Hotze to Benjamin, Aug. 17, 1863. Pickett Papers, "Confederate State Department," J, No. 38b.
45. McRae to Memminger, No. 19, Mar. 16, 1864 (enclosures). R. G. 56. Confed. Archives. Confed. Papers Box No. 96.
46. McRae to Memminger, No. 8, Oct. 2, 1863. *Off. Rec. Rebellion*, 4th S., II, 980-981.
47. Slidell to Benjamin, No. 52, Dec. 29, 1863. Pickett Papers.
48. Slidell to Benjamin, No. 59, Apr. 9, 1864; *idem* to *idem*, No. 61, May 5, 1864; *idem* to *idem*, No. 65, June 30, 1864. *Ibid.*
49. "Report on the Erlanger Loan, Feb. 11, 1865," showing proceeds of loan as of Oct. 1, 1864. *Confed. Treas. Reports*, III, 435-436.
50. Contrary to orders, Commander W. L. Maury retained the cotton certificates after his arrival in Europe. He proceeded to have them countersigned by Mason and then hypothecated $680,000 of them in order to procure naval supplies. McRae bought these up as quickly as possible with funds from the Erlanger Loan. Memminger to McRae, Sept. 15, 1863; *idem* to *idem*, Feb. 16, 1864. *Corresp. of Treas. CSA.*, IV, 520-522, 583-585. McRae to Memminger, Oct. 2, 1863. R. G. 56. Confed. Papers Box No. 96.
51. Mason to Benjamin, No. 29, Feb. 5, 1863. Pickett Papers.
52. For facsimile of a temporary cotton warrant, see Caleb Huse, *The Supplies for the Confederate Army*, facing p. 35.
53. James Spence to Memminger, Dec. 19, 1862. Pickett Papers, II.
54. Nelson Clements to Maj. S. Hart, Houston, Tex., Dec. 16, 1862. *Off. Rec. Rebellion*, 4th S., III, 566; McRae to Memminger No. 9, Oct. 7, 1863. *Ibid.*, 4th S., II, 982-985; Bulloch, *The Secret Service of the Confederate States in Europe*, II, 250-253.
55. McRae to Seddon, July 4, 1864. *Off. Rec. Rebellion*, 4th S., III, 528.
56. Hotze to Benjamin, No. 30, Oct. 3, 1863. Pickett Papers.
57. *Ibid.*
58. McRae to Memminger, No. 9, Oct. 7, 1863. *Off. Rec. Rebellion*, 4th S., II, 982-985.
59. *Ibid.*
60. *Ibid.*
61. Seddon to McRae, Sept. 26, 1863. *Ibid.*, 824-827.
62. Act of Feb. 6, 1864. *Stats. at Large*, 181-183.
63. Davis to The House of Representatives of the Confederate States of America, June 10, 1864. *Off. Rec. Rebellion*, 4th S., III, 553-555. For several months prior to the above regulations, the War Dept. had required all vessels to devote one-third of their tonnage to the Govt. Trenholm to Davis, Dec. 12, 1864. *Ibid.*, 954.
64. Trenholm to Maj. J. M. Seixas, Aug. 12, 1864. *Corresp. of Treas. CSA.*, IV, 725.
65. Lt. Col. Thomas L. Bayne to Seddon, May 2, 1864. *Off. Rec. Rebellion*, 4th S., III, 370-371.
66. Bayne to Seddon, May 2, 1864. *Ibid.*
67. The agreement, signed July 7, 1864, by Charles Kuhn Prioleau, in the name of his firm, Fraser, Trenholm & Co., and Colin J. McRae, on behalf of the CSA, is found in R. G. 56. Confed. Papers Box No. 96.
68. McRae to Seddon, No. 7A, July 4, 1864. *Off. Rec. Rebellion*, 4th S., III, 525-529.
69. *Ibid.* The contract with Alex. Col-

NOTES

lie & Co. was made for six months. The original contract is found in R. G. 56. Confed. Papers Box No. 96.

70. McRae to Seddon, No. 7A, July 4, 1864. *Off. Rec. Rebellion*, 4th S., III, 525-529.

71. Davis to H. of Rep., June 10, 1864. *Ibid.*, 553-555.

72. Act of Feb. 6, 1864. *Stats. at Large*, 181-183.

73. Seddon to The President, Dec. 10, 1864; Trenholm to The President, Dec. 12, 1864. *Off. Rec. Rebellion*, 4th S., III, 928-929, 953-955.

74. Trenholm to Davis, Dec. 12, 1864. *Ibid.*, 953-955.

75. On Mar. 8, 1865, both Houses did pass a bill "to authorize the exportation of cotton by the several States in payment for Army and other supplies and cotton and wool cards." The bill would have removed all trade restrictions, but before final action was taken on the measure the Confederacy collapsed. *Jour. Confed. Cong.*, VII, 694, 720; Owsley, *St. Rights in the Confed.*, 149.

76. Davis to H. of Rep., Dec. 20, 1864. *Off. Rec. Rebellion*, 4th S., III, 948-953.

77. Seddon to Davis, Dec. 10, 1864. *Ibid.*, 928-930.

78. The list of articles imported is taken from the report of Col. T. L. Bayne, Chief of the Bureau of Foreign Supplies of the War Dept., as enclosed in report of Trenholm to Davis, Dec. 12, 1864. *Ibid.*, 953-955.

79. *Ibid.* Trenholm fails to account for the two missing bales.

80. R. Salas to Benjamin, Jan. 2, 1862. *Ibid.*, I, 829-830.

Selected Bibliography

I. PRIMARY SOURCES

A. MANUSCRIPT SOURCES

1. *Official Manuscripts*

R.G. 56. Archives of the Confederate Treasury Department, 1861-65 (Treas. Dept., National Archives, Wash., D. C.).

This collection of Confederate Treasury records consists of correspondence, financial and accounting records, warrants, currency, customs and court records, public debt records, and records of the Trans-Mississippi (Texas) Cotton Bureau and the Produce Loan Office, 1861-65. Vast in scope and volume, they are of inestimable value to a study of Confederate finance. The collection is composed of two types of manuscripts, i.e., "loose papers" and manuscript volumes. There are 100 boxes of "loose papers" and 132 manuscript volumes. Of each type the following have proved of especial value in the preparation of the book:

Loose Papers

BOXES	DESCRIPTION
23-24	Louisiana. Cotton Transactions (DeBow's)
45	Texas. Cotton Bureau 1864-65 Papers
89	Partial Lists of Confederate Depositaries
90	Foreign Correspondence—Erlanger Loan Papers
91	Foreign Correspondence Relating to Building of War Vessels in Europe
92-93	Miscellaneous Correspondence Addressed to Secretary of Treasury Relating to Finance, Printing of Notes, Bonds, Auditor's Certificates, Cotton, etc.
94-95	Confederate Papers Relating to Sales of Cotton in Europe
96	Confederate Papers Relating to (1) Erlanger Cotton Loan (2) Building Confederate Cruisers in France (3) Fraser, Trenholm & Co. (4) Letters to C. J. McRae, Memminger, Erlanger, S. A. Duncan, et al
98	Confederate Papers Relating to Confederate Property in Europe

BIBLIOGRAPHY

- 99 Confederate Papers Relating to
  - (1) Petition of Richmond Banks for Return of Captured Gold
  - (2) Reports of F. E. Spinner and Loomis on Same
- 100 Sequestration Papers

MANUSCRIPT VOLUMES

Number	Description
45	Texas. Trans-Mississippi Cotton Bureau Memorandum Books of Letters Received
45	Texas. Trans-Mississippi Cotton Bureau Press Copy Books of Letters Sent
46	Texas. Book: "Records" Containing Organization and Transactions of the Texas Cotton Bureau in 1863—Col. W. J. Hutchins, Chief of Bureau
62B	Confederate Treasurer . . . at New Orleans
68	Record of Contracts, Civil, Military and Naval Comptroller's Office, C. S. A.
79	Record of Certificates of Stock
103	Record of Miscellaneous Warrants, Treasury Department, March 29, 1861, thru April 6, 1864
111B	Record Book of Copies of Letters of Secretary of Treasury from March 1, 1861, to October 12, 1861
115F	Record Book of Copies of Letters of Secretary of Treasury from October 17, 1864, to March 31, 1865
121A	Comptroller's Office: Letters Addressed by Lewis Cruger, Comptroller of the Treasury, March 23, 1861, to December 16, 1861
......	Letter Book B. United States Depositary at New Orleans [A. J Guirot]. Records of Correspondence and Telegrams from May 14, 1853, to May 11, 1865
......	Letters from Secretaries, from January 10, 1862, to June 11, 1863, to the Comptroller's Office
......	Press Copies of Letters, Restricted Intercourse, June 1 to 30, 1865, Treasury Dept.
......	Telegram Messages, Treasury Department: Telegrams of the Confederate Treasury Department from February 27, 1861, to July 30, 1864

R. G. 109. War Department Collection of Confederate Records (War Dept., National Archives, Wash., D. C.).

After the fall of the Confederate States of America, a large quantity of Confederate records came into the possession of the United States

CONFEDERATE FINANCE

Government by capture, donation, and purchase. In July, 1865, a unit was organized in The Adjutant General's Office for the care of these records. They include records of the Confederate Congress and of the Confederate War, Treasury, and Post Office Departments. Of those pertaining to the Confederate Treasury, the following proved to be of particular value:

MANUSCRIPT VOLUMES[1]

Chap. V — Vol. 199 (Quartermaster Correspondence with the Confederate Treasury Department).

Chap. V — Vol. 199½ (Quartermaster Correspondence with the Confederate Treasury Department).

Chap. VIII—Vol. 323 (Miscellaneous Correspondence with the Confederate Treasury Department).

Chap. VIII — Vol. 325. "Cato on Constitutional Money and Legal Tender." In twelve numbers from the *Charleston Mercury*, 1862.

Chap. X — Vol. 163 (Correspondence with the Confederate Treasury Department).

Chap X — Vol. 164. Letters and Telegrams of the Secretary's Office, Treasury Department, to Collectors of Customs, March 21, 1861, to January 24, 1862.

Chap. X — Vol. 165. Letters and Telegrams of the Secretary's Office, Treasury Department, 1861-'63.

Chap. X — Vol.189.

Chap. X — Vol. 191. Record Book B, Office of Commissioner of Taxes.

Chap. X — Vol. 207. Accounts of Receivers Under Sequestration Act, Register's Office, CSA.

Chap. X — Vol. 264. Orders and Circulars of the Treasury Department.

2. Other Manuscripts

Brown, Joseph E., Correspondence (MS. Dept., Duke University).
Cobb, Howell, Papers (MS. Dept., Duke University).
Confederate Note and Bond Album (Confed. Sts. of Am. Collection, MS. Div., Library of Congress, Wash., D. C.). A similar album is in MS. Dept., Duke University.

---

1. The chapter numbers, i.e., V, VIII, and X, preceding a volume number indicate that the volume contains correspondence between a special bureau or department and the Treasury. All volumes preceded by "Chap. V" pertain to Quartermaster correspondence with the Treasury Department; those preceded by "Chap. VIII" indicate Miscellaneous correspondence with the Treasury Department; and those preceded by "Chap. X" indicate correspondence by the Treasury Department.

BIBLIOGRAPHY

Confederate States of America, Archives 1861-65 (Acc. 378. MS. Dept., Duke University). Contains original MSS. of Confederate Acts.

Davis, Jefferson, Papers (MS. Dept., Duke University).

DeBow, James D. B., Papers (MS. Dept., Duke University).

Hammond, James H., Papers (MS. Div., Library of Congress, Wash., D. C.).

Jones, Charles C., Jr., ed., Autograph Letters and Portraits of the Signers of the Constitution of the Confederate States (MS. Dept., Duke University).

Memminger, Christopher Gustavus, Papers (MS. Dept., Duke University).

Pickett, John T., Papers (MS. Div., Library of Congress, Wash., D. C.)
Vol. I May 22, 1849-May 9, 1862
Vol. II May 13, 1862-July 5, 1867
"Letter Book," covering miscellaneous correspondence, June 12, 1861-January 13, 1867
These papers were purchased because they were believed to shed light on the missing Confederate Treasure.

Register of Acts CSA. (Original MS. Vol., MS. Dept., Duke University).

Thian, Raphael P., comp., Confederate Notes with Descriptions of Emblems, 1861-64 (MS. Dept., Duke University).

——————, Confederate States of America. Treasury Department Notes and Bonds, 1861-1865 (MS. Dept., Duke University).

Contains Confederate notes and bonds with a preponderance of notes. Listed under date of act authorizing issue. Also contains chemicograph notes by S. Straker & Sons, London, England. Included are separate typed lists of male and female signers with accompanying autographs. A duplicate album in MS. Div., Library of Congress, Wash., D. C.

——————, Illustrated Catalogue of Confederate Treasury Notes with Descriptive Letter-Press (MS. Dept., Duke University).

Trenholm, George A., Papers (MS. Dept., Duke University).

——————, (MS. Div., Library of Congress, Wash., D. C.)
Vol. I (1853-1866).

B. Printed Sources
1. *Official Publications*

Acts and Regulations of the Congress of the Confederate States, in Relation to the Customs and Officers thereof (Confederate States of America Imprints, MS. Dept., Duke University).

CONFEDERATE FINANCE

Acts and Resolutions of the Third Session of the Provisional Congress of the Confederate States, Held at Richmond, Va. (Richmond, 1861).
Commercial Intercourse with and in States Declared in Iusurrection (U. S. Treasury Department Circular, July, 1863).
Instructions to be Observed by Officers and Agents Receiving the Tax in Kind (Richmond, 1863).
Journal of the Congress of the Confederate States of America, 1861-'65 (7 vols., Washington, 1904).
Matthews, James M., ed., *Public and Private Laws of the Confederate States of America, Passed at the First and Second Congresses, 1862-'64* (Richmond, 1864).
————, *Public Laws of the CSA., Passed at the Third Session of the First Congress, 1863* (Richmond, 1863).
————, *The Statutes at Large of the Confederate States of of America* (Richmond, 1862-'64).
————, *The Statutes at Large of the Provisional Government of the Confederate States of America, from the Institution of the Government, February 8, 1861, to Its Termination, February 18, 1862, Inclusive. Arranged in Chronological Order Together with the Constitution for the Provisional Government, and the Permanent Constitution of the Confederate States, and the Treaties Concluded by the Confederate States with Indian Tribes* (Richmond, 1864).
Official Records of the Union and Confederate Navies in the War of the Rebellion (31 vols., Washington, 1894-1927).
"Petition of William B. Isaacs & Co., of Richmond, Va., Representatives of certain Banks in Richmond, Praying for 'The restoration of certain coin belonging to them now in the Treasury of the United States.'" *Misc. Doc. No. 5, H. of R., 45 Cong., 2d Sess.* (Washington, 1878), 1-94.
Provisional and Permanent Constitutions, Together with the Acts and Resolutions of the First Session of the Provisional Congress, of the Confederate States, 1861 (Montgomery, 1861).
Ramsdell, Charles W., ed., *Laws and Joint Resolutions of the Last Session of the Confederate Congress (November 6, 1864-March 18, 1865) Together with the Secret Acts of Previous Congresses* (Durham, 1941).
Report, Confederate Commissioner of Taxes, November, 1863.
Report of the Postmaster General, December 7, 1863 (in uncatalogued *CSA. Imprints,* MS. Dept., Duke University).
Reports of the Secretary of the Treasury of the Confederate States of America.

BIBLIOGRAPHY

All of the reports of the Secretary of the Treasury, CSA., are found in Thian, Raphael P., comp., *Reports of the Secretary of the Treasury of the Confederate States of America, 1861-'65* (Appendix III, Washington, 1878).

Richardson, James P., comp., *A Compilation of the Messages and Papers of the Confederacy: Including the Diplomatic Correspondence, 1861-1865* (2 vols., Nashville, 1906).

―――――, *A Compilation of the Messages and Papers of the Presidents, 1789-1897* (10 vols., Washington, 1896-1899).

Sanger, George P., ed., *The Statutes at Large, Treaties, and Proclamations, of the United States of America, from December 5, 1859 to March 3, 1863* (Boston, 1863).

Treasury Circular No. 5. Acts and Regulations of the Congress of the Confederate States, in Relation to the Customs and the Officers thereof.

Walden, P. E., comp., *Compilation of the Tariff Acts of the C. S. A.* (New Orleans, 1861).

War of the Rebellion: A Compilation of the Official Records of the Union and Confederate Armies (128 vols., Washington, 1880-1901).

2. Other Printed Sources

Ambler, Charles H., ed., *Correspondence of Robert M. T. Hunter, 1826-1876*. Annual Report American Historical Association, II (Washington, 1916).

[Anonymous] "Confiscation of Vessels." [Hunt's] *Merchants' Magazine and Commercial Review*, XLV (November 1861), 526.

[Appleton's] *Annual Cyclopaedia and Register of Important Events . . . Embracing Political, Civil, Military, and Social Affairs; Public Documents; Biography, Statistics, Commerce, Finance, Literature, Science, Agriculture, and Mechanical Industry* (New York, 1862-), I-V (1862-66).

Childs, Arney Robinson, ed., *The Private Journal of Henry William Ravenel, 1859-1887* (Columbia, 1947).

Clarke, H. C., *The Confederate States Almanac, and Repository of Useful Knowledge, for the Year 1862* (Nashville, 1862).

―――――, *The Confederate States Almanac, and Repository of Useful Knowledge, for the Year 1865* (Mobile, 1865).

Green, Duff, *Facts and Suggestions Relative to Finance and Currency Addressed to the President of the Confederate States* (Augusta, 1864).

Jameson, J. Franklin, ed., "Letters of Stephen R. Mallory, 1861." *American Historical Review*, XII (1906), 103-108.

CONFEDERATE FINANCE

Jones, J. B., *A Rebel War Clerk's Diary at the Confederate States Capital* (2 vols., New York, 1935).

McCaleb, Walter F., ed., *Memoirs, with Special Reference to Secession and the Civil War, by John H. Reagan* . . . (New York and Washington, 1906).

Martin, Isabella D., and Avary, Myrta L., eds., *A Diary from Dixie, as Written by Mary Boykin Chestnut* . . . (1906).

Mason, Virginia, comp. and ed., *The Public Life and Diplomatic Correspondence of James M. Mason, with Some Personal History* (New York and Washington, 1906).

Miller, Andrew, *Our Currency. Some of Its Evils, and Remedies for Them. By a Citizen of North Carolina* (Raleigh, 1861).

Moore, Frank, ed., *The Rebellion Record: A Diary of American Events, with Documents, Narratives, Illustrative Incidents, Poetry, etc.* . . . (12 vols., New York, 1862-1868).

Nast, F. A., "History of Confederate Stamps." *Confederate Veteran*, II (March, 1894), 77-78.

Phillips, Ulrich B., ed., *The Correspondence of Robert Toombs, Alexander H. Stephens, and Howell Cobb [1884-1885]. Annual Report American Historical Association*, II (Washington, 1913).

Pollard, Edward A., *The First Year of the War* (Richmond, 1862).

——————, *The Second Year of the War* (Richmond, 1863).

Rowland, Dunbar, ed., *Jefferson Davis, Constitutionalist, His Letters, Papers and Speeches* (10 vols., Jackson, Miss., 1923).

Thian, Raphael P., Collection (MS. Dept. and Rare Book Room, Duke University). Raphael P. Thian was Chief Clerk in the Adjutant General's Office, Washington, D. C., during the time that office was responsible "for the collection, safe-keeping, and publication of the 'rebel archives.'" Having access to these records, Thian undertook to make a private compilation of all available data pertaining to the Confederate Treasury. For more than "thirty years . . . he devoted his entire time, outside of office hours" to the compilation of the materials——the result of his efforts is incomparable. The collection consists of two types of volumes—manuscript and printed. The manuscript volumes, pertinent to a history of Confederate finance, have been cited above, and the printed volumes, as listed below, have proved an indispensable source of material in the preparation of this book. Only two copies of each of the following Thian volumes are known to be in existence. In addition to the copy of each volume found in the Rare Book Room of Duke University Library, a second copy is located in the private library of the Adjutant General, National Archives, Washington, D. C.

BIBLIOGRAPHY

———————, comp., *Correspondence of the Treasury Department of the Confederate States of America, 1861-1865* (Appendix IV, Washington, 1879).

The volume includes approximately 3,000 letters carefully selected from the letter-books and files of the Confederate Treasury Department. The correspondence embraces letters to the President, the Secretaries of War and of the Navy, members of the Committees on Finance and Ways and Means, Governors of States; and presents in full the views of the department in answer to communications from representatives of the banking, in the correspondence of the department with the several assistant treasurers, depositaries, and agents.

———————, comp., *Correspondence with the Treasury Department* mercantile, and industrial interests of the South. The operations of the Treasury Department at home and abroad are described *of the Confederate States of America, 1861-1865* (Appendix V, pts. 1 and 2, Washington, 1880).

Contains correspondence from many of the social, economic, political, and military leaders of the day concerning the financial and commercial measures of the Confederate States of America. It embraces governors' messages, resolves of legislatures, and general correspondence.

———————, comp., *Extracts from the Journals of the Provisional Congress and of the First and Second Congresses of the Confederate States of America, on Legislation Affecting Finance, Revenue, and Commerce, 1861-1865* (Appendix I, Washington, 1880) (The only copy of this volume known to be in existence is found in the private library of the Adjutant General, National Archives, Washington, D. C.).

This volume contains full extracts from the public and secret Journals of Confederate Congresses (February 4, 1861, to March 18, 1865) on the subjects indicated in the title, embracing text of bills introduced by individual members or reported by the Committees on Finance, Ways and Means, etc., with legislative consideration, amendment, and vote on final disposition.

———————, comp., *Register of Issues of Confederate States Treasury Notes, Together with Tabular Exhibits of the Debt, Funded and Unfunded, of the Confederate States of America, 1861-1865* (Washington, 1880).

———————, comp., *Reports of the Secretary of the Treasury of the Confederate States of America, 1861-1865* (Appendix III, Washington, 1878).

In addition to the regular reports of the Secretary of the

CONFEDERATE FINANCE

Treasury, this volume includes special communications to the President and the Committees on Finance and Ways and Means on various subjects of finance.

Walker, Robert J., *Jefferson Davis and Repudiation* (London, 1863).

3. Newspapers and Periodicals

(Unless otherwise noted the following publications have been used for the period 1861-1865.)

Asheville News
Atlanta Confederacy
Atlanta Register
Augusta Constitutionalist
Charleston Courier
Charleston Mercury
Columbia Carolinian
Columbus Enquirer
DeBow's Review (October, November, and December, 1861).
Feliciana Democrat (Clinton, La.).
Floridian Journal
Frank Leslies Illustrated Newspaper, XII (October 5 and 12, 1861).
Jackson Mississippian
Knoxville Register
Lake City Columbia
Lynchburg Republic
Mobile Tribune
Montgomery Advertiser
Nassau Intelligencer
New York Tribune
New York World
North Carolina Standard
Petersburg Express
Raleigh Confederate
Raleigh Progress
Raleigh Register
Richmond Dispatch
Richmond Enquirer
Richmond Examiner
Richmond Sentinel
Richmond Whig
Savannah Republican

BIBLIOGRAPHY

Selma Reporter
South Carolinian
Vicksburg Evening Citizen
Washington Herald (Feb. 18, 1914).
Weekly News (Enterprise, Miss.).
Wilmington Journal

II. SECONDARY MATERIALS

Adams, James Truslow, ed., *Dictionary of American History* (New York, 1940).
Allen, H. D., "The Paper Money of the Confederate States—With Historical Data." *The Numismatist* (June 1917-February 1919).
Bigslow, John, *France and the Confederate Navy, 1862-8. An Historical Episode* (New York, 1888).
Bradbeer, William West, *Confederate and Southern State Currency. Historical and Financial Data. Descriptions with Illustrations* (New York, 1915).
Bradford, Gamaliel, *Confederate Portraits* (Boston and New York, 1914).
Bradlee, Francis B., *Blockade Running During the Civil War and the Effect of Land and Water Transportation on the Confederacy.* Essex. Inst. Coll., LX and LXI (Salem, Mass., 1925).
Brooks, Robert P., ed., "Howell Cobb Papers." *Georgia Historical Quarterly*, V, VI (1921-22).
Bulloch, James D., *The Secret Service of the Confederate States in Europe* (2 vols., New York, 1883).
Butler, Pierce, *Judah P. Benjamin* (Philadelphia, 1907).
Capers, Henry D., *The Life and Times of C. G. Memminger* (Richmond, 1893).
Cate, Wirt A., *Lucius Q. C. Lamar, Secession and Reunion* (Chapel Hill, 1935).
Chase, Philip H., *Confederate Treasury Notes; The Paper Money of the Confederate States of America, 1861-65* (Philadelphia, 1947).
Clark, Micajah H., "The Last Days of the Confederate Treasury and What Became of Its Specie." *Southern Historical Society Papers*, IX (January-December, 1881), 542-556.
Cleveland, H., *Alexander H. Stephens in Public and Private* (Philadelphia, 1866).
Coulter, E. Merton, "Commercial Intercourse with the Confederacy in the Mississippi Valley, 1861-1865." *Mississippi Valley Historical Review*, V (March, 1919), 377-395.
Dalzell, George W., *The Flight from the Flag: The Continuing*

CONFEDERATE FINANCE

Effect of the Civil War upon the American Carrying Trade (Chapel Hill, 1940).

Davis, Jefferson, *The Rise and Fall of the Confederate Government* (2 vols., New York, 1881).

Davis, Varina Howell, *Jefferson Davis, Ex-President of the Confederate States. A Memoir by His Wife* (2 vols., New York, 1890).

Dean, H. C., *Crimes of the Civil War and Curse of the Funding System* (Baltimore, 1868).

Dewey, Davis R., *Financial History of the United States* (New York, 1934).

Dowd, Clement, *Life of Zebulon B. Vance* (Charlotte, 1897).

Eckenrode, Hamilton J., *Jefferson Davis, President of the South* (New York, 1923).

Fessenden, Francis, *Life and Public Services of William Pitt Fessenden, United States Senator from Maine 1854-1864; Secretary of the Treasury 1864-1865; United States Senator from Maine 1865-1869* . . . (2 vols., Boston and New York, 1907).

Fish, Carl Russel, *The American Civil War: An Interpretation* (New York, 1937).

Freeman, Douglas S., ed., *A Calendar of Confederate Papers, with a Bibliography of Some Confederate Publications* . . . (Richmond, 1908).

Gipson, Lawrence H., "The Collapse of the Confederacy." *Mississippi Valley Historical Review,* IV (1918), 437-458.

Gordon, A. C., "Hard Times in the Confederacy." *Century Magazine,* XXXVI (September, 1888), 761 ff.

Handy, Sara M., "In the Last Days of the Confederacy." *Atlantic Monthly,* LXXXVII (January, 1901), 104 ff.

Hendrick, Burton J., *Statesman of the Lost Cause: Jefferson Davis and His Cabinet* (Boston, 1939).

"History of Confederate Stamps," *Confederate Veteran,* II (March, 1894).

Huse, Caleb, Major and Purchasing Agent, C. S. A., *The Supplies for the Confederate Army: How They were Obtained in Europe and How Paid for* (Boston, 1904).

Johnson, Allen, and Malone, Dumas, eds., *Dictionary of American Biography* (20 vols., New York, 1928-1937).

Johnson, Robert U., and Buel, Clarence C., eds., *Battles and Leaders of the Civil War* (4 vols., New York, 1884-1887).

Knox, J. J., *A History of Banking in the United States* (New York, 1900).

Lee, William, *The Currency of the Confederate States of America. A Description of the Various Notes, Their Dates of Issue, Varie-*

BIBLIOGRAPHY

ties, Series, Sub-series, Letters, Numbers, etc.; Accompanied with Photographs of the Distinct Varieties of Each Issue (Washington, 1875).
Lonn, Ella, *Salt as a Factor in the Confederacy* (New York, 1933).
McCulloch, Hugh, *Men and Measures of Half a Century . . .* (New York, 1888).
Mallory, Stephen R., "The Last Days of the Confederacy." *McClure's Magazine* (December 1910-January 1911).
Mitchell, Wesley C., *A History of the Greenbacks, with Special Reference to the Economic Consequences of Their Issue: 1862-65* (Chicago, 1903).
Montgaillard, Comte Jean Gabriel Maurice Rocques de, *Etat de la France au mois de Mai, 1794* (a Londres, 1794).
Oberholtzer, Ellis P., *Jay Cooke, Financier of the Civil War* (2 vols., Philadelphia, 1907).
Owsley, Frank L., *King Cotton Diplomacy: Foreign Relations of the Confederate States of America* (Chicago, 1931).
————, *State Rights in the Confederacy* (Chicago, 1925).
Parker, William Harwar, Capt., *Recollection of a Naval Officer 1841-1865* (New York, 1883).
Phillips, Ulrich B., *The Life of Robert Toombs* (New York, 1913).
Pollard, Edward A., *Life of Jefferson Davis, with a Secret History of the Southern Confederacy Gathered Behind the Scenes in Richmond, Containing Curious and Extraordinary Information of the Principal Southern Characters in the Late War, in Connection with President Davis, and in Relation to the Various Intrigues of His Administration* (Philadelphia, 1869).
————, *The Lost Cause: A New Southern History of the War of the Confederates . . .* (New York, 1866).
Ramsdell, Charles W., *Behind the Lines in the Southern Confederacy* (Baton Rouge, 1944).
Randall, James Garfield, "Captured and Abandoned Property during the Civil War." *American Historical Review*, XIX (1913), 65-79.
————, "Some Legal Aspects of the Confiscation Acts of the Civil War." *American Historical Review*, XVIII (1912), 79-96.
————, *The Confiscation of Property during the Civil War* (Indianapolis, 1913).
————, "The Virginia Debt Controversy." *Political Science Quarterly*, XXX (1915), 553-577.
Rhodes, James Ford, *History of the United States from the Compromise of 1850 to the Final Restoration of Home Rule at the*

South in 1877 (7 vols., New York, 1893-1906), III (1860-62), IV (1862-64), V (1864-66).

Roberts, A. Sellew, "The Federal Government and Confederate Cotton." *American Historical Review*, XXXII (1927), 262-275.

Robertson, J. Barr, *The Confederate Debt and Private Southern Debts* (London, 1884).

Scharf, J. Thomas, *History of the Confederate States Navy from its Organization to the Surrender of its Last Vessel. Its Stupendous Struggle with the Great Navy of the United States; the Engagements Fought in the Rivers and Harbors of the South, and upon the High Seas; Blockade-Running, First Use of Iron-Clads and Torpedoes, and Privateer History* (2nd ed., Albany, 1894).

Schell, Herbert S., "Hugh McCulloch and the Treasury Department, 1865-1869." *Mississippi Valley Historical Review*, XVII (1930), 404-421.

Schuckers, Jacob W., *The Life and Public Services of Salmon Portland Chase, United States Senator and Governor of Ohio; Secretary of the Treasury, and Chief-Justice of the United States* (New York, 1874).

Schwab, John C., "The Confederate Foreign Loan: An Episode in the Financial History of the Civil War." *Yale Review*, I (August, 1892), 175-186.

―――――, *The Confederate States of America, 1861-65; A Financial and Industrial History of the South during the Civil War* (New York, 1901).

―――――, "The Finances of the Confederacy." *Political Science Quarterly*, VII (March, 1892), 38-56.

―――――, "The Financier of the Confederate States." *Yale Review*, II (November, 1893), 288 ff.

―――――, "Prices in the Confederate States, 1861-65." *Political Science Quarterly*, XIV (June, 1899), 281-304.

Sears, Louis M., *John Slidell* (Durham, 1925).

Sellers, James L., "An Interpretation of Civil War Finance." *American Historical Review*, XXX (January, 1925), 282-297.

―――――, "The Economic Incidence of the Civil War in the South." *Mississippi Valley Historical Review*, XIV (1927), 179-191.

Shultz, William J., and Caine, M. R., *Financial Development of the United States* (New York, 1937).

Simms, Henry Harrison, *Life of Robert M. T. Hunter* (Richmond, 1935).

BIBLIOGRAPHY

Smith, Ernest A., *The History of the Confederate Treasury* (Harrisburg, 1901).

Soley, James Russell, *The Blockade and the Cruisers in the Navy in the Civil War Series* (vol. I, New York, 1885).

Stephens, Alexander, *A Constitutional View of the Late War Between the States* (2 vols., Philadelphia, 1870).

Sumner, William Graham, *The Financier and the Finances of the American Revolution* (2 vols., New York, 1891).

Thiers, Adolphe, *The History of the French Revolution*. Translated with notes and illustrations by Frederick Shoberl (4 vols., New York, 1854).

Thompson, Samuel B., *Confederate Purchasing Operations Abroad* (Chapel Hill, 1935).

Todd, Richard C., "The Produce Loans: A Means of Financing the Confederacy." *North Carolina Historical Review,* XXVII (January, 1950), 46-75.

Van Deusen, John G., *Economic Bases of Disunion in South Carolina* (New York and London, 1928).

Wesley, C. H., *The Collapse of the Confederacy*. Howard University Studies in History . . . No. 2 (1922).

White, Horace, *Money and Banking Illustrated by American History* (New York, 1936).

White, Laura W., *Robert Barnwell Rhett, Father of Secession* (New York and London, 1931).

Wilson, James G., and Fiske, John, eds., *Appleton's Cyclopaedia of American Biography* (6 vols., New York, 1889).

Yates, Richard E., "Zebulon B. Vance, War Governor of North Carolina." *Journal of Southern History,* III (1937).

Index

Ad valorem duties, 123, 140, 148-149, 150
Agency of the Treasury, created in Trans-Mississippi Department, 23-24; see also Trans-Mississippi Treasury Department
Agents, purchasing, 175, 178, 179, 186, 190; for War Department, 177-178, see also Huse; for Navy Department, 177, see also Bulloch, Wilkinson, North, and Ferguson; commercial, 176, see also Avegno, Helm, Heyliger, Norman S. Walker, and Fraser, Trenholm & Co.; financial, 177, see also Spence and McRae
Alabama Loan of February 8, 1861, 25, 81
Albion Trading Company, London, England, contract for military supplies, 184
Alien enemies, 160-165
Allan, Thompson, Commissioner of Taxes, 5, 132, 144; report on money collected under tax act of April 24, 1863, 145
American Bank Note Co., New York, 216 (n. 29); declared an alien enemy, 94
Archer & Daly, lithographers, manufacture government stocks and bonds, 96; postage stamps, 96, 98; see also Archer & Halpin
Archer & Halpin, manufacture Confederate stocks and bonds, 96, 98
Army, Commissary Officers receive articles in kind subscribed to Produce Loan, 41; Quartermaster General contracts for military supplies payable with cotton, 45-46, 58; see also Impressment
Assay Office, see Mints
Assistant Treasurers, duties, 16-17; with depositaries comprise banking system of Government, 17-18; see also Depositories
Augusta Constitutionalist, opposes legal tender legislation, 119

Avegno, Bernard, Commercial Agent, Vera Cruz, Mexico, 229 (n. 27)

Baker, Bolling, Auditor, CSA Treasury Department, 5
Ball, J. C., Chief Clerk in Office of Second Auditor, 5
Ball, Thomas A., 94; see also Leggett, Keatinge and Ball
Bankers Loan, Fifteen Million Dollar Loan of February 28, 1861, 25-31, 81; effect of varying rates of exchange, 27-28; organization for increasing subscriptions, 28, 30; success of loan, 30
Banking system of Confederate Government, 17-18; operation, 18-19, 22; "New Plan" for financing purchases abroad, 22-23, 187-189
Bank Notes, amount in circulation at end of 1862, 65; during the war, 116; value of affected by suspension of specie payment, 27; used by Government until Treasury notes are prepared, 92, 94
Bank of the Confederate States of America, suggested, 19; other projects for a central bank, 20-21
Banks, cooperation with Treasury Department, 21-22, 27-28, 30-31, 76-77; attitude toward Treasury notes, 92, 94; lend specie to Government, 27-28, 29, 30-31, 82; make temporary advances of bank notes, 92; opposition to tax act of February 17, 1864, 150-151
Barksdale, Ethelbert, Representative of Mississippi, proposed amendment to Sequestration Act, 164
Barter, prevalence of, 117
Baskerville, Charles, Produce Loan Agent, comments on Government cotton after the surrender, 61
Bayne, Lieutenant Colonel Thomas L., Agent of War Department, 59, 189-190

Benjamin, Judah P., Secretary of State, witnesses opening of bids for Cotton Bond sale, 55; authorized to negotiate loan, 179; proposes a central agency to improve credit abroad, 188-189

Bermuda, West Indies, depository of funds, 22, 176, 190, 193

Blockade, 16, 21, 36, 37, 41, 46, 48, 100, 101, 103, 122, 124, 128; effectiveness, 124, 125, 130, 228 (n. 2); relationship to industrial growth, 128

Blockade-running, 22, 124, 176, 186, 190-191, 193-194; regulations for control, 189; opposition to regulations, 191-192; confined to Gulf of Mexico, 193-194

Bond issues, funded debt of CSA, 82-84; see also Funding Loans, Loans, Produce Loans, and Specie Loans

Bonham, Governor M. L., South Carolina, 114

Boyce, James P., encourages State legislatures to guarantee state payment of Confederate debt, 70

Breckinridge, John C., Secretary of War, orders specie raised by Richmond Banks Loan to be used by Army of Virginia for supplies, 82

Brewer, H. O., starts line of steamers to carry cotton to Europe, 184-185

Brown, A. G., Senator of Mississippi, urges passage of legal tender bill, 119

Brown, Joseph E., Governor of Georgia, opposes impressment, 167-168, 169

Bullion Fund, of mints, 12, 14, 157-158

Bulloch, Captain James D., Purchasing Agent for Navy Department, 177-181

Bureau of Engraving and Printing, 85

Caldwell, G. W., Superintendent, Mint at Charlotte, North Carolina, 158, 204 (n. 52)

Call Certificates, 70-71, 74, 105, 106-107, 113

Capers, Henry D., Chief Clerk to Secretary Memminger, 5; supports financial views of Memminger, 2; credits Memminger with origin of Produce Loans, 33

Certificates of indebtedness, 75, 76, 165, 170

Charleston Courier, advocates legal tender, 119; opposes embargo policy, 129

Charleston Mercury, opposes legal tender, 119; favors cotton embargo, 129; declares tax-in-kind unconstitutional, 143

Chemicograph Notes, 101

Churches, donate proceeds from day of fast to Treasury, 171-172

Cis-Mississippi Department, military supplies imported by, 192-193

Clark, Micajah H., appointed Acting Treasurer of CSA, May 4, 1865, 82

Clayton, Philip, Assistant Secretary of the Treasury, 4, 5; duties, 3-4; opposes Memminger's strict regulations, 7-8

Clitherall, Alexander B., Register, CSA Treasury Department, 5, 29; duties, 3

Clitherall, George B., makes contracts for manufacture of Treasury notes, 91-92

Cobb, Howell, Member of Congress, former U. S. Secretary of the Treasury, 4

Cockrill, Sterling R., receiver for seized property of alien enemies in Middle Division of Tennessee, 162-163

Coin, 12-14; see also Bankers Loan and Specie Loans

Collector of Customs, 15-16; requested to reduce operating cost, 121-122

Collie, Alexander & Co., London, England, blockade-runners for Government, 190

Commerce, regulated by Government, 59, 189, 191-192

Commercial Agents, see Agents

Commissioner of Taxes, 144-145; report on value of tax-in-kind under act of April 24, 1863, 148

Compulsory funding, act of October 13, 1862, 109-110; act of March 23, 1863, 110-111; act of February 17, 1864, 112-113; see also Funding Loans

Confederate debt, 64-65, 105-106, 114; payment of declared unconstitutional by United States, 62

Confiscation, of United States specie and property located in the South, 157-159; act of May 14, 1861, 158; act of May 21, 1861, 159-160; act of August 21, 1861, 160; revenue received by Confederacy, 157, 158-159; by United States, 174; of Southern debts due the North, 159-164; extent of, 164-165, 225 (n. 14); see also Sequestration

INDEX

Constitution of Confederate States of America, provisions affecting; legal tender legislation, 118-119; confiscation, 161-163; impressment, 165-166; export duties, 125, 126; protective tariff, 123, 128; direct taxes, 139, 142-143; self-supporting mints, 12, 14

Constitution of United States, 14th Amendment declares all Confederate debts illegal and void, 62, 155; tax provision similar to Permanent Constitution CSA, 142-143

Cooper, C. P., Special Agent of Treasury Department to organize customhouses on interior border, 122

Cotton, a basis for credit abroad, 43, 44, 45-46, 53, 179-186; inequality of prices paid by Government, 43; illicit trade of with enemy, 56-58; contracts for military supplies payable in, 58-59, 186-188; shipped on Government account, 188-194; see also Produce Loans

Cotton Bonds, 52-56, 177, 180, 182; see also Cotton Certificates

Cotton Certificates, 43-49, 53, 177, 180, 181-182, 185

Cotton crop, Government urged to buy, 36-38

Cotton export duty, see Export duty on cotton

Cotton exports, by Government, 38-39, 58-59, 179-194; by states, 38-39

Cotton interest bonds, 52-55, 185

Cotton loans attempted, see Erlanger Loan and Produce Loans

Cotton planters, demand relief of Government, 36-38; state relief granted to in Mississippi and Louisiana, 38-39; prefer Government pay for cotton subscribed to Produce Loan with Treasury notes rather than bonds, 43; see also Produce Loans

Cotton warrant, 185

Counterfeit, prevalence, 102, 116-117; prevention, 98-100, 101; Northern counterfeits of Southern notes, 100, 101

Crawford, J. A., Warrant Clerk, Secretary of the Treasury Office, 5

Crenshaw, Captain W. G., blockade-runner, 191; delivers Cotton Certificates to England, 45, 182

Cruger, Lewis, Comptroller, CSA Treasury Department, 5; duties, 3; opposes transfer of clerks, 8-9

Crump, William W., Assistant Secretary of the Treasury, 10; opposes conscription of all clerks under 40 years of age, 10-11

Currency, amount of Treasury notes in circulation at various times, 64-65, 71-72, 75-76, 104, 109, 111, 113, 114; lithographed notes replace engraved notes, 93-94; organization for manufacturing currency, 6-7, 85-90; difficulty in filling early contracts for Treasury notes, 90-97; obstacles confronting later production of notes, 96-98; amount of Treasury notes issued, 120; attempts to reduce inflation, 34-35, 65-66, 75, 77, 103-104, 109-110, 112-113, 136, 164; state note issues, 38, 65, 116, 133-134; city note issues, 116; private corporation note issues, 116; personal note issues, 116-117; foreign bills of exchange, 64, 175, 177; United States currency in circulation in the South, 116-117; postage stamps in circulation, 96; reversion to barter, 117; legal tender legislation opposed, 117-119; see also Bank Notes, Counterfeit, Note Issues, and Specie

Custom duties, see Tariff

Customhouses, 16-17; created under act of February 14, 1861, 121; number increased, 122; United States customhouses confiscated, 158-159, 178

Cuyler, R. R., banker of Savannah, Georgia, 27

Davis, Jefferson, elected President, 1; commends success of Produce Loan, 34; views on funding policy, 74; feelings toward Memminger, 1, 78, 79; recommendations in November 1864, 80, 115; vetoes bill for further issue of notes March 18, 1865, 115; views on constitutionality of direct taxes, 143; appoints Board of Commissioners to hear claims of confiscated property, 161-162; authorizes J. P. Benjamin to negotiate loan, 179; recommends change in management of credit abroad, 188-189; summarizes regulations for blockade-running, 189, 191,

· 249 ·

192; compares private contract system and "New Plan" for procuring military supplies, 192

DeBow, James Dunwoody Brownson, Chief Commissioner of Produce Loan Office, 5, 33; issues report of loan, 35; plans organization for collecting subscriptions, 39; resigns to become General Agent for Mississippi, 40, 45; explains inequality of prices paid by Government for cotton, 43; recommends purchasing cotton in small lots, 48; complains of heavy loss of Government cotton, 55-56; verifies claim of illicit traffic in Government cotton, 57-58

De La Rue & Co., manufactures Confederate postage stamps, 217 (n. 51)

Dénégré, James D., President, Citizens Bank of Louisiana, aids Government in getting Treasury notes produced in New Orleans, 93, 94; urges adoption of a direct tax, 130-131

Depositories, with Assistant Treasurers comprise banking system of Confederate Government, 17-18; carry out funding measures under act of February 17, 1864, 76; foreign, 22, 176, 177

Donald, John T., of Thomastown, Mississippi, approves tax-in-kind, 142

Donations to Treasury, 171-174; by churches, 171-172; by Ladies Aid Societies, 172; of jewelry and silver plate, 173; amount raised by donations, 173-174

Doswell, J. T., and Company, Subordinate-Agent-At-Large, 45

Duncan, Colonel Blanton, manufactures Treasury notes, 94, 96, 97

Duncan, Stephen, Clerk in Treasury Note Bureau, 87, 90.

Dunn & Co., lithographers, manufacture Government stocks and bonds, 90-96

Elmore, Edward C., Treasurer, CSA Treasury Department, 5, 178; duties, 3-4

Elmore, William A., Superintendent, Mint at New Orleans, recommends a new coin for CSA, 12-14; transfers federal specie to Confederate Government, 158-159

Embargo, free trade policy adopted, 127-129; see also Tariff

Erlanger and Company, proposes a Confederate bank in London, 20; establishes a line of steamers to carry cotton to Europe, 184; see also Erlanger Loan

Erlanger, Emile, 177

Erlanger Loan, 22, 48-51, 177, 182-184, 193-194

Evans, B. F., lithographer, requested to set up establishment for printing Treasury notes, 96

Evans & Cogswell, lithographers of Treasury notes, 89-90, 94, 96-97

Export duty on cotton, 26, 103, 104, 105, 107, 108, 111, 113, 182; amount estimated and actually received, 125

Exports, see Imports and Exports

Ferguson, Major J. B., purchasing agent, 177, 180

Ficklen, Major Benjamin F., goes to England to procure skilled workmen and materials for production of Treasury notes, 93-94

Finances, expenses and receipts in 1861-1862, 105-106; in 1862-1864, 149, 153

Financial agents, see Agents

Financial Operations Abroad, 175-194; plan for meeting obligations, 175-176; organization and personnel, 176-177; original plan for, 177-179; Second Plan: Use of credit instruments based on cotton, 179-186; Third Plan: Contracts made for supplies payable in cotton, 186-188; New Plan: Cotton shipped on Government account and supplies paid for with proceeds, 188-194

Food, scarcity of, 165

Foote, H. S., Representative of Tennessee, introduces resolution demanding removal of Secretary Memminger, 78-79

Foreign bills of exchange, 64, 175, 177; effect of scarcity, 178; see also Currency

Foreign Loan, see Erlanger Loan

Foreign supplies, remittances, 44-46, 53, 178-179, 180-181, 182, 184, 185-186; effect of private contracts on Confederate finances abroad, 186-188; cotton

INDEX

shipped and sold on Government account, 188-194; see also Erlanger Loan
Fraser, John, & Co., 178; see also Fraser, Trenholm & Co.
Fraser, Trenholm & Co., depository of Confederate funds, Liverpool, England, 21-22, 44-45, 49, 176, 177, 178, 182, 190
Free Trade Policy, 127-128; see also Embargo and Tariff
Funding Depository, see Depositories
Funding Loans, objective, 64; provision for funding notes in bonds avoided in early loans, 31; adopted May 16, 1861, 32, 104; renewed August 19, 1861, 35; renewed April 18, 1862, 41, 42, 106; compulsory funding proposed and defended by Memminger, 67-68, 72-73, 109-110, 111-112; Funding Act of October 13, 1862, 66-67, 109-110, 111-112; of February 20, 1863, 51, 66-67; of March 23, 1863, 70-72, 110-111, 126; of April 30, 1863, 52-56; further funding measures discussed in 1863-1864, 72-74; attitude of press, 74; Funding Act of February 17, 1864, 74-79, 112-114, 126-127; state funding acts, 38; comparable value of bonds issued under various loan acts, 54; summary of funded debt of CSA, 83-84
Funding Treasury notes in bonds, see Funding Loans and Produce Loans

Gallier & Esterbrook, New Orleans Architects, submit design for CSA coin, 13
Gartrell, L. J., Chairman of House Judiciary Committee, inquires into need for legal tender legislation, 118
Gettysburg, Battle of, effect on currency, 170
Gibbon, J. H., Assayer at Mint, Charlotte, North Carolina, 15
Gilbert, W. H., detective, comments on difficulty to convict counterfeiters, 99
Gilliat, J. K. & Co., blockade-runners for Government, 190
Gladney, J. B., Subordinate-Agent-At-Large, purchases cotton to fill contracts for military and naval supplies, 45
Glover, Lloyd, submits model for coin, 13

Gold Premium, relation to amount of notes outstanding, 72, 114, 151
Grant, General Ulysses S., 90
Gray, Dr. A. W., Clerk in Treasury Note Bureau, 87
Gray, P. W., Agent of the Treasury for the Trans-Mississippi Department, 23
Green, T. T., Chief Clerk in Office of Treasurer, 5
"Greenbacks," 116-117
Guirot, Anthony J., Assistant Treasurer, 16-17; transfers federal funds to Confederate Government, 159

Hamilton, Alexander, financial system of adopted by CSA, 3
Hanckel, Charles F., Chief Clerk, Treasury Note Division, Columbia, South Carolina, 86
Harllee, General W. W., inquires regarding forced sale of crops subscribed to Produce Loan, 36
Havana, Cuba, depository of Confederate funds, 176, 190, 193
Hayes, S. C., Superintendent of Treasury Printing Office, 12
Helm, Charles J., Depositary and Commercial Agent, Havana, Cuba, 176
Hendren, John N., Treasurer, 18; submits statement showing bonds sold under 500-Million Dollar Loan of February 17, 1864, 76
Heyliger, Louis, depositary at Nassau, New Providence, 22; duties, 176
Hotze, Henry, describes effect of fall of Vicksburg on Erlanger Loan, 50; opposes private contracts for military supplies, 187
Hoyer & Ludwig, lithograph Treasury notes at Richmond, 90, 94, 95; stocks and bonds, 96
Huse, Caleb, purchasing agent for War Department, 177; amount of supplies purchased, 179; aids in negotiating Erlanger Loan, 182; authorized to issue Cotton Warrants, 185-186

Illicit Traffic, 16, 56-58
Imports and Exports, 103; importing and exporting companies, 184-185, 190-191; importation of luxuries prohibited, 189; free trade policy, 127-128; see also Blockade, Embargo, and Tariff

· 251 ·

Impressment, 165-171; cause for, 165-166, 170, 171; organization and system adopted under act of March 26, 1863, 166-167; act amended on numerous occasions, 167; schedules of items and price bids, 166; wastefulness, 168-169; illegal impressments, 169; opposition to, 167-170; collapse of, 169-170; amount of goods impressed, 170-174; summary, 170-171

Industries, growth and development during the war, 128

Inflation, measures to prevent, 104-105, 106, 109-110, 114-115, 116-117, 119, 136; see also Redundant currency

Isaac, Campbell & Co., contract to furnish military supplies, 178, 185

Jamison, Sanders G., principal clerk, superintends issue of Treasury notes, 6-7, 85-86; appointed Chief of Treasury Note Bureau, 7, 86; reorganizes bureau, 86-87; moves bureau to Columbia, South Carolina, 87-88; friction with Assistant Treasurer over trimming notes, 88; report of October 31, 1864 on operation of bureau, 89; comments on experiment of employing ladies for work in public offices, 89; describes evacuation of bureau from Columbia, South Carolina, 89-90; recommends Treasury notes be produced in Europe to prevent counterfeiting, 101

Jonas, Major A. L., of Mississippi, writes poem, "The Confederate Note," 117-118

Jones, Charles T., Chief Clerk to Register, 4, 5

Jones, J. B., views regarding effect of Funding Act of February 17, 1864, on currency, 75

Jordan, John A., Commissioner for taking subscriptions to the Produce Loan, 34

Keatinge & Ball, lithographers of Treasury notes, 90, 95, 96, 97-98; see also Thomas A. Ball

Kellogg, George, Superintendent, Mint at Dahlonega, Georgia, 204 (n. 52); transfers federal specie to Confederate Government, 158

Kennedy, T. H., Comptroller for Agency of the Treasury, Trans-Mississippi Department, 206 (n. 104)

Kenner, D. F., Representative of Louisiana, recommends uniform tax on income, 136-137; requested to amend Sequestration Act in order to curb expanding currency, 164

Kent, Paine & Co., auctioneers, Richmond, Virginia, sell bonds of 500-Million Dollar Loan, 76

Ladies Aid Societies, sponsor drives to raise funds for Treasury, 172

Lamar, G. B., contracts with American Bank Note Co., New York, to make Confederate Certificates of Stock and Treasury notes, 90-91

Lamar, L. Q. C., comments on Erlanger Loan, 50

Lawrence, Son & Pearce, Messrs., Brokers, London, aid in promoting Erlanger Loan, 183

Lee, Colonel G. W., supervisor of detective agency for apprehension of counterfeiters, 99

Lee, Robert E., surrender of, causes specie to be moved South, 82

Legal Tender, legislation opposed by Memminger, 117-118; attempts to enact law of, 118-119; attitude of press toward, 119; proponents of, 118-119

Leggett, Keatinge and Ball, lithographers of Treasury notes, 93, 94, 95; see also Keatinge & Ball

Leitch, W. Y., Assistant Treasurer, 17; responsible for disbursing notes, 88; friction with Chief of Treasury Note Bureau, 88-89

Lester, W. W., Chief Clerk in Office of First Auditor, 5

Letters of credit, 175, 178

Lincoln, Abraham, orders blockade of Confederate coast, 124; issues proclamation for confiscation of goods imported from Confederacy, 160

Liverpool, England, depository of Confederate funds, 176, 190, 193

Loans, 25-84; Five Hundred Thousand Dollar Loan, February 8, 1861, 25; Fifteen Million Dollar Loan, February 28, 1861, 25-31, 77, 178-179; Fifty Million Dollar Loan, May 16, 1861, 30-34,

INDEX

77, 104; One Hundred Million Dollar Loan, August 19, 1861, 34-35; loan of April 18, 1862, 42-44, 106; loan of February 20, 1863, 51, 66-67; loan of March 23, 1863, 70-72, 111, 126; loan of April 30, 1863, 52-56; Five Hundred Million Dollar Loan, February 17, 1864, 74-78, 113, 126-127; loan of June 14, 1864, 77; loan of March 13 and 17, 1865, 80-82; state bond issues, Louisiana and Mississippi, 38; South Carolina, 134; summary showing funds raised by all loans, 82-84; see also Erlanger Loan, Funding Loans, Produce Loans, and Specie Loans

Lumpkins, Dr. James M., Chief Clerk, Treasury Note Bureau, 87

McCulloch, Hugh, United States Secretary of the Treasury, supervises seized cotton and tobacco owned by CSA, 61

McKinney, Thomas F., Chief of Cotton Bureau of Trans-Mississippi Department, 23

McRae, General Colin J., depositary at Paris, 22, 23, 177, 183, 184; opposes private contracts for military and naval supplies, 187; recommends a central agency for improving credit abroad, 188; plan adopted, 189-191

Magrath, Judge A. G., Confederate District Court of South Carolina, upholds Sequestration Act, 162

Mallory, Stephen R., Secretary of Navy, approves use of Navy funds for purchase of cotton, 45; requests additional means for purchases in Europe, 53

Manouvrier, J., lithographer, manufactures Treasury notes, 93, 95

Marshall, Texas, seat of Agency of the Treasury in the Trans-Mississippi Department, 23

Mason, James M., Commissioner to Great Britain, suggests use of Cotton Certificates to raise funds abroad, 44, 181; cooperates with Treasury Department, 177, 183; authorizes issue of Cotton Warrants, 185, 186; opposes private contracts for military supplies, 187

Maury, M. F., purchasing agent, 177

Maury, W. L., delivers Cotton Certificates to Liverpool, 182, 185

Memminger, Christopher G., Secretary of the Treasury, 1, 201 (n. 3); duties, 3; reports of May 10, 1861, 31, 103, 123; of July 29, 1861, 104-105; of March 14, 1862, 106; of January 10, 1863, 109-110; of December 7, 1863, 72-73, 111-112; of May 6, 1864, 151-152; resignation June 15, 1864, 78-79; favors taxation, 25, 130-131, 136, 137, 139-140, 148-149; attitude toward cotton planters, 36-37; opposes legal tender legislation, 118-119; views on bank suspension of specie payment, 27-28; on government speculation in cotton, 38-39, 40-41; attacks upon, 78-79; first to employ women in public offices, 89; applies to banking institutions for temporary loan of bank notes, 92; issues regulations for conduct of department, 7; granted authority to increase number of customhouses on interior borders, 122; orders confiscation of federal funds and property in South, 157; views regarding sequestration of property of alien enemies, 162-163; favors use of cotton as basis for establishing credit abroad, 180; recommends: state guarantee of Confederate bonds, 68-70; funding, 65, 67-68, 72-73; closing mints, 12; Produce Loan, 33; accepting articles in kind in exchange for bonds, 41; compulsory funding, 67-68, 72-73, 109-110, 111-112; establishing a Treasury Note Bureau, 86; use of interest-bearing Treasury notes, 103, 104-105; ways to improve currency, 109; tariff on imports and exports, 125-127; tax on property and income, 138-139; tax-in-kind, 139-140; ad valorem tax on land and Negroes, 148-149; reforms in tax act of February 14, 1864, 151-152; amending act to curb expanding currency, 163-164; donations from churches be used to aid wounded soldiers, 171-172

"Merrimac," steamer, purchased with Cotton Warrants, 185

Miles, W. Porcher, Chairman, Committee on Military Affairs, 11

Military supplies, see Foreign supplies

Miller, W. F., Clerk in Treasury Note Bureau, 90

Mints, Federal, at New Orleans, Louisi-

CONFEDERATE FINANCE

ana; Dahlonega, Georgia; and Charlotte, North Carolina, seized by CSA, 12; equipment sold to promote industry, 14, 158-159; use of as Assay Offices, 14-15; Bullion Fund transferred to Confederacy, 12, 14, 157-158, 178; buildings used by Confederacy, 158-159

Mitchell, Nelson, opposes Sequestration Act, 162

Moffitt, John N., purchasing agent, 177

Money, see Currency and Note Issues

Murdaugh, Lieutenant Wm. H., selects Charlotte Mint to house Navy Ordnance Department, 158

Nassau, New Providence, depository of Confederate funds, 22, 176, 190, 193

National Bank Note Company of New York, submits model for CSA coin, 13; contracts to manufacture engraved Treasury notes, 90-91

Naval supplies, see Foreign supplies

Navy Department, purchasing agents, 175, 177, 180; contracts for steamers and other supplies, 180-181; ill effect of contracts on Confederate finances abroad, 186-188; agreement with War and Treasury Departments for purchase, sale and transportation of cotton, 189-190; see also Agents

New Orleans, seizure of United States Mint in, 13, 146, 158; seizure of United States customhouse in, 159; condition of banks, 27; suspends specie payment for bank notes, 27-28; seizure of banks' specie, 165; captured by Federal forces, 179

"New Plan," for procuring supplies from abroad, 22-23, 59, 188-194; Centralized Treasury Agency created in Europe, 187-188, 189-190; regulations imposed upon foreign commerce, 58, 188-189; agreement by War, Navy and Treasury Departments for puchase, sale, and transportation of cotton, 58-59, 189-190; private contract system ended, 190; New Plan for furnishing military supplies adopted, 190-191; opposition to New Plan, 191-192; success of plan, 191, 192-194; see also Financial Operations Abroad

Newspapers, support: Fifteen Million Dollar Loan, February 28, 1861, 28; Fifty Million Dollar Loan, May 16, 1861, 33; Hundred Million Dollar Loan, August 19, 1861, 35; use of cotton as a basis for alliance with Louis Napoleon, 40-41; sale of Cotton Bonds issued under Two Hundred and Fifty Million Dollar Loan of April 30, 1863, 53-54; compulsory funding of Treasury notes, 73-74; sale of bonds issued under Five Hundred Million Dollar Loan of February 17, 1864, 75-76; take opposing sides on legal tender issue, 119; condemn Congress for failure to pass adequate tax law, 137; publish impressment schedules and prices, 166

North, Captain James H., purchasing agent, 177, 180

Note Issues, 3.65% notes of March 9, 1861, 90-91, 102-103; amount issued, 103; non-interest-bearing notes of May 16, 1861, 31, 91-92, 103-104; non-interest-bearing notes of August 19, 1861, 35, 104-105; non-interest-bearing notes and 6% call certificates of December 24, 1861, 105; notes of April 18, 1862, 41, 106; 7.30% notes of April 17, 1862, 107-108; small notes of April 17, 1862, 108; unlimited issue of September 23, 1862, 108-109; issues of March 23, 1863, 71-72, 110-111; of February 17, 1864, 74-75, 112-113; of March 18, 1865, 115; poem, "The Confederate Note," 117-118; amount of notes outstanding at various times, 65, 71-72, 75-76, 103-104, 107-108, 109, 111, 113, 114; table showing amount of Treasury notes issued, 119-120; value of Confederate and United States notes compared with gold, Appendix C, 198; state note issues, Alabama and others, 116; Louisiana, 38; Mississippi, 38; issues by private corporations, 116; see also Currency, Funding Loans, and Gold Premium

Noyes, A. B., Collector of Customs, reports on effectiveness of blockade, 124

Office of Deposit, nearest approach of Confederacy to a central bank, 20-21

Office of the Commissioner of Taxes, created, 5, 143; duties, 144; last report

INDEX

showing tax receipts under acts of April 24, 1863, February 17, 1864, and June 14, 1864, 152-153; see also War Tax Bureau

Oliphant, James, recommends low uniform prices, 168

Ott, John, Chief Clerk in Comptroller's Office, 5

"Palmetto State," gunboat donated to Confederacy by ladies of South Carolina, 172

Paris, France, depository of funds, 177

Paterson, J. T., & Co., manufacture Treasury notes, 95-97

Pay Depository, see Depositories

Pettigru, J. L., opposes Sequestration Act, 161-162

Pickett, John T., Confederate envoy to Mexico, receives tobacco in payment of debt contracted in behalf of Confederacy, 61-62

Planters' Relief, see Cotton Planters

Poem, "The Confederate Note," 117-118

Pollard, Edward A., criticizes Memminger, 2; credits Davis and Congress with origin of Produce Loans, 32-33; cites extent of Southern indebtedness to North at outbreak of war, 225 (n. 14)

Pope, Joseph Daniel, Chief Collector of War Tax for South Carolina, 6; in charge of printing Treasury notes, 6, 85-86; recommends creation of a Government establishment for production of currency, 97-98

Port Hudson, fall of, hastens creation of Trans-Mississippi Department, 24

Pressley, B. C., Assistant Treasurer, 17; receives federal funds confiscated by Confederacy, 158

Prices, as affected by amount of notes outstanding, 109-110, 137, 165; local differences, 43; maximum price laws, 166; impressment prices, 166-168; rising prices, 47, 55, 75, 114, 145; causes of rising prices, 46, 110, 165-166; attempt to prevent rise in, 51, 65, 75; inequality of prices paid by Government for cotton, 43; price control recommended, 188; prices as affected by the Funding Act of March 23, 1863, 72-73; by the Funding Act of February 17, 1864, 75; see also Impressment

Produce Certificates, 42; see also Cotton Certificates

Produce Loan Bureau, created, 16, 52; summary of its activities, 60-61; see also Produce Loans

Produce Loan Office, created, 5; duties, 6, 52; see also Produce Loan Bureau

Produce Loans, origin, 33-34; First Form: Fifty Million Dollar Loan, May 16, 1861, 31-32; Second Form: One Hundred Million Dollar Loan, August 19, 1861, 34-35; Final Form: Two Hundred and Fifty Million Dollar Loan, April 21, 1862, 42-43, 52-53; Loans of February 20, March 23, and April 30, 1863, 51, 52-56, 66-67, 70-71; State Cotton Bonds of Mississippi and North Carolina, 38; obstacles confronting Produce Loan, 36-39; organization for collecting subscriptions, 39-41; procuring articles in kind under act of April 21, 1862, 41-43; Cotton Certificates, 43-48; Cotton Bonds, 52-56; purchase, transportation, and sale of Government cotton, 1864-1865, 58-61; measures taken to protect Government cotton, 55-58; last official report of Produce Loan Bureau, 60-61; Government cotton and tobacco following collapse of the Confederacy, 61-62; summary of Produce Loans, 63-64

Protective tariff, see Tariff

Purchasing Agents, see Agents

Redundant currency, 103, 105, 107, 108, 112, 113, 115, 119, 136; see also Inflation

Reyburn, Dr. William P., Treasury Agent appointed to speed up production of Treasury notes, 93

Richmond Banks Loan, 82

Richmond Dispatch, appeals to women to donate gold and silver medals to Treasury, 173

Richmond Examiner, supports compulsory funding of Treasury notes, 74; advocates legal tender, 119; strongly urges a free trade policy, 128; criticizes inaction of Congress to approve adequate taxation, 137-138

Roane, Archibald, Chief Clerk in Charge of Produce Loan Offices, 5-6, 40; summarizes subscriptions to Produce Loan up to January 9, 1863, 46-47; promoted to Chief Clerk, 211 (n. 99); issues final report of Produce Loan Bureau, 60-61

Schmidt, Samuel, managing partner, New Orleans branch, American Bank Note Co., manufactures engraved Treasury notes, 91-92, 93, 94-95

Schroeder, J. Henry, and Company, London, England, proposes a Confederate bank in London, 19-20; aid in promoting Erlanger Loan, 183-184

Schwab, John Christopher, appraises Memminger as Secretary of the Treasury, 2; compares value of bonds of Fifteen Million Dollar Loan in currency and specie, 30-31

Seddon, James A., Secretary of War, 191; urged to pay market price for impressed articles, 168; agrees with Davis on commerce regulations, 192; reports on Government cotton exported under "New Plan," 192-193

Seizures, of funds and property by the Confederate Government, 157-171; see also Confiscation, Sequestration, and Impressment

Seizures and Donations, 340-380

Sequestration, of funds and property of alien enemies, 159-165; act of May 21, 1861, 159-160; act of August 21, 1861, 160; act of August 30, 1861, passed in retaliation to United States act of August 6, 1861, 160-161; organization for receiving property of alien enemies, 161-162; Board of Claim Commissioners created, 225 (n. 23); opposition to Sequestration, 161-162; act of February 15, 1862, 163; act of February 3, 1865, 164; amount of property seized, 162-163, 164-165; see also Confiscation

Sequestration Fund, 165

Shall, D. F., Auditor for Agency of the Treasury, Trans-Mississippi Department, 206 (n. 104)

Sherman, William T., 90

"Shinplasters," 116

Simms, William, Senator of Kentucky, opposes impressment of property, 165-166

Sinclair, George T., purchasing agent, 177

Slidell, John, Commissioner to Great Britain, cooperates with Treasury officials, 177; aids in negotiating Erlanger Loan, 182-184; opposes private contracts for military supplies, 187; recommends central agency for improving credit abroad, 188

Smith, Colonel Larkin, Assistant Quartermaster General, supervises collection of articles in kind, 145-146; report of November 30, 1863, 148

Smith, General E. Kirby, Military Commander of Trans-Mississippi Department, 23

Soldiers' Tax, 152

Southern Bank Note Company, New Orleans branch of American Bank Note Company, 94-95, 216 (n. 29)

Southern Express Company, transmits Treasury notes to depositories, 98

Specie, shortage of, in Confederacy, 27, 64; banks suspend specie payments for bank notes, 27-28; specie seized from New Orleans banks, 165; used in paying for purchases abroad, 177-178

Specie Loans, Five Hundred Thousand Dollar Loan, February 8, 1861, 25; Fifteen Million Dollar Loan, February 28, 1861, 25-31; Erlanger Loan, 22, 48-51; Loan of March 13, 1865, superseded by Loan of March 17, 1865, 80-81; Richmond Banks Loan, 82

Speculation, nature of, 164, 165-166, 171, 188

Spence, James, financial agent at Liverpool, England, 22, 49, 177, 178, 180, 182-183, 186; commission revoked, 177; opposes private contracts for military supplies, 187

State notes, amount in circulation by end of 1862, 65; state notes issued, 38, 116, 133-134; see also Currency and Note Issues

States' Rights, aroused: by Government control of foreign commerce, 58-59, 191-192; by impressment, 167, 169-170; by state guarantee of Confederate debt, 69-70; by interference with states' exporting and importing one-fourth of ship's goods, 59, 191-192; by question of constitutionality of direct taxes, 142-143

Stephens, Alexander H., elected Vice President, 1; addresses rallies in support of Produce Loan, 207 (n. 30);

INDEX

views on taxation and loans, 136

Straker, S., & Sons, London, England, contract to prepare chemicograph plates for Treasury notes, 101

Strother, Captain John M., financial agent of Commissary Department, receives specie from Richmond Banks Loan, 82

Tariff, of February 9, 1861, 121, 123; of February 18, 1861, 123; of February 28, 1861, export duty of 1/8¢ per pound on cotton, 26, 71, 125; objections to export duty, 126; tariff of March 15, 1861, 123; of March 16, 1861, 123; of May 21, 1861, 123-124, 126; of February 17, 1864, 75, 126-127; protective motives prohibited, 123-124; free trade policy, 127-128; growth of protectionism, 128; embargo policy, 128-129; amount of customs revenue anticipated, 123, 124; amount of import duties collected, 125; total export duties collected, 127; summary of tariff policy, 130

Tariffs and Taxes, 121-156

Tax Acts, War Tax of August 19, 1861, 35, 130-136; its levy, 131-132; organization for collecting, 132; its assumption by the states, 132, 133-134; amount collected, 135; act of April 19, 1862, 133; effect on currency, 136; act of April 24, 1863, 51-52, 136-148, 156; act of February 17, 1864, 74-75, 148-152; weaknesses of, 150-152; amended by act of June 14, 1864, 151-152; amount of revenue collected under acts of April 24, 1863, February 17, 1864, and June 14, 1864, 152-153; tax bills in Congress in 1864-1865, 147-148, 152; act of March 11, 1865, 154; act of March 17, 1865, 154-155; probable effect of adequate taxation on finance, 155-156; summary of tax legislation, 156; see also Tariff, Tax-in-Kind, and War Tax

Taxation, postponed in 1861, 25-26, 31; urged by Memminger, 25, 130-131, 136-137, 139-140, 148-149; reluctance of Congress to adopt a direct tax, 130-131; tax revenue in 1861-1862, 133; in 1863-1864, 133-134, 135, 152-153; constitutionality of direct taxation, 139, 142-143, 148-149; burden of taxes, 136, 150-152; summary, 156

Tax-in-Kind, act of April 24, 1863, 51-52, 136-148; plan recommended by Memminger, 138-139, 139-140; modified by Congress, 138-140; broadened to include tax-in-kind on agricultural products, 139-140; final provisions, 140-141; opposition to, 141-143; constitutionality of, 143; organization for collecting money tax, 141, 143-145; amount raised in money, 145; amount raised in articles in kind, 147-148; suggestion to continue tax-in-kind after war, 115; act amended, 147; see also Tax Acts

Taylor, Thomas, Cashier in Office of Treasurer, 5

Taylor, W. H. S., Second Auditor in Treasury Department, 5; duties, 4

Tithe Tax, 6, 142, 145-148; see also Tax-in-Kind

Trade with the United States, in Mississippi, 56-58; attempts to prevent, 56, 57-58

Trans-Mississippi Department, E. Kirby Smith appointed military commander, 23; separate Treasury Department established, 23; number of burdens increased, 24; Sequestration Act, 164-165; funds raised, 174; counterfeiting, 100; effect of act of February 17, 1864, upon currency, 112-113; customs and taxes collected, 125, 127, 156

Treasury Department, 1-24; organized, 2-3; expanded, 4, 5, 11-12, 23-24; clerical force and salaries, 4, 6-7; personnel, 4-5; regulations for conduct of, 7; obstacles to efficient operation, 7-11; military training of clerks for local defense, 9-11; agreement with War and Navy Departments for purchase, sale, and transportation of cotton, 189-190; see also Assistant Treasurers, Customhouses, Depositories, Mints, "New Plan," Produce Loan Bureau, Trans-Mississippi Treasury Department, Treasury Note Bureau, Treasury Printing Office, and War Tax Bureau

Treasury Note Bureau, 6-7, 85-90, 115

Treasury Note Division, 6-7; see also Treasury Note Bureau

Treasury Notes, 85-120; see Currency and Note Issues

Treasury Printing Office, 12

Trenholm, George A., appointed Secretary of the Treasury, 79; report of November 7, 1864, 80, 114-115, 127, 153; views on compulsory funding policy, 80, 114, 115; opposes reopening mints and assay offices, 15-16; commends banks for aid to Government, 21-22; recommends continuing tax-in-kind after war, 115; plan for improving finances rejected, 115-116; recommends increase in export and import duties, 127; criticizes system of rebates under tax act of February 17, 1864, 153-154; donates currency and securities to aid Treasury, 173; agrees with Davis on commerce regulations, 192

Tyler, Robert, Register of the Treasury, 6, 45; reports amount of Treasury notes outstanding on April 30, 1864, 113

United States funds, seizure of, 12, 14, 157-159; see also Confiscation and Mints

Upham, Samuel C., lithographer, producer of "facsimile" Confederate notes, 100-101

Vicksburg, Battle of, effect on Erlanger Loan, 50, 170, 184

Walden, C. C., of Savannah, Georgia, Special Agent of Treasury Department to investigate business at custom-houses, 121-122

Walker, Norman S., depositary at Bermuda, 22; duties, 176

War Department, purchasing agents, 175, 177; negotiates private contracts for military supplies, 186-188; agreement with Navy and Treasury Departments for purchase, sale, and transportation of cotton, 189-190; see also Agents and Army

Warder, William H., procures tobacco for a mercantile house in New York, 62

War Tax, of August 19, 1861, 105-106, 132; organization for collecting, 132; list of original chief collectors, 222 (n. 48); amount of assessments, 133; payment of tax assumed by states, 134; total collected, 133, 135; see also Tax Acts

War Tax Bureau, 5-6, 132, 143-144

War Tax Office, 5, 144; see also Office of the Commissioner of Taxes and War Tax Bureau

Watts, Thomas H., Attorney General, witnesses bids for Cotton Bond sale, 55

Whaley, William, opposes Sequestration Act, 162

Wharton, T. J., comments on illicit trade in exposed area of Mississippi, 57-58

White, Joel, Montgomery, Alabama, requested to bring Treasury note plates from New York, 91

Wilkinson, Lieutenant John, purchasing agent, 177, 180

Women, employment in public offices, 89; involved in illicit trade with enemy, 57-58; donate jewelry, gold and silver medals, foodstuffs, etc., to aid Treasury, 172-173